"Not to People Like Us"

Hidden Abuse in Upscale Marriages

SUSAN WEITZMAN, PH.D.

BASIC BOOKS

A Member of the
Perseus Books Group

Copyright © 2000 by Susan Weitzman

Published by Basic Books,
A Member of the Perseus Books Group

Designed by Rachel Hegarty

Library of Congress Cataloging-in-Publication Data
Weitzman, Susan
   Not to people like us : hidden abuse in upscale marriages /
Susan Weitzman.
      p.   cm.
Includes bibliographical references and index.
ISBN 978-0-46509-074-7
   1. Abused wives—United States. 2. Middle class women—
United States. 3. Upper class women—United States. I. Title.
HV6626.2.W43   2000
362.82′92′086210973—dc21

DHSB   05 06 07 08. 15 14 13 12 11 10 9 8 7 6 5 4

CONTENTS

This book is dedicated to my parents
Abraham and Rebecca Weitzman
in loving memory

ACKNOWLEDGMENTS

The effort of researching, analyzing, and writing a book has many phases. Some are arduous, some are simple, and all have an impact on the final form. Thankfully, I have had support and guidance from several wonderful people throughout all the phases of this major accomplishment in my life; without their efforts, input, and help, that effort would probably not have resulted in this book. I am pleased to take this opportunity to acknowledge these people.

First and foremost, I want to express my thanks to and respect for the women of the study who so earnestly and honestly gave of themselves in the most expansive ways as they told their stories. Their courage, candor, warmth, and strong survival skills ultimately were the background, foreground, and essence of this work. I would never have found these women had it not been for the kind and generous efforts of attorney Mel Sloan and his secretary, Ellen Phelps. Going beyond the call of duty, they were key in helping me gather my study sample, giving their time and energy. Attorney Stephen Schlegel was also helpful at an early stage. My transcriptionist, Natalie Hector, displayed amazing fortitude and perseverance as she pored over the interview tapes (at times painful to listen to and transcribe owing to the nature of the content), getting them back to me quickly and with extremely kind and compassionate reactions.

Dr. Daniel Lee and Dr. Judith Wittner helped me begin and then pursue my qualitative research, consistently offering support, relevant references, and thoughts and ideas. Their early faith in my research on this topic served as mighty fertilizer for its growth, as well as for my own growth.

Dr. Joseph Walsh, adviser, mentor, friend, and colleague, was an advocate of my work from its inception. His belief in its importance was a beacon of light for me, as were the insights he so readily gave me through every step of my study and beyond. Always there to take a call and to keep me on track, Joe was patient, thoughtful, and wise, and offered a sense of order at times and in situations that sometimes were a bit daunting. The birth of the study and many of its findings are in large part a result of the intelligent efforts of this staunch supporter and constructive critic. I remain amazed at his foresight and insight regarding my research, and his ability to keep rereading with new eyes each time. He skillfully guided me through many phases of my doctoral research, moving me along with humor, warmth, deadlines, incredible organizational skills, and good puns. Words truly cannot express my gratitude for his work, time, and kindness.

I want to thank Karen Teigiser for her support and encouragement during the early and momentous turning point of my journey. Attorneys Leslie Landis and David Hopkins were with me when the whole project was a mere seed back in 1992, and I am pleased that their efforts and intelligent, thoughtful spirits became part of this effort once again, in its final stages. They both have dedicated much of their life's work to helping battered women, and their dedication has been inspirational. Dr. Rosemary Parse opened my mind to rigorous research standards and the concept of "lived experience." Special thanks go to Miriam Elson for our discussions about aspects of self psychology relevant to this work. She really came through at the eleventh hour, and her insights are woven into the chapter on the men.

I thank the Chicago Mayor's Office on Domestic Violence, Deborah Tucker, attorneys Sarah Buel and Miriam Berkman, the National Training Center on Domestic and Sexual Violence, the National Coalition Against Domestic Violence, Judith Barnes, and the librarians of the Loyola University Library in Chicago. I am also grateful for the teachings during the irony of a springtime in Jackson Hole, Wyoming.

These acknowledgments would not be complete without expressing my appreciation to the women patients with whom I have worked, especially the famous and long-standing Monday Night Women's Group (which now meets on Tuesdays). Whether they realize it or not, all of these women have consistently taught me a lot, both as a professional and as a woman. They have taught me as much as I have them—with love, stick-to-it-iveness, wisdom, and grace.

Suzanne Talbott Isaacs, a woman of great strength and fortitude, introduced me to Joni Evans, my agent at William Morris, and for this, many thanks. Joni is an absolute joy, and her belief in this book was there from day one. She had the foresight to see the scope of the work and the skill and talent to know just how to best get it out to the women and culture that she believed were so deeply in need of its contents. Whether struggling with the many versions of my initial proposals, calming the anxieties of a first-time author, handling "the tough stuff," or being supportive through the sudden passing of my mother, this book's birth and its journey are a result of Joni's belief in it. I am grateful for her involvement, warmth, wisdom, and guidance.

Jo Ann Miller, my editor at Basic Books, saw the book's larger potential immediately and has been insightful, diligent, and thoughtful. She never wavered in her vision for its direction and her sense of its importance. Jo Ann is a consummate professional whom I thoroughly trust and respect. Jennifer Sherwood, Tiffany Ericksen, and Donya Levine, and Jessica Callaway, assistants to Joni and Jo Ann, were always helpful and were a delight to work with.

My appreciation goes to Susan K. Golant, the book's midwife, who spent many laborious hours poring over every word after the book had been initially composed. Her intelligence and perceptiveness opened my eyes to aspects of the work that otherwise would have been lost, buried, or unmentioned. With her quick wit and agile mind she is skilled at the microsurgery of editing and rewriting, and possesses a keen awareness of what to put where, helping to bring my thoughts clearly into the light. She has been a valued contributor and I am honored to have worked with a person of her caliber. I am also grateful to Richard Miller, my copyediting guru, who brought his insights, skills, and wry sense of humor to the final moments of the project.

Last, but just as important, I must acknowledge the significant others in my life, who supported me emotionally, psychically, and spiritually. Dr. Irma North and Dianne Plummer, the surrogate mothers, nurtured me with solid love and support and continue to do so; they are ladies in every sense of the word. Dianne was sometimes the only face I would see for days at a time, and she always greeted me with a hug and a smile during the toughest writing periods. Lady North taught me to "put one foot in front of the other," and I wouldn't have missed her "adopting" me for the world!

Thomas Gauthier, my "tough-love" friend and confidant, firmly gave me the pushes I needed, even when I didn't want them. Thom has been a part of most of the major events in my adult life and has always provided a lifeboat or lighthouse whenever I needed one. Marilyn Morris, a dear friend and colleague, listened to my ideas and offered her input on the subject years before I ever imagined it would reach fruition. Always aware of the early warning signs of emotional abuse, she has been a trusted friend and colleague. Roy Moceri brings me back to basics; his friendship and common-sense perspective on things are unexpected gifts. Sincere appreciation goes to attorney Stuart Blatt and Dr. Jonathan Scott for their input and support. Ken Robins's spirit and sensibility remain warmly present through the years and will always continue to do so.

My muse and ever-constant little companion, Shelby, was there at my side as a cuddly source of love and comic relief during every typed word and arduous hour of work, reflection, and analysis. A joyous spirit of love and happiness, he truly is a magic baby bear.

My parents, Abraham and Rebecca Weitzman, made strong contributions to who I am today. My father's warmth, humor, quiet strength, and creative attitudes toward problem solving remain at the core of my being. I wish he could have been here to read this work. My mother, the strongest of women in her own way, taught me the importance of surviving life's 'daily slings' with grit and fortitude, fighting the good fight, and ever going forward. Her spirit and love, even in death, are indefatigable, and she remains an internal force in me forever. She passed quickly and unexpectedly just months prior to this book's seeing the light of day.

Finally, the richest joy is my being able to express the deep love, respect, and gratitude I have for my soulmate and husband, Dr. Richard Goldwasser—thank you, Richard, for changing the path of my life in more ways than I could ever have dreamed possible with your never-ending love, patience, humor, and devotion.

PART ONE

Upscale Violence

1

Piercing the Veil of Silence

SALLY, A PRETTY, EDUCATED, FORTY-EIGHT-YEAR-OLD HOMEMAKER, had told no one about the violence that existed within her seemingly happy marriage.[1] When I first met her, she was stylishly dressed in a tailored navy pantsuit and white silk blouse, with spectator pumps and handbag to match. Tiny diamond earrings glinted beneath her flowing blond hair. A heavy gold bracelet and a remarkable string of black pearls completed the picture of a woman of substantial means.

But all was not well in Sally's world. Married to Ray, a highly successful businessman, she gave elegant dinner parties only to be brutally beaten afterwards for offering some of her husband's favorite dessert for admiring guests to take home. Known for her culinary skills and ability to entertain graciously, she wryly commented on her husband's post-party attack: "This is not what Martha Stewart would have had in mind."

When I met and interviewed Sally during her divorce, the facade of civility and upper-class life behind which she had been hiding had already begun to crumble. Her blue eyes brimmed with tears as she told me that she had sustained a broken jaw and severe and permanent hearing damage as a result of her husband's rages during twenty years of marriage. A large man, he would throw her to the ground and lie on top of her, screaming obscenities directly into her ear when he was displeased with her—which seemed to be much of the time—and that was just part of her "punishment." At various times during their marriage, he had dragged her by the hair, thrown furniture at her, choked her to within moments of her life, banged her head against the walls and floor, and punched her. With a trembling hand, Sally pulled back her carefully arranged coif to show me a misshapen lower jaw, the remnants of a beating she had sustained several months before. Her sad face was no longer symmetrical.

The physical abuse often followed emotional abuse—tirades and put-downs that left Sally feeling worthless. Ray had had several affairs with other women and had neglected and rejected her and their children. He had humiliated Sally in front of others and consistently blamed her for the violent incidents. "It was always my fault," she explained to me tearfully. "I provoked him. It was because of what I had done. And he never apologized. Never once during all of the abuse did he ever apologize. He never bought me anything to make up for the hurt he caused me. He was never, *ever* remorseful. It was always him trying to maintain control and make it seem as if it was all my fault. And you know, for a long time, I believed him. Somehow I thought it was my fault.

"But once our youngest child left for college," Sally continued, "I was terrified. He kept threatening me. I felt like an animal—like I was being kept in a cage in my own home. 'I'm going to get you,' he kept saying under his breath. 'Now I'm really going to *get* you. And there won't be anyone here to stop me.'"

Yet no one except her children (who had witnessed only a few of the physical and emotional attacks) knew about the abuse until after Sally filed for divorce. Not once had she called the police to report the attacks. Everyone thought that Sally and Ray had a good marriage. But within their large and magnificently appointed home, the site of the fabulous dinner events Sally staged, existed a brutal and life-threatening truth that Sally had kept hidden. It was the jarring finality of her physical losses, which she had to accept when her doctor informed her that the damage to her eardrum and jaw were irreversible, that motivated Sally to get out, get help, and "go public" about the secret torture she had tolerated for far too long.

THE HIDDEN VICTIMS

When we think of love and marriage, we do not think about domestic violence. Moonlight and roses are not supposed to turn into beatings and threats upon one's life. Yet, four million women nationwide are victims of domestic violence per year.[2] Every twelve seconds a woman suffers this sort of abuse at the hands of a husband or lover.[3]

And when we think of domestic violence, we do not think about women of means. Despite occasional sensational news stories of upscale or celebrity women falling prey to a maniacal mate—Tina Turner, for example, or Pamela Anderson—the public overwhelmingly assumes that domestic violence is confined to couples with little education and few resources. And unfortunately most statistics support this belief.

Evidence gathered by domestic violence experts indicates that although domestic abuse is not restricted by social class, there is a higher incidence of it in lower socioeconomic groups.[4] In a 1986 review of all the research on domestic abuse, Michigan psychologist Lewis Okun, author of *Woman Abuse: Facts Replacing Myths*, found that most studies seem to establish a relationship between lower-class status and a greater tendency to report conjugal violence.[5] In his highly cited 1972 book, *The Violent Home*, sociologist Richard J. Gelles, now at the University of Pennsylvania, reported 82 percent of violent husbands were of lower occupational status than their nonviolent male neighbors. His research also disclosed that wife abuse was highest among men with some high school education and then steadily decreased at higher levels of education, with an overall trend showing violent men to be less educated than their non-abusive counterparts.[6]

In a more recent research effort, Gelles and his colleague Murray Straus at the University of New Hampshire found that lower socioeconomic groups are "as expected, more violent. The assault rate of blue-collar husbands is 70 percent greater than the assault rate of the white-collar employed husbands." If the combined income of the couple was $9,000 or less, the rate of assault by husbands on their wives was 368 percent higher than in families with a more adequate income.[7] Lastly, and by dramatic contrast to those figures, percentages gathered in the U.S. Department of Justice's Criminal Statistics Sourcebook suggest that in only 8 percent of reported cases of domestic attacks by a spouse or romantic companion, the income level is greater than $75,000 per year.[8]

These numbers seem convincing, but from my experience they don't tell the whole story. Most of these findings have been based on research on lower-income battered wives. These are the women who call the police and seek refuge in battered women's shelters. But there is a hidden population of wives whose abuse is not studied—women, who for reasons I will make clear, do not report the tirades and tantrums, who refuse to press charges or even call the police despite the broken bones and blackened eyes inflicted on them by the men who purport to love them.

In this book I describe many other women like Sally, women whose suffering has largely gone unheralded and remains misunderstood. Middle and upper-class women—the wives and lovers of successful, even prominent men—have rarely been studied as victims of abuse. Indeed, it is widely believed that such women, usually well-educated with successful careers of their own, have enough money and power to extricate themselves from potentially harmful domestic situations. As a result of this belief, and the surprising fact that these women tend not to report the abuse or opt to sustain many years of mistreatment before they do, their numbers have been largely absent from the research statistics. This absence, I believe, has skewed society's perception of who exactly becomes an "abused wife."

LEARNING THE SECRETS

As a mental health professional with twenty-three years of practice experience and fourteen years of teaching experience, I first encountered domestic abuse among the upper echelons of society in my practice at the University of Chicago Hospital's Department of Outpatient Psychiatry. Many of the women I was treating were doctors' wives, professors' wives, and doctors and professors themselves. Some were married to successful businessmen. They were all highly educated, enjoyed comfortable, even lavish lifestyles, and associated with people who were much like themselves.

These women sought psychotherapy for a range of typical complaints: Some were anxious or depressed; others talked vaguely of "trouble" with their husbands. Many were bored, several complained of self-esteem issues, and some simply said they were "unhappy." But regardless of their diagnoses, I began to discern a common thread in their life stories, a thread that astonished me. Nothing in my training had prepared me for the fact that I would find that more than 50 percent of my patients were enduring emotional and physical abuse at the hands and whims of their powerful and well-educated husbands.[9] Equally disturbing, these women felt it essential to keep silent about their suffering in order "to preserve and protect personal life." This imperative may be found within the makeup of many women in our society.[10] Only with the greatest reluctance did the women I worked with reveal the abuse they had suffered, even within the safe confines of my office.

As time passed, I learned that my experience was not an isolated one. When I lectured on the subject around the country, I discovered that there was tremendous interest in abuse in this population. Hundreds of people were encountering or experiencing violence in upscale marriages but did not quite know how to understand it, categorize it, or deal with it.

When I spoke to professional groups, therapists would crowd around the lectern afterward to tell me that they, too, were seeing domestic abuse in their client populations but didn't realize the breadth of its occurrence. They were unsure how to proceed, and complained that the existing literature didn't seem to fit the patients they were treating. Perhaps even more surprising, just as many would approach me privately following a lecture and in a whisper tell me about their own experiences. They wondered what help might be available and whether their predicaments were unique or similar to those of patients I had treated.

THE CONTROVERSY

It seemed clear to me that I had identified a population that was crying out to be served. Yet at the same time my news was greeted with antagonism and opposition at these very same professional meetings. Many audience members would challenge and confront me. "Why are these women any different from other abused women of lesser educational levels and financial statuses?" they would demand. I was surprised by their hostile tone, betraying both anger and ambivalence at the prospect of learning more about abuse among the educated well-to-do.

At an international conference, a female social worker staged a vitriolic argument with me during my lecture. She kept raising her hand and interrupting explosively with comments such as: "But why should we give *these women* special favors? They aren't any better! They don't deserve even *more* privileges than they already have! The women *I* work with don't have roofs over their heads . . . what have *your* women got to complain about?"

Before I could answer, another social worker in the audience meekly raised her hand and responded for me. She turned to the first woman and said, "I was in a very wealthy marriage. And my doctor-husband battered me constantly. I was ashamed and embarrassed. As a mental health professional, I felt I should have known better. I felt I should be able to fix it myself. And I was sure this wasn't happening to anyone I knew. I felt frightened, depressed, and alone. In fact, because of my reputation in the community as well as my husband's position, I really had nowhere to go for help. I actually had less access to help than women less privileged. I'm grateful that someone is finally bringing this problem to light."

Why did the first social worker have such an extreme response to my talk? Why was one part of my audience responding with relief but another with resistance and consternation? I believe these strong responses reflect not only envy of those with wealth but also the controversial nature of exposing abuse among the educated and upper-income segments of our society. It flies in the face of the widely held myth that abuse doesn't happen to "people like us"— and this threatens a status quo and comfort zone that many of us choose to live in.

The combination of strong responses from my audiences, my increased awareness of abuse among my middle- and upper-income patients, and the sudden emergence in the media of high-profile cases of domestic violence led me to believe I was onto something that begged for in-depth exploration. News of domestic abuse in the lives of celebrities like Darryl Hannah and Melissa Rivers began to surface in the early 1990s. I embarked on an intensive course of study. By the time I was well into my research, the apparent domestic abuse of Nicole Brown Simpson by her then-husband, O. J. Simpson, so graphically explored and widely reported during his 1995 trial for her murder, placed conjugal abuse among the upper classes squarely in the public spotlight.

HOW THE CONSPIRACY OF SILENCE IS REINFORCED

Why was this group of battered women so under-represented in the social work and psychological literature? One significant reason is that these women are reluctant to seek help. They buy into the myth that domestic violence afflicts only the underprivileged. The myth becomes a type of institutionalized oppression for the upscale. If a culture's tribal rules deny a phenomenon, then it is truly bound to silence. This veil of silence imbues battered upscale women with self-blame and shame—"I must be the only person like me who is going through this"—further reinforcing their sense of desperate isolation. Also contributing to the problem is the well-documented observation that the upper-middle classes are taught that it is inappropriate to involve the police in "personal problems." A New York City suburban field study concluded that "spouse assault by wealthy and powerful men rarely leads to police intervention."[11] The same study remarked that in more prosperous neighborhoods, spacious homes and large lots made it unlikely that neighbors or friends would learn about and report the abuse. Without such legal reports, the number of abused well-to-do women has gone unnoticed.

The man of means has more resources to protect his rights, his privacy, and his "castle." Expansive living quarters are not merely luxurious; they also make for an insulated existence, affording more privacy for engaging in physical and emotional tyranny. And on the rare occasion when the battered wife involves the police or other outside authorities, the upscale husband can retain skilled legal representation to defend his actions with little retribution or fanfare.

The problem is further compounded by society's response. In case after case that I encountered, both in my private practice and while conducting research, when these women do seek assistance from the police, in the courts, from therapists, and even from counselors in women's shelters, they tend to be rejected by the very systems designed to help battered women.

Take Sherry, a thirty-four-year-old attorney who was in the throes of an abusive relationship from which she was trying to extricate herself. She was too embarrassed to tell any of her friends about her husband's mental torment, so she sought help through a Chicago crisis center for abused women that offered counseling and legal referrals to women of all economic ranks. She chose not to seek a private therapist because she thought that professionals who specifically deal with domestic violence might better serve her. When the intake worker heard her story on the phone and assessed her social situation (that is, she had a home, friends, and was well paid), she told Sherry that she would be put on a waiting list to see a counselor. Understanding the crisis center's need to triage and provide help first to those women in the most immediate danger, Sherry waited.

But over several weeks her situation worsened. Sherry called the center again, wondering when she would be able to talk with someone. The next worker she spoke to treated her rudely. "Everyone has to wait," this worker snapped at Sherry before she hung up. Sherry called again a week later, requesting the original worker, and politely though firmly inquired how long the expected wait would be before she could see a counselor. In this phone call, she was curtly told that the staff workers were advised specifically not to speak with her on the phone anymore (for no stated or apparent reason) but to just inform her that she would be called when her name came up on the list.

This was devastating. Sherry was shocked and felt ostracized for no good reason. She wondered if she had demanded too much (she had *not*) and felt utterly shamed and alone. She even questioned whether her desire to get help was warranted, in light of how she had so readily been ignored and rebuffed by an agency that purported to help abused women. Was her situation less real or serious? As of this writing, it has been more than four years since Sherry's initial call to that center, and an intake counselor has yet to contact her.

The fact is, upscale abused wives are treated differently from other women. Their complaints may be taken lightly—after all, these women do have roofs over their heads and usually pretty nice ones at that. It is not uncommon for a policeman encountering an expensively dressed woman in her well-appointed home to assume that she has the resources to take care of herself— even though her husband may control all of the credit cards and bank accounts and may have brainwashed her into believing that she and their children would not survive in the world without him.

One woman I worked with, Jennifer, a successful psychotherapist married to a Harvard graduate attorney, told me of her encounter with the police that had occurred the day after an especially brutal fight with her husband. She had requested police protection when she went back to their penthouse apartment to retrieve some of her belongings. During the long elevator ride with two officers, one of them, observing the scars on her face and her sprained arm, said, "So, honey, with a rich guy like yours, what did you do to get him *this* mad at you?"

Before Jennifer could gather her thoughts to reply, the other officer said, in what he obviously meant to be a supportive tone, "Well, at least he didn't *kill* you." Such joviality in response to an upscale battered woman's crisis is merely one type of re-victimization that she may encounter from professionals.

Alternatively, her injuries may be ignored or overlooked by professionals who are unaware of domestic abuse among the upscale or are afraid to intervene in such cases. Some professionals fear reprisal for being too intrusive from their patients and the community in which they practice. One study found that in 40 percent of the cases where physicians interacted with battered women in an emergency room setting, the physicians made no response to the abuse.[12] In another emergency department that had established a protocol for domestic violence, physicians failed to give any referral or follow-up for abuse in 92 percent of the domestic violence cases.[13] And while these studies did not specifically track any particular income groups, imagine what the statistics would be if the focus were solely on women of means. Perhaps there would be even fewer referrals and responses!

Joan, a physician I know, went alone to the emergency room of a major Chicago teaching hospital late on a Saturday night after an intense fight with her husband. Enraged with her for making plans to visit her mother on the weekend, Joan's husband smashed some of her prized glass sculptures against a wall, and one of the larger pieces became deeply embedded in her arm. As the plastic surgery resident removed the glass and stitched up Joan's arm, he never once inquired beyond the story she told him: "I was lifting a glass table top and it dropped." Although her face was tear-stained and she was visibly shaken, Joan was well dressed and a professional. No one in the ER made any additional inquiry, despite the telltale signs of potential abuse. Nor was she given any domestic abuse referral numbers, even as a precaution.

Some months later, I asked the director of this ER about the handling of spousal abuse in general terms. He said, "Sometimes the ER staff assumes that if it's a case of domestic violence, a woman will volunteer that information.

And, you know, we walk a thin line. We don't want to offend someone who is professional by asking."

What does the emergency room staff fear? Are they overly concerned about being invasive and offensive as the ER chief suggests? Do they fear litigation on the part of the abused woman if they inquire about violence in her home? Or do these professionals simply buy into the myth that abuse doesn't happen to "people like us"? Indeed, some professionals are unwilling to accept the reality of violent behavior among people of their own social class, or they wrongly assume that because of her material advantages the upscale abused woman needs little help in extricating herself from or at least coping with an abusive situation. They readily believe the facile explanations about bruises and injuries when an upscale battered wife offers them.

Where do these attitudes ultimately leave the upscale abused woman who is already reluctant to report abuse and involve others? Sadly, most likely in worse straits. Indeed, the professionals the woman turns to for assistance can actually contribute to the problem and deal a final blow. By taking the woman's abuse lightly and even blaming her for it, they make her feel ashamed and responsible for her abuser's behaviors. By ignoring or overlooking that behavior, or minimizing the potential for dangerous consequences, they effectively deny help to her. This problem was clearly presented in a poignant article in the *Journal of the American Medical Association* written by a medical resident whose physician husband subjected her to domestic violence. In this article the young woman pleaded for other physicians and helping professionals to educate themselves about domestic violence and to "realize that your actions, or lack of action, can have a huge impact on [the battered woman's] life. Be aware that by not asking whether domestic abuse is the cause of your patient's injuries, you will be closing your eyes to the fact that this woman will most likely return home, only to be beaten again . . . and again."[14]

The academic community is hardly better. When I was discussing my dissertation topic during a job interview for an assistant professor position at a graduate school of social work, the dean of that institution dismissed me. "This is not social work," the dean retorted crisply. "We deal with the poor, the oppressed, and the needy. You won't find a place for the work you are pursuing." I responded by saying that I thought "we" (social workers as well as the culture as a whole) should redefine what "need" and "oppression" were, and that lack of resources cannot always be measured economically.

I soon learned that the dean's opinion was widespread in the helping fields. The pervasiveness of this belief defines, in part, how the upscale abused woman's entrapment is markedly different from that of her lower-income counterparts. Professional and societal disavowal of her difficulties and tragedies makes her feel even more immeasurably trapped. While the lower-income battered woman struggles with similar issues, at least professionals more readily believe her when she finally seeks assistance and direct her to shelters, agencies, and resources. In contrast, when the upscale abused woman's condition is unacknowledged, no referrals are made, and assistance is denied. This is only one way in which the affluent woman's course is different. As you will see, her journey is marked by unique pathways, challenges, and turning points.

MY RESEARCH

In 1991, after leaving the University of Chicago's Department of Psychiatry to pursue teaching and full-time private practice, I continued to see more and more upscale women who shared similar stories of domestic violence. Over the past two decades, I have talked with hundreds of such women. The one fundamental element they had in common was the fact that they were living in emotionally or physically abusive marriages—*and they all felt internal and external pressures to keep quiet about it.* As one woman told me, "My in-laws keep reminding me how lucky I am to have such a good provider for a husband. My lifestyle is the envy of my friends. Who would believe me if I said I was abused? Who could I tell who would not think I was demanding too much? And what would my children and I stand to lose if I betrayed my husband and talked about it?"

In my efforts to learn more about the pattern unfolding before me, I read the sociological and clinical literature on domestic abuse. In the past twenty-five years, more than five hundred scientific papers, articles, and books have been published on this subject,[15] but I found fewer than a dozen about this particular group of highly educated, upper-income abused wives.[16] Finding this gap in the literature, I decided to research the population myself. I pursued a doctoral education at the same time, as it gave me the support of academic mentors as well as the rigorous structure that research requires. My dissertation study addressed the "lived experience" of abused wives of upper socioeconomic status—what they went through as unique individuals. Through their personal narratives, I was able to gain insight into their world. Rather than focusing on statistics, I immersed myself in the richness of their individual stories, which opened the door to their previously unreported and unstudied dramas.

In seeking my research sample, I talked to lawyers, physicians, clergy, and other therapists to discover if they were observing what I was. Many were. When I invited them to help me gather women for my study, they said that asking women directly about abuse in their lives was a "delicate" issue; it was difficult to bring up. I worried about finding women to participate. If these professionals were reluctant to help, where would I seek out my research subjects? Was I looking for unicorns? Would well-to-do battered wives reveal their secrets to me? I decided I might have a better chance of getting women to talk with me if they were already out of their situations, or in the process of ending their abusive relationships, rather than in the confused state of "living in the thick of it."[17]

Talking about the issue with my friends and colleagues evoked powerful reactions once more. It was both surprising and affirming to hear people I had known for years admit to abuse in their former marriages and relationships. Professional women, stars at Fortune 500 companies, professors, doctors, psychotherapists, publishers, lawyers—each shared a personal story when I told them about the phenomenon I was seeing. In fact, once I broached the topic, many were eager to talk to me about it. They had never shared their stories with anyone before and found satisfaction in finally putting words to their experiences. Ultimately, my networking efforts paid off. Between 1996 and 1998, screening at least fifty prospective study participants, I interviewed and extensively analyzed the narratives of fourteen candidates.[18] The women who participated in my study ranged in age from twenty-four to sixty-two years old. They were well educated, with an average minimum of a bachelor's degree and 1.5 years of graduate school education.

As these women talked about their relationships, it became clear that they wanted desperately to understand what had caused the abuse to occur; to make sense of a loving relationship that had gone sour; to figure out what could have been done to prevent the abuse; to find out if such abuse happens to others like them; and to help women in similar situations who were suffering in silence.

A NEW LENS

This book draws on my years of experience in a therapy practice devoted to relationships and women's issues, as well as on the results of my research. It provides a new lens through which to view the lived experience of domestic abuse. One of my major discoveries is that the upscale abused woman actually makes *choices* along this path—choices that are pivotal in the unfolding of her marriage and her participation in it. While these choices might have led her further down the path toward injury and despair, they were the very best choices she could make at the time, given the information she had and the social milieu in which she lived. This perspective gives rise to an entirely new way of assessing and dealing with violence and sheds new light on why and how women stay in these relationships.[19]

Recognizing these paths, patterns, and coping strategies can help women who are on the brink of entering an abusive relationship and want to protect themselves from future abuse, women who are seeking a way out of an abusive marriage, and women who want insight and validation about the experience from which they have extricated themselves. In addition, I offer a much-needed corrective to the broadly held and pernicious misconception that spousal abuse doesn't happen to "people like us." I suggest theories as to why our society colludes with this myth. By exploring domestic violence from the perspective of the upscale abused woman and demonstrating that it *does* exist among this population, I also hope to change the commonly accepted face of domestic abuse and make sense of the issues and mysterious bonds that keep an upscale abused woman in a destructive relationship.[20]

I also focus on the revictimization of upscale abused wives when they seek help. Far too many women internalize the reactions of legal, medical, or mental health professionals by doubting their own perceptions, and they wind up either blaming themselves or finding their own solutions, unsupported, in an emotional vacuum. Their fears of reporting the abuse are legitimized when putatively helping professionals do not respond to any of their pleas for help.

I challenge the accepted belief that the patterns gleaned from studying lower-income populations apply to all women.[21] The theories we depend upon to understand and treat abused wives do not suit all classes of women equally well.[22] Consider these traditional theories of domestic abuse:

- *Learned helplessness* suggests that abused women learn to become helpless under abusive conditions; they are powerless to extricate themselves from such relationships and/or unable to make adaptive choices.
- *The cycle of violence* describes a pattern that includes a contrition or honeymoon phase. The abusive husband becomes contrite and apologetic after a violent episode, making concerted efforts to get back in his wife's good graces.
- *Traumatic bonding* attempts to explain the inexplicable bond that is formed between a woman and her abusive partner.

- *The theory of past reenactments* posits that women in abusive relationships are reliving unconscious feelings from early childhood scenarios.

My research results and experience with patients do not conform to these concepts. I have found that the upscale abused wife is not a victim of learned helplessness. Rather, she makes specific decisions along the path to be involved in the abusive marriage, including silent strategizing as she chooses to stay or leave the marriage. Nor does the upscale abused wife experience the classic cycle of violence, replete with the honeymoon stage, in which the husband courts his wife to seek her forgiveness. As in the case of Sally and Ray, the man of means actually does little to seek his wife's forgiveness after a violent episode.

Further, the upscale abused wife voices more attachment to her *lifestyle* than the traumatic bonding with her abusive mate. And very few of the abused women I have met over the years experienced abuse in their childhoods or witnessed it between their parents. In fact, it is this *lack* of experience with violence, rage, and abuse that makes this woman even more overwhelmed and unclear about how to cope with something so alien to her and the people in her universe.

In Chapter 7, I offer some typical profiles of the upscale abusive husband.[23] In my study, the majority of the husbands expected their wives to be obedient and to fit into a certain wifely template of looks, behavior, and style "appropriate" to the lifestyle the man was leading. These men felt entitled to their tempers and outbursts in exchange for the financial support and material accoutrements they were providing—even in cases where the women were also high-earning professionals themselves. In some cases, the men repeatedly impressed upon their wives that they were "bought and paid for."

And how do the children figure into the equation? In Chapter 8, I look at the complex relationship between a battered upscale woman and her children. On the one hand, her concerns for their future may keep her in an intolerable relationship, on the other, any threats to their well-being is what ultimately pushes her toward leaving her abusive mate. I speculate about how the woman's silent style of coping and the value she places on maintaining the upscale home life affects her perceptive youngsters.

In Chapter 9, I explore effective therapeutic interventions for women who find themselves in an abusive situation. Chapter 10 examines how help can sometimes hurt, especially within the therapeutic, medical, and legal systems. This chapter also includes recommendations for what to do if someone you know is an upscale abused woman. In Chapter 11, I cover life after the upscale abusive marriage.

A unique aspect of this book is the *inclusionary* dimension of targeting battered women of means. This focus is not a claim that this population needs special attention. Rather, it is an attempt at specifically *including* upscale wives who have been overlooked in the larger group of abused women. All women are entitled to help in dealing with domestic violence. None should be seen as deserving of "special" treatment.

The women I have had the privilege of interviewing and working with were bright, educated, and personable. They approached their participation in this study with great earnestness and determination. They had suffered in silence for many years, and ultimately it was the piercing of the veil of silence that finally set them free. They wanted their stories to be heard, and they wanted to help other women in similar straits. This book is the result of their honest and generous involvement.

2

"This Doesn't Happen to People Like Us . . . "

M Y HUSBAND, HE WAS ALWAYS TELLING ME what he'd like to do to me," Janice, a willowy thirty-seven year old marketing consultant, confided to me during our interview, "how he was going to stab me or shoot me or put his hands up inside me and tear out my organs and laugh while he watched me bleed to death. . . . In the last four months of our marriage, he increased the level of emotional abuse to the point that I couldn't take it anymore. On the outside, he was being the doting little husband, buying me a diamond and ruby necklace and a flashy new BMW, but when his rage was triggered, he always talked about how violently he was going to kill me."

Janice's revelation, disturbing as it was, troubled me even more for her seeming inability to face her life-threatening situation squarely. "At no time," I asked her, "did it cross your mind to seek professional help specifically for abused women?"

"Oh no," she replied quietly, shaking her head and then picking at a small piece of lint on her finely tailored skirt. "I didn't think that was for me. I wasn't going to the hospital. I wasn't having broken bones. It wasn't like someone you see on TV. I wasn't *hurt* enough.

"Look," she said with a shrug, finally meeting my gaze with her soft brown eyes. "I believed in my marriage. I really loved this guy. And this sort of thing didn't happen in my family. Nobody treated a woman like that. You know, it just doesn't happen to college-educated, upper-middle-class people. You don't call your mom and dad and tell them that your husband just *hit* you. It was a shameful thing. . . . No, I'm *not* a battered wife," she said resolutely. This even though her husband, in addition to the emotional abuse, had at various times in their twelve-year marriage smacked her face, choked her, and backhanded her across a room. "What happened to me, it doesn't have a name."

"Not yet!" I responded.

Indeed, in the course of my research, I have coined the term *upscale violence* to characterize exactly what happened to Janice, Sally, and other women who find themselves in this difficult situation. And I believe that our society's lack of imagery and terminology to describe spousal abuse in its upper socioeconomic echelons has helped reinforce the isolation that many of these women feel. Clearly, many affluent abused wives, like Janice, don't identify with the media-generated portrait of the "battered woman." And since they don't have words or images to put to their experience, they come to perceive that their torment lacks validity—as if it never really happened, or it wasn't all that bad, or it wasn't really "abusive." This diminishment, in turn, feeds their ability to compartmentalize the experience—until the mistreatment spirals out of control and reaches wildly dangerous levels that they are no longer able to keep secret or deny.

As Kathleen, a forty-three-year-old physical therapist, told me in depicting the first of many violent episodes with her real estate tycoon husband, "It was just a little punch—like a hit or a push. I was denying it more than he was. I thought, 'I'm too intelligent to be abused.' I didn't want to be that person who was being hit. It was too humiliating. I'm a pregnant woman who is being hit. *How* can somebody *do* that?"

What did Kathleen mean when she said she was "too intelligent"? I asked her, and she replied, "Well, people who are abused are low-income and stupid. I've seen the shows, and domestic violence is when the guy points a gun in your mouth. He's got tattoos on his body, he's in an undershirt, he's drinking beer, and he's whamming you around the house. That's my idea of domestic abuse. As far as I was concerned, what I was going through at that point in my marriage was a *communication* problem, not abuse." According to Kathleen's mindset, "a kick here, a punch there, a shove into the wall, and Stuart throwing the remote control at me on a regular basis" did not constitute abuse.

I asked Kathleen whether she thought it would have made it easier for her to identify what was happening in her relationship and to act on it if there had been an expression like *upscale violence* in the culture. She replied without hesitation and nodded ruefully: "Absolutely, absolutely."

WHAT IS UPSCALE VIOLENCE?

In my research, I applied the term *upscale violence* to married women who endured multiple or continued episodes of emotional and/or physical abuse within the marriage and also met at least three of following criteria:

- *Income:* A combined marital income of at least $100,000 per year.
- *Residence:* Marital residence in a neighborhood ranked in the top 25 percent of its statewide area according to U.S. Census Bureau data; or, in some cases, neighborhoods highly ranked according to commonly held reputation.
- *Class Status:* A self-perception of being upper-middle-class or upper-class.
- *Education:* A minimum of a bachelor's degree.

As I've noted, women who fit these criteria fall between the cracks when it comes to the filing of police reports, the computation of statistics, and the pursuit of research studies on domestic violence. My investigation focused on this group in the hope of bringing to light the shadowy, mostly hidden spousal abuse in the upscale population. Using a qualitative perspective, I sought to understand exactly what the experience of being an upscale abused wife feels like.[1] That is, I examined these women's experiences and aspects of their internal worlds of thoughts, images, and emotions, all which create a richer view than simply compiling statistics.

As I pursued my analysis, many questions became apparent. I wanted to know:

- What personality traits do these women have in common?
- What is similar in their childhood and marital experiences?
- How do these traits and experiences, as conveyed in their stories, differ from what we already know about the dynamics of domestic abuse among other socioeconomic groups?
- How would a woman know if she were involved in and suffering from upscale violence?
- Is there something about the inner landscape of these women that is different from that of affluent women who are not abused?
- Why would women with "so much going for them" stay in such terrible circumstances?

While upscale women may not be the most disenfranchised sector of society, they are nonetheless people with specific experiences and needs. I only began learning about those experiences and needs when I met Julia and her husband, Marc.

JULIA'S STORY

Julia was a thirty-nine-year-old painter and teacher (with several advanced degrees) and mother of four when she first came to see me fifteen years ago. She felt inexplicably sad and believed that things were "not going smoothly" with her husband. She was intelligent and attractive, small yet solid, with long dark curls that framed her classic features. Julia's expression was colorfully intense, but when she talked about painful aspects of her marriage, it darkened dramatically with sadness and fear as if a storm cloud had passed across the face of the sun.

An ambitious woman, Julia was fluent in five languages. She was actively involved in raising her small children, while at the same time producing an entire body of work for a one-woman show that traveled throughout Europe and parts of the United States. Her budding success in the art world, as well as her skill as a mother, was unquestionable. But when it came to her relationship with her husband, she felt she was a failure.

Marc was a professor in the sociology department at a local university. He was well published and greatly admired and respected by his colleagues. Marc was a native of Germany, and Julia came from Italy. They had met while both were in graduate school in Massachusetts. Their courtship, at a time when Julia was feeling particularly homesick, was swift and romantic. Marc was handsome and brilliant, and they had fun together. In addition to their many shared interests, Marc's European background gave Julia a sense of familiarity with him and quenched her yearnings for her family in Italy.

They had one breakup during their courtship, which Marc had incisively initiated. He was fiercely devoted to his work and spent long hours and weekends at the university. Julia, lonely, wanted to have more time with him. She felt a strong bond, heightened in part by their similar backgrounds, and she had little interest in pursuing relationships with other men who might have been more attentive. She tried to feel satisfied with their sporadic times together, but inevitably she wanted more. In various ways Julia would entreat Marc to participate in activities with her, but he would be consistently unavailable or irritated by her requests. This theme of discord persisted throughout their marriage.

After several months of dating, Marc angrily and abruptly ended their re-lationship, blaming Julia for being unsympathetic toward his work. It was not an impassive breakup. The arrogance and cruelty of Marc's words stung her like sharp slaps in the face. "I could never be with a woman who is so selfish and withholding," he announced coldly. "And you're not as great an artist as you think you are. Besides, there are many other women out there who would appreciate my talents and ambition and would be more supportive of my ca-reer." Julia was crushed. She berated herself for not being the kind of woman Marc wanted.

Several weeks passed, but Julia couldn't tolerate the separation. She con-tacted Marc and pleaded with him to try again. "I care about you and your ca-reer. I promise I'll be more supportive and encouraging," she sobbed on the phone. She convinced Marc to spend the day with her. It was one of the days in their relationship that she fondly remembers. "We passed the day drinking espresso, walking through the park, going to stores and trying on hats, and just being silly. We laughed and laughed, more than we ever did or have since. Shortly after that, we got engaged and married."

Although Julia was able to win Marc back, a pattern had been established. Marc knew he could be cruel to her and that in response she would double her efforts to please him and make the relationship work. She neither ac-knowledged nor comprehended that the way Marc had ended their relation-ship was indicative of his ability to be mean, rejecting, and callous.

I met Julia after she and Marc had been married for eight years. I had no sense of any physical or emotional abusiveness in their relationship. Julia and I worked together for many months exploring the impact of the marriage on her moods and the ways it might mirror relationship patterns from her past. Marc came in for a few sessions, and we discussed improving communication skills and developing ways the couple could be more demonstrative of sup-port and love. Nothing that this couple told me about their lives together nor any of their behaviors in my office suggested that I should ask about abuse or violence. They appeared to be a well-matched pair, with typical complaints about feeling unattended to and unloved within a relationship that existed alongside very busy individual daily lives.

Over time there was some improvement in Julia's moods as well as in the marriage. Both spouses made efforts to compromise and mend the cracks. Marc agreed to spend more time at home, and they began to eat at least two dinners together as a family each week. Julia disciplined herself not to com-plain when Marc worked long hours. Marc made efforts to call her when he knew he would be late at work. They went out on dates twice a month. Their married life was becoming acceptable, as each saw that the other was making efforts to show affection and improve the situation.

But this positive interlude did not last. Julia unexpectedly became pregnant with their fourth child. During the course of her pregnancy she stopped treatment for a while, but then returned. This time she slowly revealed the abuse and violence that had been taking place within her marriage since they had wed. She told me in an emotionless voice that Marc bolted her and the children inside their house, that he ripped the phones out of the wall so she couldn't call for help. It was these episodes, I later learned, so frightening to her and her children, that had brought her to my office in the first place.

Julia went into great detail about how Marc would beat her when he was disappointed in her actions toward him. At times she seemed detached from her narrative, as if she were speaking about some other family, her voice flat as she revealed events that were utterly horrifying. At other times tears welled in her eyes as she recalled how he would roughly force her to have sex. When he was angry, he would kick her in the vaginal area so hard that she feared she might miscarry. She thought Marc was angry that she wanted to keep the baby they hadn't planned on. He didn't believe in abortion and was unhappy about having another child.

Whatever his motivation, I was surprised to learn all this and quite taken aback. I imagined what it must have been like in her home as she was locked inside with her children and no phone. I feared for their safety. I visualized the house and wondered what kind of person could conceive of putting locks on the outside. As Julia's story was sinking in, I was stunned and perplexed. I asked myself, "Why did I never even think to ask about domestic abuse? How did this get by me?" The answer: Julia never alluded to it, and she and her husband seemed attractive and intelligent. They were educated, well spoken, and highly regarded—people who could have been friends had they walked through a different door when we met.

I handed her some tissues. When she stopped crying, I said, "It sounds absolutely horrific." I felt protective of her and was revolted by her husband's actions. I probed a bit further. "What did you do? How did you get out?" She explained that she cried for about twenty minutes and then went to play with her children so they wouldn't detect that something bad was happening. She then returned to her studio to paint and waited until Marc got home to be released. In the future, unbeknownst to him, she kept a cell phone with her and always left a ground floor window ajar.

"Why had you never told me any of this before?" I asked.

"I had considered telling you at first," she replied, " but I felt ashamed and decided to keep it to myself. I kept thinking it would pass. Besides, I really thought I had instigated the abuse."

"This is a lot to have kept all to yourself," I said.

"I know—but it was tolerable until he started kicking me while I was pregnant."

Julia covered up the abuse by telling herself that "the marriage was just not going smoothly." She justified his bad behavior by blaming herself for being an inadequate wife, which echoed Marc's complaints.

At first, abused women typically deny the severity and even the existence of abuse within their marriages, and often blame themselves for their mate's abusive actions. But one of the hallmarks of upscale violence is the great pains to which these battered wives will go to hide it. My lower-income patients have come right out and said that their husband's abuse was why they had come to see me seeking help. Rarely do abused wives from affluent homes give this as their reason for coming to therapy.

The majority of upscale violence is emotional rather than physical, but it is often the physical aspect that brings the woman to treatment (even though, paradoxically, she won't speak about it). By comparison, in research studies on reported cases of wife abuse among lower-income families, the physical assault tends to be more prominent and more readily identifiable.

The violence in Julia's marriage grew insidiously. It started with emotional disparagement. Marc was sporadically sullen, indifferent, distant, disdainful, and angry. His coldness and abrupt temper escalated over the years to include episodes of physical violence. Like most of the battered upscale women I've met, Julia insisted that the effects of the emotional onslaught were far worse and longer lasting than any physical assaults she had endured. Indeed, previous research on domestic violence reports that emotional violation can be just as destructive and even more pernicious than physical abuse.[2]

Julia returned to me for help when Marc's violence threatened her children's well-being, but even then she struggled against revealing the violence in her marriage. Marc's last atrocity—kicking her in the groin while she was pregnant and jeopardizing the health of their unborn baby—was the reason she decided to admit what seemed unthinkable: she was a battered wife.

Julia was sure that her friends wouldn't believe her. She kept making excuses for her husband's emotional assaults, convincing herself that they "weren't that serious." She knew that colleagues and friends saw Marc as sensible, reliable, affable, and honest, and saw Julia as the sensitive and emotional "artiste." When she tried to confide to friends about the fights she and Marc had, they dismissed them as a product of Julia's intense temperament, which was more apparent than Marc's temper.

Julia's fears of coming forward about the violence were based on anticipated as well as actual responses from friends and acquaintances. I also recognized Julia's introverted and moody side, but I knew she wasn't capable of inciting her husband to kick, choke, and lock her in her home like a caged animal. Besides, considering how she was being treated, it was not surprising that she seemed moody, sensitive, even depressed. More important, nothing any woman could do could justify such behavior.

When Julia told her parents about the fights, they urged her to try harder to make the marriage work. She once broached the subject with the minister at her church. He lectured her about the sacredness of the bonds of marriage. "As a good wife and a good Christian," he told her kindly while patting her hand, "you should bring more love, patience, and understanding to your relationship with your husband." Again and again, Julia could garner no validation or support from significant people around her. And when she finally came to therapy, I "helped" her sort out her emotions within the marital situation and worked on facilitating the couple's improving their communication skills. Yet I, like her parents, friends, and minister, had missed the point.

Julia's story was my introduction to upscale violence, and it marked the beginning of my journey to unveil the dynamics of domestic abuse in this population. I, too, had to acknowledge that marital abuse happens to "people like us." And as I treated and spoke with increasing numbers of women, I began learning more about the pattern of upscale violence. These women's stories coalesced into common themes that created a larger picture of what happens in the life of the upscale abused wife.

COMMON THREADS

The experiences of affluent abused women are marked by features and themes unique to their circumstances. In fact, they can explain some of the dynamics that lie behind the intense secrecy surrounding the abuse.

Isolation and the Fear of Being Disbelieved

"I didn't want to tell anyone about what was going on in my house," one woman confessed to me. "They all thought I was living this Cinderella life, and they just wouldn't believe it." Isolation is one of the most conspicuous predicaments in which abused affluent women find themselves, and this sense of utter aloneness can be traced, ironically, to their social milieu. When a woman meets her friends at the country club or a business or professional event, or even when she lunches with colleagues or clients, there is little opportunity for these kinds of disturbing and intimate confidences.

Even though the affluent wife next door might also be enduring humiliation, beatings, and worse, her silence about the abuse makes it seem to the sufferer that hers is a unique experience. Thus, the woman feels unspoken pressure from those around her to keep private about what is happening to her. As one woman said to me, "I never told anyone. I isolated myself from *everybody*. And at my job, it was easy to keep a secret. I mean, I compartmentalized!"

Almost all the women I worked with stated that their silence was due to the fear that others would doubt their stories because "marital abuse doesn't happen . . . to people like us . . . with education . . . in this neighborhood." In my study, every woman expressed some version of this sentiment:

- Lynne, a law student, said, "It's a class thing. . . . I didn't know anybody that this happened to. I had kind of an elitist belief that it didn't happen to women like me—you know, professional women living on the North Shore. It happens to a *client*, but it doesn't happen to us. I knew about clients who had been abused. A couple of them were homeless; a couple were on public aid. But I didn't know any women in my situation who were emotionally abused."
- Amy, a successful accountant, explained her reason for keeping silent: "It just was unacceptable. And I wouldn't want the neighbors to know. I wouldn't want our friends to know. The stigma associated with it was awful. I thought that lower socioeconomic classes would accept physical violence. I didn't think anyone I knew was ever going through anything like this. I thought I was clearly the only person on earth who was experiencing this in our circle of friends. It doesn't happen here."

It is difficult for any woman to admit that her husband abuses her, but women with a lower income level seem to worry less that people won't believe them. Domestic violence is not unheard of in those communities. For the upscale, other rationales are offered to explain the complaints. When one woman lamented to her mother-in-law that her husband was beating her, the mother-in-law responded, "Well, maybe it's because of his job pressure. Are you sure my son *hit* you?" And Julia's friends were quick to attribute her problems with Marc to her temperament, in effect discrediting and undermining her reports about his unbridled rages.

Embarrassment and Shame

Many of the women with whom I have spoken expressed a deep sense of humiliation about having been abused. Living a life perceived to be foreign to the experience of one's peers typically gives rise to emotions like shame. Sally told me, "I was embarrassed by it. When he would hit me, I would become embarrassed. I would be humiliated." Another woman, Alice, strongly asserted, "No, you're married, for better or for worse. You can't tell anybody, and the reason you can't tell anybody is: it's *embarrassing*. It's a very shameful thing." And Jennifer said, "I didn't want anyone to know that about me; I didn't want them to think that of me. I wanted them to think, 'She's wonderfully happy; she's wonderfully successful; she's a good wife.'"

Shame revolves around several issues. Some of the women had been high achievers in other aspects of their lives, but ironically these very strengths and competencies influenced their decisions to keep silent about and remain in their abusive marriages. A number of the women were familiar with achievement, goal attainment, and success throughout their lifetimes and were well able to create opportunities in their professional worlds. They worked in large corporations, major law firms, highly ranked universities. They were published, interviewed, and quoted in the media. Julia was the focus of an international art show, Lynne had made law review, and Jennifer was a consulting psychologist for several television shows. For these successful women, an abusive marriage simply did not fit in.

These women ignored their inner voice that questioned whether it was their husbands who were actually at fault. Many came to swallow whole their spouse's diatribes—that they were unworthy wives and the cause of the distress in the marriage. Jennifer wanted to be seen as a "good wife," as if she had been brainwashed into believing that she wasn't. Another woman, who had scratched her husband's arms while fighting off his attack, was mortified by her own defensive actions. "The next day, he took off his shirt and showed me the marks," she told me, sobbing. "He said, 'See. You're the one who's violent.' And then he left. At that point, I was so ashamed he had those scratch marks. I thought he was right. I was violent, and I couldn't tell anybody what happened."

These battered women believe that revealing or discussing the abuse is in effect an admission of failure. Carol, who her whole life had been described as an all-American girl and an overachiever, wondered whether "other successful women had a thread of fear of failure. I had pretty much succeeded at anything I had ever put my mind to, and here's a strong fear of failure at work with this marriage that is supposed to last forever."

While battered wives of all socioeconomic classes wish to rid their marriages of abuse and often view it as a personal failing, the inability to put an end to the violence is publicly judged and criticized unequally among the classes. It seems likely that the women who report domestic violence more frequently have greater opportunities to discuss their problems with others in the same situation—especially in women's shelters or domestic violence court. However, because many in an upscale battered wife's neighborhood may take a dim view of the abuse, she may choose not to seek help or report the incidents. Blaming the victim of upscale abuse marginalizes the problem, maintains the myth, and keeps the observer safely at arm's length from the problem. Thus, the upscale abused wife chooses secrecy and denial rather than face what she perceives as a personal failure, and thereby remains out of touch with others who are experiencing similar abuse.

For well-educated women, the sense of shame can also relate to the notion that they "should have known better" or "should have been smart enough to read the signs." They are afraid of looking foolish, stupid, or ignorant at having "chosen" an abusive husband. Lynne, the law student, explained to me that she was too embarrassed to tell anyone about her husband's first violent episode. "I was ashamed that I had picked somebody who was so. . . you know, so awful," she said with a sigh.

It was as if these women had experienced their husbands' abusiveness and the deterioration of their marriages as personal failures. And that attitude further contributed to their sense of shame, embarrassment, and isolation.

Anticipated and Real Rejection

Upscale abused women also experience the fear of being ostracized and rejected. Many of those I interviewed anticipated (with very real justification) that their friends and family would shun them when they spoke out about their torment. One woman I worked with was married to a minister who beat her regularly. She put off telling anyone about the abuse because she feared that the people who loved and depended on her husband would disbelieve and disdain her. Her worst fears were realized when she finally did talk about the domestic violence in her home. Her community turned on her, loyally supporting her husband through their divorce. This battered wife not only was the bearer of bad news that contradicted the congregation's views of their beloved minister, but she also became a pariah.

Irene, who was married to Carl, a successful entrepreneur, was also ostracized when she spoke out about her marriage. Carl and Irene were high school sweethearts who married in their teens. Carl was the first and only man Irene had ever loved. They had four grown children. When I met her, Irene was in the midst of divorce and was trying to rebuild her life. She expressed overriding and realistic concerns for her safety because of her husband's threats. I could tell she was preoccupied with these fears but at the same time overtaken by melancholy at losing a man she had once treasured.[3] A tall, elegant, graying woman in her late fifties, Irene had fulfilled the role of homemaker and mother that her husband had prescribed for her. She spoke softly and clearly, but an air of sadness pervaded her otherwise friendly and cooperative manner. Weariness seemed to defeat her, and tears dampened her eyes as she revealed to me in one sitting the problems in her former marriage.

Carl's abuse was always of an emotional nature. He lied about his whereabouts, cheated on Irene frequently, and even forbade her from asking him where he was going when he left the house. He was a charismatic and fascinating businessman involved with groundbreaking business deals and negotiations who had intricate political connections in their community. After pulling off a financial coup, he would usually "celebrate" with one of the many women "friends" who made it their business to hang around him.

Irene protested Carl's increasing distance from her and the family. When she would ask where he went, he would become gruff and distant. The more she tried to get close to him or make efforts to address their marital troubles, the more he would insult and degrade her. Occasionally, he "rewarded" her by staying home or taking her and the children on a glamorous vacation. But overall, Irene had settled into a pattern of being the good homemaker and mother, always thinking that Carl would treat her nicely again as soon as the stress from his work receded. Of course, he never did.

Once the children were out of the house, Irene began to stand up to Carl, and became involved in activities on her own. But her increased independence engendered Carl's rage. He began making threats on her life. He would say in total earnest, "You know, if I had you killed"—which he had the means and connections to do—"I would save a lot on divorce fees and alimony."

On one occasion, Irene attended an important business luncheon where Carl was to give a keynote address to hundreds of members of his industry. He took the opportunity to humiliate her in part of his speech. "My wife doesn't like my working out of town," he said, "and whenever she is unhappy she gets in touch with her attorney." He then followed that with a "take my wife—please" joke. Irene was enraged. At the end of her husband's speech, she stood up and, with grace and courage, said: "I gather my husband has a penchant for telling just one side of the story." The audience fell silent, and she left the banquet hall in tears. What was most sobering about this event was that no one in the audience seemed to believe she had a side to tell. They knew Carl as charming, generous, and kind, and some thought she must be going through a severe menopausal phase that caused her to distort the wonderful marriage she probably had with this wealthy, all-around good guy, Carl.

After this event, many of Carl's business acquaintances were cold and disdainful toward Irene. Neighbors and friends who had gotten wind of the story began to pull away from her as well. Irene confessed to me that she felt like a burden to her husband, but now she was also feeling like a disreputable outcast within her community.

Only her grown sons stood by her her. It was they who helped her to break free of her abusive marriage. They reassured her that they believed in her and that they thought their dad had treated her horribly. One son, in a display of anger and support, stopped talking to his father for almost a year. Actions like this not only validated Irene's experience but also gave her the support to act in ways that were self-protective and in her best interest. She got in touch with a high-powered attorney and filed for divorce.

Although Irene was glad to be free, she regretted that she had chosen to keep silent in order to be part of a community that ultimately turned against and shunned her. Yet at the same time she recognized that had she kept quiet about the abuse in her marriage, she would still be an accepted and respected part of that community.

These types of rejection contribute to the unique ways in which upscale wives stay silent. And it is the strong hidden nature of upscale abuse that gives it a different flavor and spirit from domestic abuse among lower-income abused women. The lower-income battered wives I worked with often told me about afternoons spent comparing stories of husbands' abuses while waiting for their children to come home from school. Moreover, the majority of women in domestic violence shelters and related agencies are from lower-income families, and these refuges provide ready venues for discussing the atrocities the women experienced.

By contrast, the upscale woman rarely discloses the abuse to her friends because she fears being rejected and disbelieved. Nor does she typically go to the shelters. She can afford to stay at a hotel or to take a quick get-away trip with her children without revealing her situation. Her financial resources afford her anonymity—which, paradoxically, contributes to her isolation and her torment.

Disavowal of Self-Worth and Resources

Of the women who were part of my research study, 71 percent had a college degree and 50 percent had attained an advanced degree, including J.D.s and Ph.Ds. In fact, these wives had on average 1.2 years more education than their husbands. Yet rarely did they rely on their education, work successes, and other personal achievements when they searched for solutions to their abusive predicaments. Not one woman recognized her accomplishments as the only resource she would need to help her move beyond her abusive marriage.

How is it that competent and capable women can doubt their abilities to get by without their abusive partners? Why, with so much going for them—education, professional status, money—do they feel stuck and helpless in abusive marriages? These women's feelings of entrapment seem unfathomable to those of us who are not in their situation. But indeed they do feel trapped, and often they stay in the destructive relationships for far too long.

A puzzling commonality among these women is that they fail to appreciate and lay emotional claim to their talents, accomplishments, and abilities. And the way in which an upscale abused woman inadequately assesses or even acknowledges her capacities and strengths dramatically affects her efforts at securing help. As a woman sits with feelings of isolation, embarrassment, and shame, as well as fears of being disbelieved and rejected, she discounts her personal resources. Ellen is a prime example. A successful health-care lobbyist, she thought a divorce would force her to leave the well-to-do suburb where she and her husband resided. She completely ignored the reality that she was nicely paid at her job at a major consulting firm. When I dug deeper into these issues, I found that these women discounted their achievements. Many of my interviewees described themselves as having had little faith in themselves when they met their husbands-to-be. They found their wealthy, powerful suitors to be self-assured and exciting and believed the men would compensate for what they felt they lacked.

As Allison explained, "I was feeling vulnerable and low at that time. I had a devastating breakup with a man I thought I would marry, and I was thinking that maybe I was incapable of having a lasting relationship with anyone. I was also struggling in my graduate program. I was treated like a peon, and I wasn't sure what I was doing. I had this feeling that everyone else knew what they were doing except for me, and if they found out about me, they'd kick me out. *But Robert had what I didn't have.* He was eight years older; he had been through law school at an Ivy League university; he was so sure of himself; and he came in and swept me off my feet."

Sadly, many of these women believed that their mate would provide for them the parts of themselves that they felt were missing. But, paradoxically, the very men who were supposed to support the women's weakened sense of self eroded it even further.

It is important to note, however, that when it comes to financial status, sometimes outward appearances can be deceiving. Although some of these women had all the trappings of affluence and success, they were personally impoverished. Allison, who had a Ph.D. in English and wrote for prestigious journals, worried how she would find the money to feed her new baby if she left her husband. "After he tried to smother me, I locked myself in the closet, sobbing and sobbing," she told me. "I knew it was over, but I kept thinking, How am I going to take this child and leave? He's only seven weeks old. I had no writing assignments, Robert had taken away all my money, and we only had one family car. I kept thinking, What would life be like without Robert? Can I do this? Would I be able to handle this baby without Robert even if I don't have a job?" Allison did eventually find the means to get herself out, but it took several months of planning and fortifying self-talk in order to do so.

Fear of Change in Socioeconomic Status

One of Allison's deepest fears was that she would not have the wherewithal to support herself and her baby. Not surprisingly, many of the upscale abused wives with whom I spoke had similar fears of impoverishment, or at least loss of socioeconomic status. And yet, although the income levels of the women I studied did decrease after they left their marriages, 85 percent of them were not forced from their surroundings. Most remained in neighborhoods where the median family income was at least as high as in the neighborhoods they lived in while married. In fact, these neighborhoods all fell into the top quarter of metropolitan and suburban neighborhoods in the area (see Appendix A). In this regard, the women's fears that their lifestyle would dramatically change after leaving their upscale marriages were worse than the reality. The fear of change in socioeconomic status can compound a woman's feeling of being stuck in a destructive marriage.

Limited Possibilities for Getting Help

The more I learned about upscale violence, the more I came to see that traditional avenues for help—shelters, hotlines, the court system, clergy, friends,
family, and in some cases clinicians—do not suffice and can even increase a
woman's reluctance to reveal marital abuse. Often the upscale abused woman is
turned away, or she senses that she won't fit in. I had given Julia phone numbers for several shelters in case Marc's violence escalated and she needed to
escape with the children. But she told me in no uncertain terms, "A shelter is the
last option I would ever consider," and offered a story to explain her attitude.

At one time, prior to her treatment with me, she had called a few domestic violence hotlines connected with shelters. "The hotline volunteers put me
off when they learned of my resources," she said angrily. "They assessed that
I probably didn't need to leave the house. Most told me to find a private therapist, and only one gave me the number of an agency." Julia's claims match
those made by many of the other upscale battered wives I have met. Sherry,
the attorney mentioned in Chapter 1, did contact a domestic violence agency
but never received any assistance. The volunteers at the agency made her
ashamed of her efforts to seek help, and technically she is still languishing on
their waiting list.

It is most likely that if a woman in economic distress had called with the
same concerns as Julia, she would have been offered more support. According
to Leslie Landis, a Chicago attorney and Domestic Violence Projects manager
with the Mayor's Office on Domestic Violence:

> When these women who are not poor seek services from identified domestic
> violence programs, they encounter the following: A lack of appreciation of the
> feelings these women experience around the loss of status/money due to the
> fact that many women receiving services at these programs never had or likely
> will not have that status or money and are working on basic survival issues.
> Women grieving the loss of the relationship and the fear of changes which will
> lower their standard of living are sometimes viewed as less "worthy" victims.[4]

Agencies offer support to affluent women less readily because we are typically unprepared to comprehend the problem of marital abuse among the upscale. Unfortunately, a privileged lifestyle does little to evoke sympathy from
others, despite one's emotional difficulties. As Jennifer told me, "How can I go
to a domestic violence shelter, sit in a group of women who are worrying about
a roof over their heads and food for their children, and say, 'My husband broke

my wrist after he put our jet in its hangar?' These women would also shun me if I told them I was trying to put my kids through college!"

When abused upscale wives do go to domestic violence venues, they tend to attract a lot of attention. Irene recounts her experiences in court: "During the divorce process, I felt the judge didn't believe me because here I was, this lady with millions of dollars. There was this kind of disbelief like, 'Why would you divorce this guy?'"

Ellen, the health-care lobbyist, told me about her disastrous faux pas in domestic violence court. "It was an extremely cold winter day. Most of the other women there looked poor and in need of warm clothes. Everybody looked at me. Some angrily. I was wearing my fur coat because it had been so bitterly cold. I hadn't thought about what my wearing that coat would look like down at court. I was awkwardly conspicuous and keenly aware of these other women's material needs as opposed to mine. And yet, my eye was just as blackened as the woman standing next to me, waiting her turn to be called."

The traumas sustained by Nicole Brown Simpson, Pamela Anderson, Roseanne Barr, Darryl Hannah, Melissa Rivers, and Farrah Fawcett have demonstrated to us the difficulties that high-profile celebrities who have suffered domestic abuse and dating violence have in seeking help. Any action they take to deal with domestic violence results in media frenzy, a total disregard for their privacy, and scant support. The public felt little sympathy for the scars Nicole Brown Simpson received in her marriage because they were simultaneously bombarded with pictures of her perched on her new Ferrari or partying in a glittering evening gown.

On September 29, 1992, a report appeared in the *Chicago Tribune* reporting on actress Darryl Hannah's filing of domestic abuse charges against her live-in boyfriend, singer Jackson Browne. The Abuse Awareness League, an organization I cofounded to increase public awareness of the prevalence of violence against women, submitted a letter to the editor criticizing the *Tribune* for its flippant treatment of this instance of domestic violence. The three-sentence paragraph in the paper's "Newsmakers" section was headed "Put Up Yer Dukes."[5]

The frivolous fashion in which the paper reported this act of violence served to reinforce the public's misconception that when wealthy or privileged people are abused, it is just part of the "Hollywood scene." Hannah's beating was not presented as a criminal act but rather as a cute "down home couple's feud." Browne, like other abusive men in high-profile cases, was not reported to have exhibited any remorse or to have suffered any major legal consequences. In many of the upscale domestic abuse cases I worked with, the legal system treated the abuser with great leniency owing to his reputation and standing in the community. Whether this is due to the judge's identification with the abuser, who is usually of a similar economic and educational standing, or the court's skepticism about abuse among the upscale, is difficult to discern. This tolerance is yet another factor that differentiates upscale violence from that among the lower classes.

THE EMPEROR'S NEW CLOTHES

The upscale abused woman lives within a perplexing, self-perpetuating trap. Her feelings of isolation come from her belief that her experience is unique. She and society buy into this myth, supported by the lack of reports of upscale abuse as well as an absence of language to even describe the experience. The woman's isolation is then fueled by the very real fear that no one will believe her and that she might be rejected if she speaks up—a fear that further compounds both her silence and her isolation. By maintaining secrecy, she avoids being perceived as a failure, but at the same time she paradoxically disavows and undervalues her strengths and capacities to survive outside the marriage. Having no one to challenge her underassessment of herself, she uses her inner resources to survive as best she can within the marriage.

Clearly, the time has come for us to incorporate the concept of *upscale violence* into our lexicon. As feminist theorist Carol Gilligan has observed, women learn non-aggressively, interactively, and relationally.[6] That is, they might say, "This is what I know or have experienced. How does it fit with everyone else?"[7] However, since no one else gives voice to the experience of upscale violence, the abused woman may doubt her own reality. The lack of external validation—even in the form of terminology—pushes her toward denying what has happened to her.

Moreover, women have been socialized to place the needs of others above their own—especially when it comes to protecting the family unit. If a woman is experiencing violence in her home and knows that talking about it will destroy her family while at the same time those around her are denying that such violence can exist, she may feel compelled to deny reality and keep the abuse secret to maintain the family's integrity. By using the term *upscale violence* we legitimize this woman's experience. Like the naïve young boy in "The Emperor's New Clothes," we say the unsayable and make plain what has been hidden in full sight.

The traditional view of psychotherapy holds that once you sort out your inner conflicts, your behavior will change. Insight precedes action. But when it comes to the abused upscale wife, I have found that *outsight*—the validation that others bring from the outside by concretizing the experience with words and recognition—precedes insight, which in turn precedes action. Validation must occur before the woman will recognize what is happening and take action on her own behalf. Until there are words and images to describe her experience, she has trouble making meaning of it and protecting herself and her children.

The silence that typically surrounds upscale violence takes a terrible toll. It dooms the woman's course of action in five ways:

- It keeps her isolated and prevents her from seeking validation from others.
- It limits her motivation to seek help.
- It keeps her from receiving feedback from others confirming her worth and ability to survive outside of the marriage.
- It prevents her from utilizing existing avenues for help, which are geared toward lower-income women, further limiting her options for getting relief.
- It confirms the myth that abuse does not occur among the upscale, because the violence is rarely discussed or reported.

Consequently, the upscale woman's silence, which is her misguided attempt to adapt and cope with her circumstances, reinforces her staying trapped in her predicament. Hers are indeed dangerous secrets—secrets that are kept by "people like us."

3

Why Do Women Stay in Abusive Marriages?

HOW CAN WE MAKE SENSE OF A MAN denigrating, beating, or choking a wife he claims to love, and how can we understand a woman tolerating such grievous mistreatment? Baffling as these questions are, they become even more puzzling among the upscale. Why would an otherwise intelligent and accomplished woman—one with the means and financial resources to escape an intolerable situation—remain in an abusive marriage?

In truth, every battered woman, regardless of her social standing, is plagued with a multitude of conflicting emotions. Rarely is there a single, clear-cut reason for her to tolerate abuse from the man who purports to love her. Her motivations for staying can be varied and complex. The well-to-do, highly educated abused wife is no exception.

Theories abound to explain the paradoxes of a destructive marital bond. Feminists depict the problem of spousal abuse as societal, based on power imbalances between men and women. Sociopolitical studies point to the effects of the media as well as the family system, both of which serve as a learning ground for abusive behaviors toward women. Psychological hypotheses largely address the dynamics within the relationship and the inner mental landscape of the woman who tolerates abuse.

Are these and other accepted theories and explanations relevant to the upscale abused wife? I believe that other factors may be at work here. But before we examine such theories, we must first understand that conventional wisdom regarding why women stay in abusive situations is born of an extensive and substantial history of abuse and violence against women.

HOW LONG HAS THIS BEEN GOING ON?

Any sense of spousal abuse as a criminal and immoral act only came into awareness in the late nineteenth century, spurred primarily by the advent of the women's movement. This lack of attention obscured a long tradition of male supremacy, discrimination, and abuse toward women since biblical times.

The Bible implies that the female of our species is the source of suffering and evil and must be chastised. Eve, who was created "for man from man" to relieve his loneliness and serve him (not vice versa), demonstrated her "weak nature" by succumbing to the serpent's exhortations to eat the forbidden fruit of the Tree of Knowledge. This "original sin" resulted in devastation and curses to all future generations, and as a consequence all women were punished with the pain of childbirth.

Seen throughout the ages as emotional, difficult, weak, vulnerable, and unstable, women have always felt great pressure to enter into marriage. They had few alternatives: the only sanctioned roles for women included those of wife, mother, priestess, prostitute, or concubine. Unmarried women lost the only totally legitimate and therefore socially unproblematic position that was open to them. Moreover, women often chose marriage as a way to protect themselves from rape.[1] The male and female roles were legally mandated, not just perpetuated through informal socialization.[2] Such prescriptions, however, did not protect women from harm within their marriages.

Some abusive customs that originated in Rome, for instance, continued through the twentieth century. In 753 B.C., soon after Rome was founded, laws were instituted to render the husband the sole authority and head of the household. Each husband was granted *patria potestas*, a custom directed at protecting his rights and powers. Wives remained under their husbands' guardianship and were viewed as possessions; they did not exist as legal entities in their own right.[3] A husband even had the power to sell his wife and children into slavery or put them to death.[4] In fact, the Latin word *familia* means "servants in a household," signifying the totality of slaves belonging to a man. Women had no property rights, even as widows.

Under the law of chastisement, a Roman husband had the right to discipline his wife physically for various, often unspecified, offenses. The law of chastisement justified its barbarism as follows: since man and woman were considered one under law and a husband was responsible for his wife's crimes, he could use physical punishment to prevent her from engaging in criminal behavior to protect himself from prosecution. In fact, he could chastise, discipline, divorce, or even kill his wife for the very same behaviors (such as adultery or drinking wine) that were not defined as illegal for him.[5] These laws protecting men's authority established a tradition perpetuated in English common law and in most of Europe.[6]

The situation did not change until 202 B.C., when the Punic Wars improved social conditions for women. Widows could be legally recognized as property owners, laws against wives' infidelity were made less severe, and women could sue for financial compensation for unjustified beating. In fact, by the fourth century A.D. excessive violence by either spouse was legally recognized as grounds for divorce, although it is not known whether this law was ever enforced.

But while Roman law was becoming more liberal in its treatment of women, the advent of Christianity did little to better women's lot. Indeed, early Christian doctrine reinforced traditional patriarchal authority.[7] For the next eleven centuries, women held a singularly subordinate status: they could be burned at the stake for engaging in adultery, prostitution, sodomy, masturbation, and lesbianism, for miscarrying in childbirth, and for talking back or refusing favors to a priest.[8]

In medieval Europe the wives of feudal lords were symbols of their husband's power, commodities exchanged in order to increase wealth or influence, solidify bonds, or serve as peace offerings. Marriages were often arranged to fulfill these obligations, and men could lock their wives in chastity belts to ensure fidelity. Once a woman married, all her goods became her husband's property.[9]

The medieval concept of courtly love, while seeming to elevate women, actually contributed to their subordination. Wives and daughter became objects to be admired, enjoyed, and coveted—as long as they were young and pretty, standards defined by men. Indeed, the Age of Chivalry did not help a woman's cause; the chivalric code advised men to honor and serve women at any length, yet physical abuse was also deemed acceptable.[10] According to Lewis Okun, "Raping and/or abducting a virgin of noble birth was an effective and fairly common method for a knight of low status to gain a marriage above his station."[11]

The coming of the Renaissance also did little to improve women's lot. In the fifteenth century, Friar Cherubino of Siena wrote in *The Rules of Marriage*:

When you see your wife commit an offense, don't rush at her with insults and violent blows. . . . Scold her sharply, bully and terrify her. And if this still doesn't work . . . take up a stick and beat her soundly, for it is better to punish

the body and correct the soul. . . . Readily beat her, not in rage but out of char-
ity . . . for [her] soul, so that the beating will redound to your merit and her
good.[12]

And another prelate exhorted his male parishioners to "exercise more
compassion for their wives by treating them with as much mercy as they
would their hens and pigs."[13] In sixteenth-century France, Abbe de Brantome
maintained a man's right to kill his wife (which persisted in some areas until
the twentieth century).[14] And by the seventeenth century, the rise of Puri-
tanism in England had led to the so-called golden age of the rod, which was
used against women and children.

In 1641 the first American reform against family violence was included in
the Massachusetts *Body of Liberties*, which declared that no assaults were per-
missible except in self-defense. According to Elizabeth A. Pleck, a historian at
the University of Illinois, Urbana-Champaign, although wife beating was "the
single most common case of family violence in the Plymouth courts," those
courts still "placed family preservation ahead of physical protection of victims."[15] Wives had fewer rights than slaves, who, according to Lewis Okun,
could "refuse their masters the 'final familiarity.'"[16] Women had no right to
consent or refuse to engage in sex with her husband. It was not until the
mid–1970s that the invoking of conjugal privilege would be defined as marital rape.

Throughout Euro-American history, wife beating enjoyed legal status as an
accepted institution in Western society.[17] The familiar aphorism "A man's
home is his castle" assured a husband's dominance, his right to demand sexual pleasure, domestic privacy, and the preservation of the family system. And
within this castle the "rule of thumb," which descended from the law of chastisement to British common law, was observed: a man could beat his wife
with a rod or switch as long as its circumference was less than that of the base
of his right thumb. Wives were never accorded reciprocal rights.[18]

The first substantive sign of change occurred in the 1874, when a representative of the Society for the Prevention of Cruelty to Animals (SPCA), acting as a private citizen, was instrumental in having a maltreated child
removed from her parents on the grounds that as a member of the animal
kingdom she was entitled to the protection guaranteed by laws against animal
cruelty. This was followed by the creation of the Society for the Prevention of
Cruelty to Children (SPCC) in New York; prior to this, no formal institutions,
other than secular or church courts, aided victims of family violence. Sadly,
no Society for the Prevention of Cruelty to Women was ever formed.[19] And

the budding women's rights movement focused primarily on suffrage, not on abuse.

In the second half of the nineteenth century, starting with the temperance movement, which linked domestic violence to a husband's alcohol use, wife beating became the subject of public discourse. In 1869, words from John Stuart Mill's *The Subjection of Women* sparked concern for the plight of battered women, accelerating the perceived need for laws to control wife assault in England.[20] Mill wrote:

> When we consider how vast is the number of men, in any great country, who are little higher than brutes, and that this never prevents them from being able, through the law of marriage, to obtain a victim, the breadth and depth of human misery caused in this shape alone by the abuse of the institution swells to something appalling. . . . The vilest malefactor has some wretched woman tied to him, against who he can commit any atrocity except killing her, and if tolerably cautious, can do that without much danger of the legal penalty.[21]

Eventually, laws were passed in England making life-threatening wife beatings grounds for divorce.

Various rules of law were slowly made by United States courts as well. The Fourth Amendment to the Constitution secured the privacy of the home, but it was left to case law to determine whether America would uphold the tradition of the law of chastisement. In 1864 a North Carolina court overturned the "finger stitch rule," by which a husband could be criminally prosecuted for domestic violence only if his spouse's injuries required stitches.[22] In 1871 Alabama and Massachusetts courts overturned men's rights to chastise their wives, and many states followed by passing laws forbidding wife beating. In 1882 Maryland became the first state to pass a law punishing brutal wife beating: convicted husbands were sentenced to public whipping. Alabama and New Hampshire followed with legislation prohibiting wife beating. In 1884 the Brooklyn SPCC defined cruelty to wives as the infliction of needless and wrongful physical pain, endangerment of life or limb, and neglect of food, shelter, and well-being.[23]

And yet despite the passage of these laws, efforts at policing domestic violence were seen as potential violations of civil liberties that encroached on the privacy of the family.[24] For instance, in the case of the finger stitch rule, the court also advised that it would be best to "draw the curtains" on domestic interactions so the parties could "forget and forgive."

HOW THE HELPING PROFESSIONS FELL SHORT

After World War I, the precept of social workers who interacted with the courts and the family guidance system was to return the family functioning to the status quo, keep the castle private, and educate women to be better wives. The focus was on the victim as someone needing repair, rather than on the batterer. Unfortunately, this attitude facilitated the maintenance of marriages that were often brutal prisons for women. The couple was told that neither spouse was to blame,[25] but the wife was identified as the client. She was deemed "more influenceable" since she was willing to go for counseling.[26]

Although the battered wife received empathy in such counseling, social workers made few interventions that would encourage her to leave the abusive situation or even to confirm that spousal abuse was wrong.[27] Indeed, after a court hearing, the social worker often advised the battered wife to "be attractive and keep a nice home."[28] The trend in the courts and agencies during the first thirty years of the twentieth century continued to be toward reconciling the couple and mending the home.

In an oft-cited case, a woman with bad teeth prepared soft foods for most meals so that she could eat with her family. A judge saw this as suitable grounds for the beating to which her husband had subjected her. The recommended remedy involved having social workers teach her how to keep a good home and cook better, as well as referring her to a dentist to repair her teeth. This was considered a just handling of the case because social workers believed that they were best serving the family by keeping it intact. The mother was financially unable to support herself and her children alone. [29]

During World War II more women entered the work force and, coincidentally, the divorce rate rose. After the war, as the country turned toward recovery, many women returned to the home front. The psychological theories of Sigmund Freud, geared toward explaining and maintaining the passivity of women, gained popularity. Psychoanalysis, which expressed the concept that "anatomic differences resulted in differences in personality,"[30] contributed to what Freud deemed the defectiveness of the female personality. A woman's penis-deficient state caused her to envy men and created unresolved oedipal dilemmas that affected her character.

Psychoanalysts adopted Freud's belief that urges and desires of which human beings were hardly aware governed their actions.[31] Helene Deutsch, one of Freud's disciples, developed a theory of masochism that she applied to women who had been beaten or raped. She maintained that girls, enraged because they were without a penis and driven by unconscious desire for the missing organ, wanted to be raped and impregnated by their fathers. This transmogrified into the notion that masochistic women desired their symbolic fathers—their male partners—to rape them.

Unfortunately, Deutsch's theory became the dominant psychiatric explanation of why women became victims of domestic violence and why abused women remained with their assailants. Psychiatrists believed that such women secretly enjoyed the pain that was inflicted on them, and some were thought to consistently seek out men who would mistreat them. Further condemning women, the theory held that any female who behaved counter to the traditional passive female prototype suffered from a masculinity complex and was therefore unable to properly fulfill her role as wife, child-bearer, and mother.[32]

It is easy to see how this theory worsened the plight of battered wives by explaining away violence against women.[33] An abused woman's psychological stability was always questioned, and the victim always bore the burden of proof.[34] Explanations contrary to Deutsch's theory of masochism, such as Karen Horney's view that masochism was rooted in misogyny, women's economic dependence on men, and the exclusion of women from public life, gathered few adherents.[35]

THE CULTURAL CONTRIBUTION

Deutsch's theory offered the comfort of male dominance and control to a post-Depression country in which the male's ability to provide for his family had been threatened. This reassurance could also be found at the movies, which showed that under their strong, independent, assertive ways, women secretly yearned for submission. Often a brutish male mastered an overeducated and prudish heroine. We need only think of Katherine Hepburn and Humphrey Bogart in *The African Queen,* where the heroine's very survival depended on the leading man's street smarts and physical prowess, to see that this was a predominant theme in American culture.

Other psychodynamic theories of that era also tended to be male-centered and to foster men's power. Mother-blaming was a basic tenet that reinforced negative self-concepts in women while strengthening the dominant role model for men who could readily view women as toxic agents.

During the 1950s and 1960s, in an effort to deal with the social upheavals engendered by World War II, society focused more intensely on a stable family life. The concept of "the happy home" was born. Women opted to be homemakers, a propensity that was both reflected in and modeled on television. June Cleaver, Donna Reed, and Harriet Nelson were perfect nurturing parents who always had time to help solve their children's problems, offer support and praise, or provide effective and nonintrusive advice on moral dilemmas.

The developing "feminine mystique" about domesticity supported the emerging postwar conservatism, as well as the dominant school of Freudian psychology. Women were deemed to be truly fulfilled only if they embodied the passive role of the soft, receptive wife and mother. Steeped in the popular magazine culture of *Good Housekeeping* and *Ladies' Home Journal,* they learned how to be happy housewives who fully lived up to their destinies as females. They were to care little about the outside world and politics but simply were to focus on their wifely and motherly duties. According to Betty Friedan's estimate of this mystique, "Women, in their mysterious femininity, might be interested in the concrete biological details of having a baby in a bomb shelter, but never in the abstract idea of the bomb's power to destroy the human race."[36]

Such concepts and popular images deeply affected what was viewed as normal behavior. Women were responsible for making happy homes. As a consequence, contact with a helping professional made the battered woman feel even more isolated and blameworthy for her own and her children's fate.[37] Reporting domestic abuse would be destructive to the idyllic home life that the woman was supposed to maintain. This added an element of psychic abuse to an already physically beaten individual.

It was not until the turbulent and revolutionary 1960s and 1970s that the issue of domestic abuse began to be recognized. Growing unrest over large social issues such as the war in Vietnam, poverty, discrimination, and civil rights awakened public awareness of violence in American culture. C. Henry Kempe and Mary Edna Helfer's work on the battered child syndrome in 1963 refocused society's attention on the problem of family violence. Most important, the burgeoning women's liberation movement began to open the door on injustices to women both at home and in the job market.

In 1971, in the small English town of Chiswick, the world saw five hundred women and children (and one cow!), led by British feminist activist Erin Pizzey, demonstrate against wife beating. Pizzey, the originator of temporary residences for battered women, was no stranger to violence. Interned in a Japanese prisoner-of-war camp during World War II, she was raised by a father who was emotionally abusive to her mother. Though her father never beat her, Pizzey grew up watching him browbeat and bully her mother. In

1974 she helped to found Chiswick's Women's Aid, a place that provided women with child care and housing.

Chiswick readily attracted women who had been battered and had received little assistance from legal and social services. Any woman could obtain emergency safe shelter there when no one else would take her in. She could escape from loneliness and isolation, and seek help with problems such as domestic abuse, divorce, poor housing, and alcoholism. Pizzey championed the model that explained domestic tyranny as a cycle of violence, and worked at aligning with professionals who would be more sympathetic to the battered woman's plight.[38]

In the United States, the women's movement cleared the way for various establishments to help women who had been abused. 1972 saw the creation of the first rape crisis hotline in Berkeley, California, which became a model for the battered women's movement.[39] Women, such as the acclaimed poet Maya Angelou, began writing about personal family violence, a term coined in the 1970s. In 1973 the National Organization of Women's (NOW) established its first task force on abuse. The task force began as a self-help group seeking to reform police practices and improve legal aid for victims. NOW volunteers accompanied battered women to court.

In 1974, in England, Erin Pizzey published the first book on wife abuse, *Scream Quietly or the Neighbors Will Hear,* while in the United States the movement was gathering its own groundswell of support. That same year the first American safe house for abused wives, Women's Advocates, was founded in St. Paul, Minnesota. Beginning in 1975, a number of American women charged with murder were acquitted in landmark verdicts on grounds of self-defense and temporary insanity after having claimed that they had been abused and battered by their husbands.

It was in the 1970s that explanations of wife abuse took on a feminist perspective. A 1976 *Ms.* magazine article made it clear that wife battering was occurring to the "woman next door." In 1979, in *Violence Against Wives,* Rebecca Emerson Dobash and Russell Dobash, professors in the School of Social Work and Social Policy at the University of Manchester, argued that marriage was an institution based on the subordination of women and that wife beating was an extension of male dominance and control.[40] The Dobashes discussed the power of myth in disguising wife abuse. In 1979, in *The Battered Woman,* Lenore Walker of the Domestic Violence Institute in Colorado introduced the concept of the "cycle of violence," which soon became a central tenet of theories about abuse.

Public focus began to turn from protecting the family to protecting the victim. Most theoretical explanations, however, still implied that women were either helpless or inexplicably paralyzed by internal conflicting forces that doomed them to remain in abusive relationships. An abused woman was the victim of either a male-dominated society, or the media, or her husband's mood swings, or her own intrapsychic conflicts.

WHY WOMEN STAY: CURRENT THEORIES

Since the 1970s, many theories have arisen as to why an abused woman tolerates domestic violence. She stays for the children's sake. For economic security. Because she has low self-esteem and believes she doesn't deserve better treatment. In the hope that she can change her husband's abusive behavior. Because she is a masochist, or a victim of society's norms and expectations. And on and on. Let's look at some of these explanations more closely.

The Feminist Perspective

Feminist theory, which suggests that abuse is a reflection of unequal power between men and women, points to the historical precedent of male supremacy.[41] The socially constructed conditions existing in a male-dominant culture produce and reinforce abuse against women. Thus a woman stays in a violent marriage because she is part of a society that politically and ideologically makes the abuse possible.[42] This outcome is supported by an inefficient and inequitable criminal justice system, which provides few consequences for men's violent behavior toward women.[43] The institution of marriage, historical attitudes toward women, the economy, and inadequacies in the social service systems also come under attack as contributing to the cause and perpetuation of wife abuse.

In addition to society's compounding abuse against women, the feminist view posits that a woman develops her sense of self very differently from the way men learn about themselves—and this difference contributes to why she might stay in an abusive marriage. Jessica Benjamin, a psychoanalyst, asserts that a woman learns about her voice in the world and develops her self-concept based on a public self and a private self, by what is and is not shared with others.[44] Silence is one way women adapt to a world where they feel overpowered.

The woman in a violent relationship hides the abuse in an attempt to accommodate to an overpowering situation. She feels she will get little help;

going public will only worsen her situation and may even engender further mistreatment. Ironically, however, her efforts to adapt and cope serve to tighten the bonds to her tormentor. As we have seen, concealing an abusive marriage restricts her access to support from those who could penetrate the private sphere where the indignities occur. According to this view, liberation from this process involves "unlearning not to speak."[45]

From a feminist perspective, a woman is trapped by the male-dominated society in which she lives (one that condones abuse toward women), and her way of adapting to this society (by silencing herself) contributes to her staying with the batterer. This framework holds the abuser solely responsible for his actions but often labels him as "ill," excusing his behavior while explaining it.

Sociopolitical Theory

Sociologists expanded on specific ways in which the cultural norms and values of the Western world reinforced the right of men to use violence and the inability of women to escape from abusive situations.[46] Sex-role stereotyping and sexism, especially before the 1970s, and cultural acceptance of violence as a form of discipline all contributed to the abused woman's feeling trapped. Although the situation has certainly changed as more women have entered the work force, for many years this image seemed embedded in our communal psyches. Women were expected to fulfill their roles as mothers and wives; men were granted the privilege of ruling the roost. According to this theory, before the women's movement society cast females in well-defined roles to which they became subjugated. As Betty Friedan observed, women were relegated to being the "happy housewife" and doomed to follow stereotypic paths on the domestic front. If they deviated from these sociocultural norms, they were confronted with prejudices in their communities, in the workplace, and in society.[47] What options besides staying home and raising children did a woman have who was untrained in a profession and unwelcome in the work force? Dependent on her husband for financial support, she was forced to tolerate whatever tyrannies he might mete out.

Moreover, violence and aggressiveness have been and continue to be glamorized in our culture. Most movies and television shows bombard us with enormous doses of often-gratuitous brutality that is aimed to excite. The cumulative effect is to normalize cruelty. But this is not new. In the popular 1950s sit-com *The Honeymooners*, Ralph Cramden's repeated threats against his wife—"To the moon, Alice!" and "One of these days . . . *pow*, right in the kisser!"—brought laughs to living rooms all over the country. Perhaps Ralph and Alice were meant to be seen as a loving couple whose history of playful banter meant the threat would never be carried out, but the words—and the not-so-subtle sense of danger they imparted—became part of our culture. Earlier, in *Public Enemy* (1931), actor James Cagney demonstrated that "dames" need to have a grapefruit shoved in their face to keep them in line.

Because our society viewed the American male as tough and rugged, enjoying violent sports and war stories that depict him as a strong but rough hero, the husband who was violent at home was not seen as a criminal. He was simply acting out his dissatisfactions in the way that a manly man did.

Cure and healing in both the feminist and sociological rationales require the revamping of mammoth social structures and ideologies. And these efforts, though worthwhile for the culture as a whole, don't offer ready paths for a battered woman to extricate herself from her troubles. Should she attempt to leave, she is up against a legal system that doesn't work on her behalf. Even if she is successful in separating herself from her abuser, she remains a member of the same culture that helped create the situation she is fleeing, so the likelihood is strong that the abuse will be repeated. For lasting as well as more immediate change, exceptional shifts must occur in the inner mental landscape of the abused woman.

Psychological Theories

Popular psychological theories—the cycle of violence, learned helplessness, traumatic bonding, and the reenactment of childhood issues—help us see that inner landscape. They have been applied to women from all socioeconomic strata.

The Cycle of Violence. In *The Battered Woman*, psychologist Lenore Walker describes a three-stage cycle of violence to explain a husband's pattern of abuse:

- The tension-building stage: pressure mounts in an abusive husband during daily interactions with his wife.
- The explosive stage: the destructive behavior occurs.
- The honeymoon stage: the abuser is contrite, loving, and engaging in order to soothe his wife's hurt feelings and become emotionally reattached to her. However, as this stage wanes, tension begins to build again.[48]

This cycle of violence becomes a fixture in the relationship when the woman forgives her abuser during the honeymoon stage. Once she takes him back, he implicitly knows she will accept his behavior. The woman must not succumb to the sweetness her husband displays in this last phase if she is to escape the cycle of violence.

Learned Helplessness. Psychologist Martin Seligman's theory of learned helplessness is drawn from studies of caged rats subjected to several different situations as they approached food: electric shocks that they could evade, inescapable electric shocks, or no shocks at all. The rats that received no electric shocks continued their lives peacefully. Those that could escape learned to jump away when pain was inflicted. But the rats that were placed in inescapable pain-inflicting situations failed to learn how to flee. Indeed, after repeated exposures to the inevitable shock, this group of rats made no attempt to leave their cages, even after the shocks were no longer administered.[49] They had learned to be helpless.

When Seligman conducted similar experiments with dogs, those trapped in the inescapable situations stopped leaving their cages, even when the doors were left open. They had given up all hope of escape. The experimenters had to drag the animals out of their cages to help them escape the shocks. It took time for these dogs to learn to overcome the effects of learned helplessness. Seligman found that the earlier in life the dog acquired the trait of learned helplessness, the longer it took to learn to respond voluntarily again. Once taught to respond appropriately, however, the helplessness was eradicated.

The theory of learned helplessness teaches us that when one learns that one's behavior cannot improve a painful situation, one's motivation to change the environment diminishes. Consequently, one becomes passive, submissive, and compliant.[50] In humans, it is not just behavior that is limited and compromised. People who feel trapped in abusive situations become depressed and anxious and begin to doubt their own abilities. Learned helplessness undercuts their motivation to leave the abusive situation.[51]

Learned helplessness can befall all types of women—even independent, successful professionals—partly owing to the power imbalance inherent in male-female relationships,[52] which often contributes to a woman's feeling of powerlessness. Change occurs when the abused woman is helped to see that she has safer and less painful options than staying with the abuser.

Traumatic Bonding. Donald Dutton, a social and forensic psychologist at the University of British Columbia, offers the concept of traumatic bonding as a partial explanation for why a woman stays in an abusive marriage. According to this theory, strong emotional ties develop between two people when one of them intermittently harasses, beats, threatens, abuses, or intimidates the other. There is an addictive quality to this interaction, especially because it is cyclical, alternating with loving behavior.[53] Psychobiologists Harry and Clara Harlow developed this theory in earlier studies with monkeys. They replaced mother monkeys with "evil" surrogate mothers—food-providing wire structures that were spiked, delivered noxious blasts of air, and were capable of hurling baby monkeys to the floor. Yet surprisingly, none of these factors disrupted the infant monkeys' bonding behavior and maternal attachment. In fact, the attachment proved most powerful when the negative behaviors were interspersed with warm and friendly contact.[54] In any casino, you'll find people who can't break away from their favorite slot machine, which takes all their money and rarely returns the jackpot. Monkeys—and people—will usually stick with a situation even when it seems self-defeating, so long as there is a chance of a reward or payoff. In this type of addictive attachment to a bad situation, which I call *slot machine love*, the woman has already invested much time, energy, and emotion in the relationship, and it intermittently pays off when her husband responds to her in a loving way. This keeps her ever ready, ever hungry, for the moment she can hit the jackpot with him again. [55]

Traumatic bonding is a bit like the Stockholm Syndrome, in which hostages deny the continued danger and brutality of their captivity.[56] After a period of time, they begin to sympathize with the terrorists' motives and even become attached and grateful to their captors for keeping them alive. According to Donald Dutton, "In a life-and-death situation with a powerful authority figure, the ego identifies with the aggressor-authority to avoid punishment and anxiety."[57] Rather than attributing an abused woman's tenacious loyalty to the abusive relationship to an internal masochistic trait, Dutton ascribes her return to a batterer to the traumatic formation of strong emotional ties and feelings of dependency. It is only long after the woman leaves the abusive bond that her fears of and hidden attachment to her abuser begin to subside.[58]

A woman may have a predisposition to bond traumatically if such relationships remind her of childhood attachments in her family of origin.[59] Change occurs after the woman recognizes the destructive nature of the abusive relationship and uses this awareness to break her connection to it.

Psychodynamic Impact of the Past upon the Present.   According to Freudian psychodynamic theory, early childhood (the first five or six years of life) is divided into stages of development in which various tasks are to be mastered. If conflict or arrest occurs in any one of these stages (because of trauma or family dysfunction), personality development can be impaired. In fact, such early conflicts or arrests can shape an adult's character and style of interaction.[60] This belief system asserts that people tend to reenact situations over which they have not achieved mastery.[61] Self-defeating behaviors may derive from conscious or unconscious causes.

Psychodynamic theory holds that what is learned first is learned best.[62] For the abused woman, earliest environment and dysfunctional family relationships become the overarching forces that explain why she remains in her difficult situation. Unconscious connections with her earliest caregivers mean that she easily reenacts the role of being "smaller" than her aggressor, as she was in childhood.[63] In an effort to master earlier abusive traumas, she is predisposed to repeating the situation. She feels familiar with states of abuse characteristic of dysfunctional families in which abused women are reared.[64] Although she may have been unable to influence her parents' behavior, the abused woman holds fast to the belief that she can get her partner to give her what she so sorely needs and make him become a loving and protective caregiver. This longing to *right an original wrong* can last forever.

Some psychoanalysts propose that in an abusive relationship, a battered woman would be so familiar with the feelings that arise from her dysfunctional interactions with her partner that she would feel dissonance and discomfort if placed in a healthier but unfamiliar emotional environment. Indeed, they believe she would experience enough unconscious tension and anxiety over the sense of strangeness that she would be driven to re-create the earlier dysfunctional state. She would undertake such a reenactment, not because she enjoyed being in a painful situation, but to release tension, manage anxiety, and maintain her internal equilibrium.[65]

Moreover, if helped to leave her situation, the woman might feel great loss in not having her husband, even though he abused her. In fact, she might continue to yearn for the destructive environment to which she was accustomed.[66]

According to this theoretical framework, change occurs when an abused woman gains insight into internal conflicts that would influence her to remain with an abuser and to repeat dysfunctional patterns. Interpretation and insight are essential in order for the woman to free herself from the unconscious ideas that determine her self-defeating actions. With insight, the primitive mental and emotional states can lose their strength, and she can choose healthier attachments or leave the abusive relationship.

While all these theories have appropriately been applied to abused women, I have found that other pertinent patterns emerged among the abused women I studied. In Part 2 I describe these patterns, which form a distinctive path that reveals a dramatically different picture of the upscale abused woman. I then offer alternative ways of understanding not only why an upscale woman stays in an abusive marriage, but also how she got into it and how she eventually can bring herself to get out of it.

PART TWO

The Wife's Path In and Her Way Out

4

Getting In:
"He Was So Sexy, So Powerful—
He Swept Me Off My Feet . . . "

THE UPSCALE ABUSED WIFE MAKES DECISIONS throughout the course of her marriage. Some of these represent significant turning points that entrench her more firmly in her abusive relationship with her husband. Her first steps on the path of upscale domestic violence begin when she meets her future husband. What happens during the courtship and engagement that makes her believe she cannot live without this man?

A susceptible young woman feels as if her boyfriend has swept her off her feet and she has been allowed access to a world previously closed to her. Indeed, 79 percent of the women in my study were impressed by their suitor's prestige, power, charm, and charisma. In some cases the men were as much as eight years older than their wives and seemed worldly and sophisticated. In fact, despite their educational attainments and life experiences, there was a certain naivete among this population of women. Half the abused wives I studied had held Cinderella-type beliefs about love and marriage. They had fantasized that their man would take care of them—as if landing the prince could actually enhance and enlarge their girlhood dreams.[1]

Yet when I asked abused upscale wives whether they had detected early warning signs of their future husband's abusive temperament prior to the marriage, 71 percent reported they had, and the figure rises to 80 percent if we include only women with advanced degrees. The most prominent early clue was the men's verbal bullying of the women and others. But though these women had noted the disturbing behavior, they found some way to ignore the inner voice that warned them of danger, and they explained away the aggressiveness. Indeed, they all married despite this foreshadowing of violence.

As I highlighted and analyzed the similarities among the women I interviewed, a certain path emerged that helps illuminate how an upscale woman becomes involved in such a troubled marriage. While each person's story is unique, Allison's experience is emblematic.

ALLISON'S STORY

Allison was warmly engaging during our first phone call, and she expressed great willingness to participate in my study. A science writer with an advanced degree in English, she was "well aware of the importance of research efforts." When we met, I found her to be an attractive, slim thirty-six-year-old woman, dressed casually in gray pants and a soft pink cashmere sweater. Her sturdy frame led me to surmise that she had been outgoing and athletic as a teenager. She had cut her neatly groomed chestnut brown hair in a bob. Her complexion was clear and she wore little makeup, exuding a clean, fresh, unadorned all-American beauty. Hers was an intelligent face, and her direct eye contact with me was comfortable. Yet beneath it all, I sensed a certain yearning. It seemed to me as if she wanted someone to hear her, affirm her experience, and tell her, "Yes, this does happen to other women who are intelligent."

I asked her to recount the history of her relationship with her husband. Allison cleared her throat and let out a sigh, then began by describing her experience in her Ph.D. program. "At that time in my life all I could do was question what direction I wanted to go in," she explained. "I might not stay in research. I was debating whether I should continue the Ph.D. or just cut it short. My project at school wasn't going very well. It was at a low point." Although she had capably immersed herself in her work, Allison doubted her abilities to be a "star" graduate student in her department.

In addition to her troubles at school, Allison was devastated by a breakup with a longtime boyfriend. Fearing that she was unlovable, she withdrew from social interactions. That, of course, caused her to become lonely, even though she kept to herself by choice. But one night her situation changed. A roommate convinced her to go to a blues club with a group of friends. "I remember wearing baggy old sweats," she told me, "because I had no intention of meeting anyone. I didn't care much about my appearance." She mingled with a large group that night, including one man, Robert, who showed particular interest in her. Robert was eight years older than Allison, but the age difference was insignificant to her. She liked that he was bright and had completed a law degree from a prestigious university.

Still, Allison was not ready to get involved. "My friend told me that Robert wanted my phone number, but I refused to give it. I just wasn't into it. A month went by, and my friend brought it up again. 'He just wants to have lunch with you,' she told me. So I said, 'Okay, what's the harm in having lunch?'"

Their first date a week later took place at a chic, upscale though understated French bistro in the heart of the trendiest part of town. "It was a nicer place than I would have gone on a typical lunch date," Allison explained. Robert chose to take her there because he wanted to impress her. Allison felt intimidated, as if she had to watch which fork she was using. "I was very uncomfortable. . . . It just seemed very strained, and I felt as if there were some sort of standard I was trying to achieve. I didn't feel like myself."

When I asked her about this notion of a standard, she offered, "There seems to be a social set of rules that you're supposed to follow when there's money involved. And I didn't even know what the rules were. I've learned some of them, like how you hold your fork, or what you say and what you don't, how you dress, and who you speak to and who you don't. Certain subjects are taboo, and you just don't talk about them."

Although such expectations are not necessarily suggestive of abuse, Allison immediately had an intuitive sense that life with Robert would include many social pressures. "He asked me all these personal questions at lunch like, 'So how many children do you want to have?' and 'Do you think you could ever be spontaneous enough to go from a catamaran to a black-tie dinner in one day?' and 'What business is your dad in?'" She suspected that "he had a criterion or check list in his head of what he wanted in a mate, and he was wondering if I was going to fit it. That made me a little uncomfortable, but I also took it as a challenge." Allison was drawn to Robert's self-confidence, but at the same time she felt insecure being around someone she viewed as so powerful. She also found him charming, if a bit arrogant—an educated and well-traveled man who seemed to know a lot about the world. Graduating at the top of his class, he was poised to be working in a boutique law firm. He had already started to carve a niche for himself in a specialized area of business law.

With some irony, Allison noted that she ended up falling for Robert despite her initial gut feeling that he was full of himself and would not make a caring, romantic partner. She also felt, though, that he had the self-confidence and savior faire she was lacking. And she thought he saw her as an asset to his career, his image, and his standing with his family. Bright, educated, attractive, and unaffected by the nuances of wealth, she provided him with a depth and sincerity that he found appealing and that fueled his pursuit of her.

"He came in and swept me off my feet," Allison told me. She said she felt transported to a new world. "Part of it was the money, part of it was the social, the persona . . . He took me on an adventure to places I had never been before. My world was sheltered and closed. I was very academic-minded, so I didn't have a good sense of how to meet people socially. It wasn't like I was a social misfit, but I'm more introverted. I'd rather be alone. He seemed to be outgoing, a party-person who surrounded himself with a lot of friends. They all had money, too, and it seemed like there was *power* in it, a mystique. I wanted to know what it was—it was intriguing."

"And he was very flattering," Allison continued. "I didn't have a lot of money at the time. I was in graduate school, and I was living on less than $12,000 a year. And here's this person who could take me out to dinner and to plays!" Even though money was not an important factor in Allison's choice of partner, the benefits that money brought were alluring to her and were a part of the relationship she began to enjoy.

Their many dates after that first lunch included outings at country clubs, polo parties, cross-country weekend trips by jet, and visits to his parent's lavishly decorated home. Allison experienced these dates as Robert's screening tests to see if she would "qualify" for the role of his girlfriend. Having been "shown off" to his friends and family, she felt an odd sense of accomplishment for "passing" and moving forward with him. "I was a Ph.D. candidate," she explained, "so that was a big deal for him. I was someone who was attractive, smart, and who he thought was outgoing . . . this model find. I was something no one else had. And so he was showing me off."

Allison's self-description made her sound as if she were Robert's latest acquisition. Yet she found him to be genuine in his affection for her, and she began to fall in love with him. But she also noted that she was slightly anxious all the time. "I don't know if fear was quite the word," she explained. "I was in awe of him . . . he seemed so much more powerful than I was. And his interest in me, it pulled me up a rung and made me feel as if I had a secret entree into this world. Now I was part of it. If he was the prince, then I must be the princess. And everybody wants to be the princess!"

Allison and Robert's whirlwind courtship lasted several months. He took her on extravagant dates to plays and new restaurants, often with his group of exciting friends. The glamorous time Allison spent with him was markedly different from the hours she struggled as an impoverished, unappreciated graduate student. She felt that their dates were an oasis to which he whisked her away from her tedious and tiresome existence.

Still, Allison had reason to believe that Robert could be controlling and demanding. Several incidents before their wedding tipped her off to the darker side of his personality. The first was when Robert asked her to move in with him. She declined because she wanted to keep her own place as a way of maintaining her sense of self. "I was very worried about losing my identity in this relationship," she explained. "I had done that with my previous lover and had gotten very hurt, so it was important for me to keep something of my own."

Robert responded angrily—more than one might expect given the depth of their relationship and the situation. At first he ignored Allison, which she found unnerving. He read the paper or watched television when she tried to talk to him. "His coldness could get me to do things that I didn't want to do because I felt so *rejected*," she explained. "I wanted him to love me again." He would not respond to any of her overtures to ameliorate his hurt feelings or defuse his rage. One evening, on their way to dinner, he drove his Ferrari at eighty miles per hour in a residential neighborhood. Allison, terrified, pleaded with him to slow down. But he wouldn't listen.

They regained their equilibrium only after she agreed to give up her own place in a few more months and then move in with him. But the towering anger he could muster against her neither vanished nor diminished. Several weeks later on a holiday camping trip, Robert humiliated her in front of his family. Allison had taken a walk on her own in the woods without telling Robert where she was going. When she returned, she saw that her sleeping bag and clothes had been flung out of their tent and into the middle of the campground. Again, his "punishment" seemed larger than her "crime." Apologetic, she begged him to let her back into the tent, but Robert refused. His family, who witnessed the scene, sympathized with her but didn't interfere. Robert's sister later told her, in a warm and concerned way, that he had a history of problems with women and that the family had long ago realized that he could be temperamental and difficult to be around.

Robert finally did let Allison sleep in the tent, but he never apologized for his actions or the embarrassment he had caused her. She was grateful that his tirade had stopped, and she agreed that she was wrong for not having told him she was leaving the campsite for a walk. Because his family had said nothing about it, she convinced herself that his level of rage must have seemed overblown in her own mind, and that his anger about her wandering away was only protectiveness—a sign of the extent of his love. In the end, she wrote off his controlling behaviors to his being a powerful man.

A few months later, Allison and Robert married in what Allison called a *Sound of Music* wedding. "But," she added, "the wedding was a dream, but the marriage was a nightmare."

Robert's anger became more pronounced after they wed, but Allison could not ascribe it to protective urges. At the start of their honeymoon he became enraged when an airline put his luggage on the wrong overseas flight. He ranted and raved, demanding that they turn around and go home before the honeymoon had even begun. Because Allison's aunt, a travel agent, had planned the trip, Robert blamed any problems they encountered on her, but he also directed this fury toward Allison. She spent the whole honeymoon trying to placate him. Her honeymoon, her first trip abroad, had turned into a disaster. Robert refused to have sex with her and belittled her everywhere they went. Allison was frightened and confused. Abandoning the honeymoon or traveling alone in a foreign country where she didn't speak the language seemed unthinkable. What's more, she didn't have enough money to buy her own return ticket or to pay the penalty for changing the return date on her existing ticket. She decided to tough it out, rationalizing to herself that "maybe all honeymoons are just a mess."

They managed to get through the trip, but when they returned home, the pervasive mood of the failed honeymoon persisted. Neither of them discussed Robert's behavior. Allison continued to accept the condemnation he heaped on her. She held to the belief that her husband was a smart man, and she could not fathom that he would randomly get angry without good cause. But she also could not understand why he alternated between iciness and fury toward her. She became depressed and blamed herself for his behavior. "Maybe I am not pretty enough, or thin enough, or a good enough partner," she lamented. She made excuses for him and rationalized his acrimony: "He's nervous about his work. He's very stressed out right now."

In trying to be understanding, Allison didn't realize that she was justifying, tacitly allowing for, and ultimately perpetuating Robert's abuse—abuse that would only escalate in the coming years.

THE POWER IMBALANCE

Allison's story shows many of the landmarks on the path into an upscale abusive marriage. Many of the women I interviewed felt that their prospective partner's interest in them increased their social status, even if they had been successful in their own right.

Implicit in this dynamic is the fact that these relationships house a power imbalance from the beginning. As one woman put it, "I remember not being insecure in myself and my ability to attract someone like Thomas to me, but it just seemed that he had the upper hand from the beginning." As these women allow themselves to become increasingly dependent on the man's stature and wealth for their own identity and sense of self-esteem, they become fearful that he will withdraw his affection, destroying the magical enhancements he provides. For many women, this notion is consistent with childhood fairy-tale images: Cinderella is rescued from her lowly rank as a "girl of the cinders" and elevated to princess because Prince Charming has fallen in love with her.

The power imbalance increases when a woman feels vulnerable owing to emotional losses in her life. During courtship and the early phases of marriage, mutual attraction is present in varying degrees for any couple. According to psychologist Erich Fromm, often the strength of such attraction is determined or mediated by the depth and duration of disconnectedness or loneliness that the person experienced prior to encountering the new sweetheart.[2] The transition from a dissatisfied or negative emotional status to a feeling of connection with someone adds to the intensity of falling in love. This pattern applies to the women I studied.

In fact, when it comes to the upscale abusive relationship, the man most readily gains his place with the woman when she is in a vulnerable transitional phase in her life. Allison had recently ended an intense relationship and was questioning her suitability as a partner. Other women also experienced major life transitions such as the death of a parent, the loss of a job, or graduation. Julia, mentioned in Chapter 2, was lonely because she was so far away from her home in Italy; Kathleen was homesick in Europe during her junior year abroad when she first connected with her abusive husband-to-be. "It's such an 'away from home' experience for people," she explained, "that there's even a history of how many couples have gotten married from this particular European program. Essentially you're alone; your parents are gone, your families are gone. People who go there make intense relationships." She turned to her new man for comfort and ego enhancement, as well as a sense of belonging and security at a time of psychological vulnerability.

PSYCHOLOGICAL VULNERABLITY

In the early 1960s Chicago psychoanalyst Heinz Kohut, diverging from Freudian dogma, developed a new psychoanalytic theory called self psychology. One of its basic tenets is that the self becomes strong and cohesive as a result of positive experiences with significant others during infancy and childhood. Self-esteem and well-being rest upon how others respond to these needs. These affiliations, which contribute to what will become the core of a person's character and personality, are referred to as *selfobject* experiences. A selfobject experience occurs when we sense another person as part of ourselves.[3] When that person says or does something that we would do, when he or she echoes sentiments that we share or demonstrates in words and deeds a deep knowledge of ourselves, he or she becomes a selfobject, helping to validate and shore up our sense of self.[4]

The selfobject experience also provides us with a sense of being valued and admired by another. It contributes to how we feel about ourselves and how we soothe ourselves and regulate our thoughts and emotions in order to feel internally consistent, solid, and together. When we feel whole, we take it for granted, like the air we breathe.

People who had good selfobjects in their earliest relationships have learned ways to provide themselves with feelings of well-being.[5] When they are scared or lonely, they don't feel as if they are falling apart. They can call a friend or entertain themselves with a book or movie. They know how to use a type of self-talk they have internalized from parents and caregivers that makes them feel safe and confident that things will turn out all right. Those who did not receive good selfobject experiences at an early age may be dependent on others to fill their emptiness and make them feel okay.

There is no evidence that the personalities of the women starting down the path into an abusive relationship were not fully formed owing to early negative selfobject experiences. However, most were feeling unsure about themselves when they met their future husbands, whether because of difficulties at school or in romance, their youth and naivete, the death of a parent, homesickness, or career dissatisfaction or transition. When these women met their husbands-to-be, their core sense of themselves was vulnerable and they were endangered. As one insightful study participant pointed out, this needy state attracts abusive men. "Narcissistic people like my ex-husband are *predatory*," she told me. "They look for people who are dependent."

A woman who is in a deficit state and needs positive selfobject experiences is at a disadvantage when it comes to creating and sustaining a healthy partnership. When she is unable to bolster her own flagging self-esteem or to reach a state of balance, she is significantly more dependent on others to fill her up and sustain her temporarily. The abuser may be acutely tuned in to the woman's sense of self. Perhaps he is able to understand how to make her feel that he knows her deeply and is connected to her. Such shrewdness may have made him successful in business, but he can also use it to woo a vulnerable wife. And while his purposes with her may be nefarious, she can view his seeming generosity as exciting and pleasurable as she begins to idealize the image of who she hopes he will be.

CINDERELLA UNDONE

Especially susceptible to this type of pursuit are the women who hold Cinderella-like beliefs about courtship and marriage. These are the women who truly yearn to be transformed through a magical connection with Prince Charming. More than half of the women in my study voiced sentiments that reflected a longing for a handsome prince to rescue them. Ellen, who held a Ph.D. in chemistry, told me that her husband-to-be took care of her. "I think that's what started our relationship," she explained. "I didn't have my dad around a whole lot, and I had been extremely close to him. I believed that my husband would take care of me. And he did." Sally had similar feelings. "I was always attracted to older men, possibly because I lost my father at such an early age," she told me.

Most of the women readily idealized their men and described them in fairy-tale terms. They used phrases such as "tall, dark, handsome, and fit," "the Clark Gable–Harrison Ford look," and "Rhett Butler suaveness."

For some women, the man's prestige—being the smartest in his class, the best athlete, the most popular, the best looking—had as much impact on their affections as did his wealth. Allison admitted to being in awe of Robert. "He seemed to be so much more powerful than I was." Sally noted that Ray "had a level of success, was a little older. I was just so young, and so flattered that he wanted to marry me. I really thought that no one else would ever come along." When the woman had a more affluent socioeconomic status and lifestyle than her future husband, her idealization focused on his other traits.

One woman I talked with, who earned significantly more than her husband, was spellbound by his talent as an rock musician and the way he electrified a roomful of people, even though his albums sold sparingly.

The man with charisma, power, and financial resources is the Prince Charming who offers the woman a new and glamorous lifestyle, whether actual or perceived. She idealizes him along these lines. His courtship behaviors are larger than life, and she sees him in those terms as well, further enhancing his ego. He consciously uses his power, talents, and money to bring her many glass slippers, and he takes her to many fancy balls, influencing how she feels about him and the new relationship.

INGRID'S STORY: THE FINANCIAL SEDUCTION

Sometimes the psychological vulnerability combines with financial difficulties to create a perilous situation. Allison found that Robert's money brought with it pleasures she couldn't afford on her own. It was not crucial to her existence—she had managed before she met him, albeit modestly—but his wealth certainly made her life more interesting. For some women, however, the financial need is more pronounced and more enticing. Ingrid, a beautiful twenty-nine-year-old African American electronics engineer, was employed by a high-profile computer corporation when I met her. Now happily remarried, she has little contact with her abusive ex-husband, although they have a four-year-old son. Still, her recollections of her first marriage clearly evoked painful memories and feelings.

Ingrid was a lively and popular nineteen-year-old college student at a well-respected East Coast university who already had a boyfriend when she met Bill. He had lived near her family, and they met when she came home to work as a waitress at a diner the summer after her freshman year. Fifteen years her senior, Bill was a history professor who was politically active and well regarded in the state legislature. He was tall, handsome, and had a powerful demeanor that, Ingrid told me, "made people stop and take notice."

"My ex-husband is an extremely handsome man," she admitted. "He's just drop-dead gorgeous." He was so intensely proud of his business status that he even offered to show her his resume to impress her with his credentials and accomplishments.

Bill pursued Ingrid with great vigor that summer. She was taken with his looks, his intensity, his political drive, and his ambition, but at the same time she felt he was moving too fast. "It's like you wait your whole life for somebody to come along who is self-directed and knows what he wants," she explained to me. "But it scared me. You know, it was just too much, too soon." Besides, she was young and not ready to commit to such a serious relationship.

As Ingrid prepared to return to college that fall, Bill laid everything out before her. He asked her to show his resume to her mother in order to prove his sincere intentions, and he told her to forget about returning to school. She could stay with him as his career took off. Then he would take her to Paris in the spring and arrange for her to attend school at the college where he would be teaching the following year. "It was almost storybook," Ingrid explained. "Here was this attractive guy who had his head on straight. And he had this look in his eye that said he really, really admired me."

At the time Bill's persuasiveness did not strike Ingrid as odd or controlling; rather, she thought this was the way an older, established man might express his interest. She turned down his offer but believed he earnestly wanted her to be part of his life. She offered to correspond with him while she was back in school, but he flatly said no. It was an all-or-nothing deal for him.

Ingrid returned to college and watched Bill's career from afar. That year, when he was appointed by the governor to a high-ranking position, Ingrid sent him a congratulatory note. She never heard back from him. But at the end of her sophomore year, Ingrid's life changed dramatically. She learned that she would no longer receive financial support from her family. Her mother had come upon a unique opportunity to buy a valuable house about to be auctioned in her birthplace, and she had decided to invest all her money there. This was an unkind blow to Ingrid's academic future, but she recognized that her mother had sacrificed for her children and the chance to buy a landmark home like this would probably never come again.

Ingrid applied for student loans and worked hard that summer, holding three part-time jobs. But it was fast becoming clear that her financial arrangements were insufficient to keep her at school. She spent spring break desperately contemplating how unhappy her life would be if she had to transfer to a local city college. Ingrid called Bill, naively thinking it would take her mind off her worries.

Bill welcomed Ingrid's call in a way she had not expected. He asked to see her, and she consented. As he was now living in the state capital, he sent her an airline ticket so she could meet him for dinner. Being flown somewhere just for supper seemed exciting to her. During their meal, she updated Bill about her life, her plans, and her crushed dreams of finishing school as she had originally hoped. He then did something for which she was unprepared.

He proposed. He told her in clear terms that if she married him, he would take her on incredible vacations and she could attend his college at no charge. She was unsure how to respond. Was he talking about a financially backed romance? Or was he just being kind in wanting to share his financial success with her?

Ingrid still wasn't ready to wed, but she wasn't ready to reject Bill again either. So she offered a compromise. "I told him, 'I'm not interested in getting married yet. If you want to date, we can date. I would even be open to living together. Still, you need to know that my main concern is finishing school.'" He jokingly asked if she really wanted to be a "kept" woman.

But the emotional yearning that motivated Ingrid's decision had roots deeper than the concept of being kept. The fathers of most of the upscale battered wives I have known and interviewed were not violent toward their wives or children. However, Ingrid's father beat her mother and verbally abused Ingrid and her siblings. He had never supported her financially throughout her childhood. She welcomed Bill's willingness to show his affection in this way with heartfelt longing. While she was not at all sure she viewed him as a husband or thought of herself as ready to become someone's wife, she was impressed with his position and the power and excitement attached to it. "The man I was going to marry was giving me a luxury I didn't have as a child," she explained. Being able to finish school also sounded tempting.

So Ingrid dismissed any concerns she might have had that she was "selling" herself—and she moved in with Bill the following week. They married within the year and traveled a great deal, as he had promised. She was happy to be able to finish school. Reflecting on how it felt at the time, she said, "You know, I didn't see how it could get any better than that. You have somebody; you want to be the cat's meow. And I *made* it. I was there. I was able to go on to finish school. I didn't have to worry about finances. I didn't have to think *stress*. That's what he gave me." Of course, all this came at a very great price, as Ingrid would soon discover.

ROMANTIC DREAMERS OR GOLD DIGGERS?

Let's look at these women. They are resourceful, educated, and bursting with career potential. In some cases, they are already wealthy and successful, yet at the moment of contact with their future husbands they are emotionally vulnerable. They are drawn to their mates on many fronts: the men are handsome, sexy, powerful, and successful, and they're usually able to provide resources or experiences many of the women believe themselves unable to acquire on their own. Often the men's hot pursuit ameliorates the women's wounded sense of self. It distracts them from the pain of their present transition while refocusing their emotional energies. Being with such men may also encourage others to see them as more worthy.

Attraction includes finding desirable and appealing qualities in one's potential partner. New lovers are usually impressed with certain attributes their partners possess, and they are overtaken with the hope of what being with this person might mean for their future. This is a typical courtship pattern.[6] However, unlike lower-income abused wives, women who find themselves in upscale abusive marriages overly idealized their men.[7] This idealization largely revolves around the man's socioeconomic status, career potential or accomplishments, and prestige.

The women I interviewed were not gold diggers. They didn't set out to find and marry a wealthy man, although some of them came from lower-income backgrounds or, like Ingrid, were facing a financial crisis. It is important to realize, too, that the men used their financial edge as part of the courtship process. They came on strong and made the women feel like princesses being swept off their feet.

Bailey, for instance, was neither a gold digger nor a romantic dreamer. She had no need to become part of the "rich and famous" since she already belonged to this set, nor with the ever-burgeoning success of her career, did she need to have a man provide for her. A strikingly glamorous fifty-three-year-old woman, she was highly respected in the New York advertising world. She was known not only for her achievements, but also for being warm and kind, funny, gracious, and generous.

Still, Bailey found her future husband's power electrifying. "I remember feeling a charge the moment I met Peter," she told me. "This man was sexy and attractive even though he wasn't handsome. He had so much energy. And he was so fearless. I was instantly excited by him. I thought, 'This guy is fabulous.' He was dazzling."

The lifestyle that accompanies a powerful and wealthy man can be a subtle yet tremendously persuasive force. This force is compounded if the woman has just experienced an emotional trauma that left her feeling needy and craving nurturing. Sometimes material demonstrations—lavish gifts, luxurious trips, fancy dinners—may imitate or even reflect the real feeling of caring and affection shown during courtship. And although Bailey did not need such accoutrements, Peter was able to provide the excitement her current marriage was lacking.

"I FELT TRANSPORTED . . . IT WAS MAGICAL"

What does the upscale batterer do in the early days of dating that influences the woman's perceptions and affections? Many of my interviewees expressed a sense of magic as they became more deeply involved in their relationships. Their suitors' desires and abilities to make formidable, irresistible larger-than-life gestures intensified this magical feeling. Many of these men were highly self-confident. They took quick and effective control of situations. They could mesmerize an audience or charm a crowd. They had a presence, and others around them—not just the woman—saw them as special. Like Allison, all these women referred to the phenomenon of *feeling transported.*

Such transport was often literal, as suiters took the women on glamorous trips all over the world. One woman told me, "When we went to meet his family, it was the first time I had ever been on an airplane. And that's when I realized they were much wealthier than I had imagined. I was from a small town and very naïve, to say the least. And he paid for the ticket." Like Allison, Sally reported that her husband-to-be wined and dined her in grand style. "We did more things downtown, plays and theaters and fancy restaurants. He bought me a lot of gifts. I was very young." For some, the transport had more to do with moving up a rung or two in class status, which felt utterly new and intriguing, as Allison made clear. Calling herself a princess, it was obvious that she had felt like Cinderella at the ball.

If the man did not instantly transport the woman to a new reality—perhaps because he was just launching his career—his potential for creating a new lifestyle was obvious from the outset. One upscale wife said of her future husband, "He was very intelligent, very articulate, very sure of himself, and it just seemed as if he had unbelievable promise. He had the most potential for really building a successful career." In all cases, the man's actual or potential power and wealth held a substantial mystique.

The resources of such men become instrumental in the courtship pattern. The women become used to the comforts of their lavish lives, which include the future husband's career status and accompanying power. This potential *wifestyle* becomes part of the woman's identity, part of how she sees herself in the world—which adds to and seems to fulfill her romantic dreams.

Of course, none of these factors is an indicator of what is to come. There are many wealthy, powerful, charming men who are kind and devoted. So what can be gleaned from these dynamics? What else was embedded in these women's narratives that could have predicted the abusive future of their relationships?

WHAT WAS SEEN AND IGNORED

Nearly three-quarters of the women in my study noticed early warning signs of their future husband's abusive behavior prior to marriage. Interestingly, I found nearly the same proportion in my clinical population as well. These women reported "knowing" early in the relationship or at least before they married that there were problems, but they overlooked, ignored, or justified them. And they told no one about their suitor's ominous behavior.

Allison's husband abused her verbally before the marriage, but she married him anyway. Ingrid saw clues as to how manipulative her partner could be. She had a sense that marrying Bill "came with a price," and not long after the wedding she began to see it. "There were signs," she explained, "like the way he would speak to people. He was usually very short with them, and he blew them off. He didn't make a lot of eye contact. I noticed that."

Other women remarked that their lovers were nasty to others, but they soothed themselves with the thought that the rage was never directed at them. Sally remembered Ray becoming irate when a friend missed a dinner meeting. "He began screaming and totally chewed out his friend. I remember thinking, 'I'd never want to be on the receiving end of *that!*' Up to that point, I never had; his temper was never directed at me before we were married." The intensity of Ray's rage frightened, intimidated, and confounded Sally. This furious person was radically different from the mild-mannered Ray she had grown to love. In fact, he was usually so demure and polished that many of his friends called him Gentle Ben (after the playful bear of the television series) because usually he was "overly kind."

Kathleen told me, "I fell in love with this guy over my own objections. I was attracted to his self-assuredness, which I now see as arrogance. But I thought early on that he was a real jerk somehow." And one of my patients had qualms as she observed her future father-in-law and husband dominate, bully, and condescend to her future mother-in-law. "Jim acted as if there was nothing wrong with this picture," she told me. "I didn't know his mother, but I thought, 'There's something terribly wrong here.' That's the first time I recognized that abusive and domineering behavior was like water off a duck's back for him and his father."

Perhaps no one was as thoroughly forewarned as Bailey, the advertising executive. She was familiar with Peter's reputation for ruthlessness long before she met him, and she knew in advance what she was getting herself into. "Peter was a legend in the advertising community," she explained. "He was notorious for being shrewd and impulsive, with a nasty temper that knew no bounds. He was real smart, real strong, and everyone sort of hated him. They called him 'a killer' because he would immediately fire people who could not pull their weight." Although she swore she would never become involved with him, once they met she found him physically attractive and was drawn to his power.

Peter was the principal at a large up-and-coming ad agency. Although people in the business feared him, they also respected him because of his success at acquiring smaller agencies, utilizing talent, and engineering innovative approaches to marketing and sales. He had a sense of adventure and daring and probably too much self-confidence for his own good. All combined, he was making a lot of money for his clients, his employees, and himself. He helped his agency rise to new heights of power and acclaim, and he acquired much of that power to use for his own best interests as well.

Peter wanted to hire Bailey and invited her to lunch to woo her to his firm. Bailey was torn about this meeting, but at the same time she was thrilled at the thought of having lunch with such an influential player. She believed she might gain some leverage for advancement at her own firm as a result of it. They ate at Windows on the World atop the World Trade Center. Bailey felt attracted to Peter instantly. "During lunch I thought, 'This guy is not a horror, like people say he is. He's really fun.'" They sparred and talked about nothing personal. He was married at the time and so was she.

Over coffee Peter offered Bailey a coveted vice presidency in his firm at twice her current salary. But he demanded that she give him a response on the spot. "I need time to think about this," she protested, but he wouldn't relent. Finally, Bailey took a deep breath and said, "Okay, I'll take it."

"I'm so glad you're interested," was Peter's curt reply. "But I have many other people to interview. I'll get back to you."

Mortified by this manipulative move, Bailey left the meeting in a rage. "That action was a metaphor for who the man was," Bailey reflected. "I was blindsided and went home furious."

Two weeks later, insulted that she still had not heard from home, she called his agency to announce that she was withdrawing her name from the list of contenders. Peter called back within minutes. Again he offered her the job, saying, "Anyone who wants the position so badly that they can't wait has spirit—I like that! The vice presidency is yours." The advertising community was stunned that "good, sweet Bailey" would work for "Killer Peter." And yet she found it exhilarating and took him up on his offer. Peter's behavior, while still only a business proposition, foreshadowed what was to come in their relationship. He forcefully courted her for his company and eventually seduced and married her using similar strong-arm tactics.

Bailey chose to ignore hundreds of signs that appeared as early as a first en-counter and as late as the honeymoon. Women like Bailey turn off their an-tennae and proceed headlong into relationships. In hindsight they understand the cost of ignoring their intuition, for once abusive behaviors begin they only escalate. These early warning signs are crucial for identifying and preventing upscale violence. They arise in the initial phase of the relationship and con-tinue throughout courtship, engagement, and early marriage. The women in my study recognized nagging feelings of discomfort and unease. They started to see signs that the coach in which they were being transported was really a pumpkin. But because the rest of the package looked so enticing, they wanted to find reasons to believe that what was "too good to be true" was real.

These early warning signs included the following behaviors and circum-stances on the part of the man:

- The man dominated the woman verbally, criticizing and belittling her, throwing her off balance or causing her to doubt her own worth and abilities.
- He made all plans, neither inquiring as to the woman's desires nor gathering input from her.
- He alone set the sexual pace, initiating all contacts and rejecting any of the woman's sexual approaches.
- He made most of the decisions about the future and announced them to the woman instead of including her in planning and deci-sion-making. He refused to compromise on major decisions.
- He was moody, making it difficult for the woman to predict what the next encounter with him would be like. Allison, for instance, con-stantly wondered what she had done to cause Robert's foul temper.
- He was chronically late without apology or remorse.
- He determined when the couple could discuss issues, if at all; he re-peatedly justified this control by claiming that he "hated conflict."
- He was hostile toward others as well as his future bride: unjustified rage, arrogance, controlling behavior, pouting and withdrawal of af-fection, and sudden coldness and rejection.
- His father was abusive to his mother.
- He demanded control over the woman's contacts with friends and family and over finances.
- He publicly humiliated the woman. This sometimes began as put-down humor, but rather than apologizing when she protested, he urged her to "get a thicker skin" or "lighten up."
- He slapped, pushed, or hit the woman.

By far the most common indicator of future domestic abuse in the upscale marriage was the man's verbal dominance over the woman. Verbal dominance is one of the earliest warning signs of controlling behavior that an upper-income, educated woman would tolerate. It easily blends in with the man's powerful persona, and she can convince herself that this is the sign of a self-possessed man who will not be intimidated by her brains, strength, or competence. At last a winner, not a wimp, is interested in her.

BABES IN THE WOODS?

What would make bright, educated, resourceful, and capable women go forward with marriage plans when they saw so many signs predicting a rough road ahead? Why did they ignore these potent indicators?

The women were hardly unworldly waifs. Their average age was 43.8 years when I interviewed them, and they were on average 26.2 years old when they wed. The younger the woman was when she walked down the aisle, the longer she tended to stay in the marriage. In fact, the women who wed under the mean age of 26.2 were married 20 percent longer than the other women in the study. This may be related to the level of development of the woman's identity and sense of self prior to her bonding with her husband.

A less mature woman may grow more dependent on the relationship with her husband to attain a sense of identity. Her perception of their mutual experiences as an integral part of her burgeoning female identity (which usually solidifies in the young adult years) may attenuate the pain she feels within the marriage as it becomes abusive. In fact, if her identity is enmeshed in her connection with her husband, he and the marriage—violent or otherwise—are harder to discard. To do so would mean closing the door on a primary sense of the self.[8] A young woman in that position wouldn't fully know who she is without her man and would be terrified to find herself alone.

Nearly half of the women in my research were virgins when they married. Perhaps an inexperienced young woman might bond deeply with the first man with whom she engages in sexual intercourse. Maybe she envisions that she becomes "his." This intense sense of belonging to someone may provide her with the conscious or unconscious feeling of protection and safety she may have longed for, especially if traumas and other life changes had made her vulnerable. Perhaps she sees herself as being obligated to the man she believes protects and possibly possesses her, rendering her more willing to tolerate the abuse. In addition, this "first one" status may indicate a type of ownership that the man exploits.

Most of the women I studied saw early warning signs of the potential for abusiveness in their husbands. Did their disregard of these signs reflect their under-developed perceptions of their partners? This might be true if the women didn't know their husbands well enough or long enough. But according to the study results, the women had dated, lived with, or otherwise interacted with their husbands-to-be an average of 2.5 years prior to marrying. This figure rose to 2.8 years among the women who reported detecting early warnings. This would certainly refute the commonly held belief that abusive marriages usually emerge from a quick courtship and an innocent rush to the altar.

If the woman's age and the length of her courtship don't tell us why she ignores the danger signs, we must look further for explanations. Psychoanalysis posits that childhood events leave an indelible mark that spurs us to repeat the experiences in order to correct them or run in the opposite direction. While some therapists and researchers believe that abused women have a family history of abusive behaviors that predisposes them to repeat such relationships, my research suggests otherwise. Except for these six women who were virgins,[9] the abused upscale wives I have known had no exposure to domestic violence in their childhoods, especially between their parents. Paradoxically, their innocence stems from *this very lack* of experience in early childhood. And, even for those who were sexually inexperienced, the abuse they described was not between their mother and father.

Moreover, few of the women had ever encountered abuse in previous relationships. Indeed, for most of the women the verbal and physical assaults from their fiancés were entirely new experiences. This innocence was shattered by the first instance of abuse. The women simply did not know how to recognize any of the early warning signs. They were clueless about how to heed or act on them and were even further stymied from taking action when the abusive behaviors emerged full blown. In her recent book, *I Closed My Eyes: Revelations of a Battered Woman*, Michele Weldon a well-known journalist whose husband, an attorney, had beaten her, gives voice to this experience:

Some people say to me, innocently, that for me to have become a victim of domestic violence, I must have been raised in a home with it . . . but that's a myth. I come from a family where my father was very loving and passive. I don't mean a pushover, but he was not aggressive, and we kids were never afraid of him. I never heard my father yell. And, in some weird way, coming from that kind of background hurt me because I thought that every man would be as wonderful as my father. It wasn't that I tolerated domestic violence because I was used to it—violence was so foreign to me that I denied it was possible.[10]

Kathleen remembered feeling utterly bewildered the first time her husband hit her. "I was just sitting there crying, thinking, 'What am I supposed to do? Am I supposed to pack up my bags and go home? Am I supposed to call someone in my family and tell them that my husband just hit me?' This didn't happen in my family. No one ever treated a woman like that."

Most of these women were shocked to see their partners as cruel, mean, or violent. Their initial reaction was denial—they didn't believe what they were experiencing. And they doubted that whatever their men were doing could be labeled abuse.

Many of the women I have worked with not only married very young but were raised with a distinct set of expectations about specific traditional gender roles within marriage. This was especially the case with women over fifty. This group was most likely to believe that the home was the man's castle, and they were more apt to point to economic concerns as reasons to stay in the upscale marriage. Unlike their younger, post–women's movement counterparts, they tolerated misbehavior on their husband's part for the sake of preserving the "happy home" and keeping the family together "for the children." They more readily ignored early warnings and were prepared to put up with disappointments and increasing assaults. They stayed married longer and therefore suffered more years of mistreatment. Irene was in her fifties when I interviewed her and had been married to Carl for thirty-five years. But Allison, in her thirties at the time of our interview, remained in her marriage only five years.

These younger women, even if they were insecure in terms of romantic relations or worldliness, still had positive regard for themselves before their marriages. They were often viewed as the star of their classes—the all-American girls, the overachievers, the ones who could succeed. Denying that their husband could turn his rage on them somehow fit into their sense of mastery. In a misguided application of their own sense of power and efficacy, these women believed on some level that even if the man's rages were turned on them, they would be able to fix the marriage and triumph again. Others would see their amazing effectiveness, they could once more reaffirm it to themselves, and they might even have an appreciative audience as they had had at other points in their lives.

Allison was accustomed to excelling in all her endeavors; she was sure she could figure out how to curb Robert's explosions. But she never could grasp the pattern to his outbursts, so it was impossible to predict how to stop them.

Bailey, a master at her own work, was unselfconsciously prideful when she told me, "I knew Peter was an angry man with moods, never directed at me, of course. The moods would come in rants that were irrational, where he couldn't stop yelling. I became the facilitator. I thought the traumas he sustained as a result of being Killer Peter were sad, so I tried to soothe him. I would go to the person he was yelling at and smooth things. I became the patch between him and his reality."

THE PATH IN

Within each woman's narrative of the early phases of courtship, there were tiny turning points along the way that pushed her more deeply into the relationship. These small decisions, almost indiscernible to others as well as to the women themselves, reached a critical mass and became the couple's tacit agreement about what was to come. Bailey accepted Peter's insulting and manipulative job offer against her better judgment. Allison moved in with Robert, although he had demonstrated on several occasions that he was difficult. Ingrid noticed that Bill was cold and dismissive toward others but married him anyway. Sally witnessed one of Ray's terrible tirades yet assured herself he wouldn't behave that way with her. Any of these behaviors should have raised a red flag of warning, which somehow these women chose to ignore.

Indeed, despite their misgivings, the women made the decision to marry the charismatic, wealthy, but potentially dangerous men who were pursuing them, and the stage was set for a disastrous future. Usually the path they took featured these stepping stones:

- *Susceptibility:* Many factors can predispose a woman to falling prey to an upscale abusive mate. She may have experienced intense loneliness or a major life change. She may have had little or no history of parental spousal abuse and so is unused to such behavior or naïve about it. She may be worried about money (or may have come from a lower-income family) and may believe in Cinderella stories about romance, love, marriage, and being taken care of.
- *Excitement:* She meets a sexy, charismatic, rich, powerful man (often many years older than she) who sweeps her off her feet. She idealizes the magical feelings he evokes as well as the man himself. She feels transported, taken for a wild ride by the man's power, prestige, personality, money, and material possessions.

- *Power imbalance:* The woman continues to feel inferior to the man and/or believes that being with him will increase her own esteem or status. If she is sexually inexperienced, this may further the bonding effect.
- *Denial:* She denies or ignores or fails to recognize early warning signs.
- *The abuse begins:* More tangible emotional and physical abuse often begins around the time of the engagement or marriage, perhaps because the man then feels more confident that he has "secured" the woman. The affronts may be mild at first—a put-down, a slap, a push, a pinch, driving dangerously, pulling hair, destroying the woman's property—but eventually they escalate.
- *The woman decides to keep silent:* Stunned, ashamed, confused, self-blaming, the woman keeps her dangerous secret to herself. She perseveres and goes along, which unfortunately seals her fate. She has now purchased her ticket for a perilous ride.

The Path of the Upscale Abused Wife: Getting In

Predisposing Suspectibility: Prior to meeting the man, the woman goes through major life changes or feels internal emptiness

Woman feels lonely and is alone (away from home, parent dies, career blues)	She has little history of being abused or witnessing spousal abuse	She has money concerns or comes from a lower-income family of origin	She holds strong beliefs in cultural narratives about fairy-tale romance (Cinderella fantasies)

Excitement: Woman meets future husband who is sexy, powerful, rich, often older; she feels "swept off her feet"

Man aggressively and vigorously courts her	Man is charming and charismatic, offers money, power, personality, prestige, material things; woman feels "transported"	Woman idealizes him and has magical feelings about him

Power Imbalance: Woman feels inferior to the man

Woman feels more complete when she is with him	Woman believes his power and prestige increase her social standing and esteem	Woman approaches first sexual intercourse with him naively, leading to strong sense of attachment and belonging

Denial: Woman sees and ignores all these early warning signs or does not detect them and goes ahead with plans to marry the man

Abuse Begins: Shortly after the engagement or wedding, emotional and/or physical abuse starts

Decision to Keep Silent: Woman decides to tell no one about the abusive incident(s)

Woman begins the journey of an upscale abused wife

5

Staying the Course:
"I Made My Bed . . . "

R AY STRUCK SALLY FOR THE FIRST TIME right after they left a realtor who had shown them a house she'd fallen in love with. They had been married less than a year. The blow came out of nowhere during what seemed like a peaceful discussion. Sally knew Ray was particular about finances, and she had advised the realtor how much they were willing to pay. Although Ray was doing extremely well with his coffee franchises, he firmly believed in living beneath one's means, and the house Sally loved was well within that range. As they sat in the parked car discussing their options before driving to her mother's house (where they had been living), Ray abruptly shouted, "We're not buying a house now!" And he lunged at her.

He ripped from her neck the gold and diamond heart necklace he had given her as a wedding gift, punched her, and pulled her hair. He choked her with such force that she thought she would pass out. As he released his hands, Sally, stunned, yelled at him to get out. He continued to shout at her and push her as she shoved him against the door. He finally left the car, but not because Sally had forced him out—he weighed eighty pounds more than she did.

Although Sally was screaming hysterically in the car, no pedestrians stopped to help her. She drove to a friend's house, crying. She felt she could not let her mother see her with a bleeding lip and a bruise forming on her cheek. But even her sympathetic friend didn't advise her to leave Ray. It never occurred to either of them that what had taken place could be considered domestic violence. They did not think of contacting the police, a battered women's shelter, or a hospital. They talked about the incident as if it were a newlyweds' spat, one that got a bit rougher than usual.

"I must have found it acceptable in some way," Sally explained. "I was in no way ready to leave our marriage. I told myself, 'You've made your bed, and now you have to lie in it.' I had heard that expression all my life. Once you make a decision you stick with it, you are committed in a relationship. I hoped I could change him, that I could make him recognize what he did was absolutely unacceptable." Sally had grown up in a loving, peaceful environment, so she could not begin to comprehend Ray's violent rage.

Sally turned, as so many women do, to blaming herself. "I thought maybe I *was* asking for too much. Maybe I should reassess my values and just live the lifestyle Ray wanted—which was different from what I had expected and from what he had promised." She had no idea that the attack in the car would be the first of many. She cleaned herself up, pulled her hair down over her bruised cheek, and went home, telling her mother that they had had a fight and that Ray would not be coming back for a few days. She never revealed the abuse to her mother—until years later, when her son reported it.

Ray stayed away for several days, but then called to ask if he could come home. Rather than apologizing, he explained to Sally that she had provoked his temper and that she shouldn't do it again. "He told me, 'I didn't *mean* to hurt you, but I had to because you were out of control—you wanted that house so much, and I had to show you that you were not going to have it.'" Against her better judgment, Sally accepted this explanation. She allowed Ray to return but warned him that if he ever touched her again it would be the last time. Ultimately, however, she did not enforce her threat. Sally wanted her marriage to work. She loved Ray, so she made a decision to let the incident become a distant memory.

Curiously, Sally was never able to find the necklace that Ray had torn from her neck. "Symbolically, he ripped my heart out," she said ruefully. And he never offered to replace it. In fact, Ray, like so many of his upscale counterparts and unlike abusive men in the honeymoon phase within the cycle of violence that Lenore Walker outlines, never bought Sally any gifts or flowers and did nothing to win her back after such incidents. Even when his beatings eventually landed Sally in the hospital, he never apologized. "He was never emotional about any of the abuse," she explained to me. "And afterwards, he never showed any remorse. *Never*. It was always somehow my fault."

HARDLY A NEWLYWEDS' SPAT

The early days and months of any marriage are a period of adjustment: the couple learns to adapt to one another, to negotiate the power imbalances that inevitably arise, and to live alongside their beloved. Committed to a lifetime together, newlywed spouses figure out how to compromise and accommodate to each other's needs. But once married, the women I have studied had to contend with more than these typical marital adjustments. Early in their marriage (and for some during their engagement) abusive behaviors became evident or worsened. It was exactly one week after their honeymoon that Bill publicly humiliated Ingrid by shouting "Shut up!" at her in front of another couple. This shocked her; no one had ever spoken to her that way before. They were out on a double date. Bill became lost driving in a neighborhood that Ingrid knew well. When she tried to give him directions, he yelled at her and then pushed her. His behavior alarmed the couple in the back seat. But, in Ingrid's words, "I just kind of let it go."

All the women in my study suffered abuses that if they had simply occurred as isolated incidents, could have been taken for a couple's fight or a husband's bad day. But for these women an abusive pattern quickly established itself, and the onslaughts intensified as time went on. It is important to note that it is not just physical abuse that can result in severe damage. Mental or emotional abuse can be just as injurious. Not only destructive, the emotional onslaught from a loved one takes many a woman off-guard. As with Sally, the violence was a new experience for most of these women. And with the exception of Ingrid and a few others I have encountered, the abused wives I met had never seen domestic violence in their family of origin. But they soon learned to live with it on a regular basis.

SETTLING IN

When there is no intervention, abusive patterns become entrenched over time. Sally's overriding need to feel taken care of blinded her to all else and kept her bound in a destructive marriage. She subtly convinced herself that if she could be "good enough" and not make Ray angry, she would reap the benefits that her handsome, wealthy husband could give her. She worked harder at being the good wife and mother, which entailed her ignoring his neglect, his unreasonable demands, and his episodic though increasingly virulent attacks. Each time she explained his behaviors away.

But this took its toll on Sally's health. She developed a spastic colon and was often sick. She felt tired and sad. She sought psychiatric help, but Ray accused her of wasting money and berated her for being dumb enough to believe in the concept of depression. Eventually, he forbade her to go. Perhaps he thought the psychiatrist would advise her to leave him. Sadly, that wasn't the case. Sally told the doctor about Ray's behavior and even showed him an enormous bruise that her husband had inflicted, but the psychiatrist merely chalked it up to her inability to have a satisfying life. He never discussed abuse with her, asked about her safety, or even wondered if Ray should be talking to someone about managing his anger.

After the birth of their second child, Ray and Sally moved to a nicer home in an upscale neighborhood. Part of her dream was coming true, but her health was failing. She was sick and frail after this birth, and Ray heartlessly criticized her when, because of her illness, she had only enough strength to take care of their children. He was especially irate that she did not have supper on the table for him when he arrived home from work. His cruel attacks just made her redouble her efforts to please him.

She became a talented cook and learned how to entertain. She derived great pleasure from the friends she would see when she threw elegant dinner parties. She continued to love Ray. And even though she felt lonely at times, she rationalized that all marriages were probably not loving and idyllic like her mother's. She tried to make herself feel content, but during her interview for my study she expressed feelings of defeat. "When I look back on my life, I see that I was young and fragile," she wept, "and he just abused me so. I accepted it, and I ruined my life." She realized that she had wasted precious years with a cold and vicious man—a man who had begun to hit her regularly.

Renewing her efforts to feel in control of what ultimately proved uncontrollable, Sally began to categorize Ray's physical attacks. She knew there would be regular short beatings monthly and at least one severe beating a year. And she learned to prepare for them. The beatings would usually come when Ray had had an exceptionally tough day at work. Sally learned to tell when they were coming. Ray had a crazed look in his eye similar to Jack Nicholson's look in the movie *The Shining*, where Nicholson played a deranged killer who murderously stalks his wife and child.[1] Sally would brace herself and pray that Ray's attack would end quickly. And after a few slaps and punches, it usually did. But the bruises lasted far longer, both physically and emotionally. And what started as stinging slaps became punches that by the end of their marriage had left blood clots, damaged an eardrum, and broken her jaw.

Sally continued to endure all this in secret, consciously deciding it was better that way. Her reasoning was threefold: she could not raise her two children without Ray's financial support, she and Ray occasionally had good times together, and she felt too ashamed to tell anyone. She thought, "Well, the psychiatrist saw the bruises and he didn't suggest anything dangerous was occurring, so maybe I need to relax about this." They did get along pretty well when he wasn't violent. Their friends even spoke about them as a "darling couple."

Sally felt stymied by the stigma associated with her situation. "In the sixties no one talked about domestic violence. It was just unacceptable, I thought. I mainly didn't want the neighbors to know. I was so embarrassed by it. I kept it from everyone—until ultimately someone was directly involved and saw it." Her embarrassment was not solely related to the fact that the abuse was occurring; she was ashamed that she had done nothing to stop it or to escape from it. Thus the double bind: telling no one made her feel even more embarrassed and humiliated, further thwarting her desire to get help.

The first turning point occurred when her four-year-old son witnessed a beating. It was an awful fight. Ray pushed on her hand so hard he broke her finger. This was a new low: it was the first time one of his attacks had necessitated medical intervention, and it was the first time anyone had witnessed the abuse. Sally was mortified. She thought about hurting Ray, having him arrested, or leaving. It was so bad that her little boy called his grandmother while she was at the hospital. That's how Sally's mother first discovered what was going on at their home.

Her mother only added to Sally's shame. She called that afternoon to ask Sally what she had done to cause Ray's temper to flare. She admonished Sally to keep his attack a secret. These remarks affected Sally deeply and made her feel even more isolated with her deadly secret. The doctors at the hospital simply called Ray a jerk. They never referred Sally to the police or a domestic violence center. But Sally admitted to me, "Even if they had sent me somewhere, I wouldn't have gone." She was more and more frightened and began to recognize that Ray's abuse was a pattern she was living. Her self-esteem spiraled downward as her shame and self- blame increased. Forced to wear a splint on her hand, for the first time Sally made excuses to conceal the battering.

Sally never left Ray or had him arrested. She resigned herself once again to sleeping in the bed she had made. And when he became angry, Ray reinforced her choice by reminding her that she was "bought and paid for." Accepting the violence as her fate, she took solace in knowing that her children were living a life of opportunity and privilege. As Ray's income increased, however, so did the violence. He bought more stores and his income spiraled upward to more than $500,000 a year, and his brutality intensified to a point Sally could never have predicted.

She had thrown Ray a wonderful surprise birthday party during the fifteenth year of their marriage, with marvelous food and with all their friends in attendance. She had baked for days. At the end of the party she offered their friends leftovers to take with them. When Ray learned that Sally had given away the rest of his favorite cake, he hurled a table at her, followed by the tirade directly into her ear. Ironically, Ray's assault literally helped her turn a deaf ear to his verbal attacks. He had injured an eardrum, permanently damaging her hearing. Even after suffering this loss, she still found ways to maintain her life within the marriage.

EMOTIONAL ABUSE

Like Sally, all the women in my study reported that their husbands subjected them to emotional abuse. The most frequent types included:

- neglect
- extreme selfishness (including sexual selfishness)
- secretiveness as to his whereabouts
- rage attacks and criticism, especially about her abilities as a wife and mother
- bullying and controlling behavior
- public humiliation
- threats to her well-being
- destruction of her property or the family's property (although a physical act, such destruction is meant as an emotional assault)
- *shifting sands*—the husband sends out conflicting and contradictory messages and changes his mood and emotional positions frequently and unpredictably, so that she has no clear idea of what is coming next or what she has done to evoke such behaviors
- extramarital affairs
- inducing fear, such as angrily driving at high speeds when she is in the car or making death threats

Besides physical outbursts, Ray's abuse often took the form of emotional neglect. Sally first became pregnant the year they bought a tiny home near one of Ray's coffee franchises. While the house was not all Sally had hoped for, it was within a good school district (her one demand that was honored), so she settled into life there with Ray and their baby. But shortly after their child's birth, Sally became ill with severe bronchitis. She was so weak she couldn't leave the bed.

Ray refused to help, because he viewed caring for the baby as Sally's job. "It was awful," she said, weeping. "I had to call a neighbor to come over and give the baby a bottle. And then he came home from work and demanded his dinner. He couldn't believe that I couldn't get up. But I was too sick to even feed my own baby.

"He never ever helped me out, whatsoever," Sally continued tearfully. "I was always subservient to him; I was always waiting on him." When she could not fulfill her duties as a wife to his satisfaction, he became cold to her. Indeed, it was around this time that he began the first of many extramarital affairs. But Sally justified his distance and unwillingness to help as aspects of his personality. He had never been very warm toward her, even though she initially thought he could be a caring husband. And he was always forceful about getting his way, never doing anything he didn't want to do. Ray felt he did not need to perform any chores related to the home or baby because he worked hard to fulfill his role of good provider. And from a material perspective, he had. But emotionally, he provided very little good and mostly pain.

Irene, the older woman whose husband humiliated her publicly, was constantly in the dark about his whereabouts. "I never raised my voice at Carl," she told me, "unless he was walking out the door. Then I'd ask, 'Where are you going?' And he would turn around and say, 'You are never to ask me that when I walk out the door.' And I would say, 'But why? I just want to know where you're *going to be*,' but he'd answer, 'That's none of your concern.' He would raise his voice at that point, and I would *shrink* and say, 'Well, okay.'"

For Kathleen, the physical therapist, the emotional abuse at first was verbal. Stuart would berate her. "I used to love to play tennis," she told me, "but one time we went to play and he started criticizing me and yelling at me so that I couldn't do anything right. It was the sort of character assassination I had heard him do with other people, but never to me. That first time I was devastated. I came from a family where my parents didn't even fight, and here he was dumping on me over a *tennis game!* I remember I was scared, alone, and on his turf in Manhattan. We were surrounded by his friends, and all this contributed to my doubting myself. Besides, I was totally unprepared to deal with anyone's anger. I didn't even know the difference between healthy anger and that kind of total put-down. I was sure I'd done something wrong. I didn't feel angry; I felt guilty. And I was afraid of him because he was so mad."

Although they were not yet married, Kathleen didn't have the courage to sever the relationship. "I thought maybe I shouldn't marry him, but my parents had already mailed the wedding invitations," she explained. "I went home a month before the wedding, so there was some safety in that." But in time they married, and the tirades worsened. "Eventually," Kathleen continued tearfully, "he would just dump on me to the point of his convincing me that I didn't have a *right* to be alive. He told me everybody hated me and that people put up with me because they liked *him*. That really hurt. I could feel my heart breaking when he was saying that."

Stuart's emotional battery continued throughout the marriage, and because Kathleen's spirit was broken, she did little but acquiesce to his malevolence. At the end of her third pregnancy, she was at home in labor when he decided to throw a party. "He wasn't happy with my last delivery because I couldn't tolerate pain," she explained. "So this time he invited over the woman who he was having an affair with and a group of people. They snorted cocaine and had a barbecue. I learned later that he was screwing his girlfriend in our swimming pool—we had a big house by then—while I was in bed, *in labor*. And do you know what I did? I asked my midwife to move me into my daughter's bedroom [at the other end of the house] so my difficulties wouldn't hurt their party or stop the fun." Her decision to change rooms was also a volitional act, aimed at removing herself, although feebly, from the pain of Stuart's cruel indiscretion. Later in the relationship she was able to make stronger choices and became less tolerant of his antics.

Bullying and controlling behavior often revolves around financial issues. After a particularly violent episode Ingrid tried to leave her husband. But when he heard her getting out her suitcase to pack, he yelled, "When you leave, you leave everything I ever gave to you. You leave the car keys, you leave the checkbook, you leave the credit cards." Because Ingrid had accepted what she had previously thought was a loving offer to take care of her, Bill, in fact, had purchased most of what she currently possessed. It was wintertime and she felt a coldness both inside and out. If she walked out the door, she wouldn't even have enough money for cab fare, so she decided to stay and make the best of it.

Advertising whiz Bailey began her marriage to Peter with prenuptial agreements in which she pledged to carry 50 percent of their expenses. But she never anticipated that she should have put a cap on the agreement, or that Peter would expect her to pay based on his income, which was more than five times her salary. In retrospect, she concluded that he purposely drained her assets in order to control her and keep her with him—drained them in ways that were permanent. By Peter's design, her contribution paid for everything but equity—housekeepers, gardeners, decorators, furniture—a loophole Peter would later use against her in court. Despite her financial success, he kept a tight rein on her, making her as financially vulnerable as an unemployed wife dependent on her husband's income would be.

As Peter became increasingly powerful in his industry, he also became meaner. He spent more time away from Bailey, and his temper flared more quickly and forcefully. But now these scenes were also directed at her. He became intensely critical of her, even as she garnered acclaim for her own successes. He took credit for all her accomplishments, including decisions she made on home purchases. He acted as if he were in fierce competition with her. She grew weary of his tirades at waiters and secretaries and began to feel unhappy with the way he treated her as well.

As he became "too important for his own good," Peter grew colder and colder. He began to humiliate Bailey in public. When he was upset with her, rather than pulling her aside to talk with her he would shout, "Bailey, you're such a cunt. How could you do that? Don't you dare ever do that again!" Humiliated, she dealt with his vituperations by lying to herself. "It must be my fault because I'm not sleeping with him anymore," she told herself. "I realized I was trapped in an ivory tower," she recalled later. But she also was terrified to let anyone else know. Her work, home, resources, indeed her entire life was entangled with this man. She didn't know how to extricate herself.

Women like Bailey report a common type of emotional abuse that I call *shifting sands*. The husband creates a constantly but unpredictably changing emotional reality that has a "crazy-making" and dominating effect. He sends conflicting and contradictory messages and changes his mood and emotional positions frequently. Shifting sands is different from "gaslighting," named for the movie *Gaslight*, in which the lead character comes to doubt her sanity as her reality is deliberately manipulated. As Ingrid said of Bill, "He was always very hard to please. I never knew what was going to come through the door." And Bailey said, "Peter was very demanding. And *irrational*. There was no *pattern* to what the demands were. The expectations were never clear. They would always change, and there would always be a good excuse for him to start a fight."

As a consequence of her husband's shifting sands, the woman has no clear idea of what is coming next or what she has done to provoke such behaviors. If she cannot validate reality—and this was true for most of the abused upscale wives who were living in self-imposed isolation—she relies on her husband's version of what has occurred and what is acceptable behavior on her part.

Kathleen's shifting-sands ordeal had an extremely harsh and critical tone. Stuart would act as if he loved her and wanted to save the marriage, and then just as quickly, and without any warning, he would turn on her and deride her viciously. Since Stuart had isolated Kathleen from her friends and family, she had only his feedback about her to go on. He was literally shifting the very ground on which she stood; she lost faith in her self, her strength, and who she was in the world.

Often the men used the shifting sands for their own unsavory purposes. Julia's husband, Marc, the sociology professor, berated her for not supporting his work, which entailed long hours at the office. He called her selfish when she complained that he didn't come home for dinner. But he was using the shifting-sands strategy to cover up an affair with a graduate student. He would hold Julia's hand one night and say the marriage meant everything to him, then unaccountably become disgusted with her the next day and announce that he was working late, acting as if the conversation of the night before had never occurred.

Linda's husband stormed out in a fury on Fridays and returned on Mondays. Although he blamed Linda for making him angry enough to leave, it is noteworthy that he would always become enraged on Thursday nights. He made Linda believe that she was prompting his behavior, but he neglected to tell her whose house he ran to each weekend or about the steamy hours he spent there. When she learned the truth, Linda finally pulled the sand out from under her husband and restored her own dignity. He came home one Monday morning to find that she had changed all the locks, and she never allowed him back into their home or her life again.

Many of the well-heeled husbands created shifting-sands scenarios around money. When Bill told Ingrid, "When you leave, you leave everything I ever gave to you," he changed the rules of their relationship right before her eyes. In fact, most of the women indicated that their husbands used money as a form of manipulation and an arena for shifting sands.

PHYSICAL ABUSE

More than half the women I studied endured physical abuse, including:

- pushing and shoving
- choking and strangling
- hair pulling
- pinning the woman down
- punching, hitting, throwing her against a wall or down the stairs

Ingrid experienced a significant violent episode just two months after her wedding that left her "walking on eggshells" for the rest of her difficult marriage. Bill attacked her on her birthday. She had been working at a job for training purposes related to her major. She was hurt that Bill didn't call or send greetings or flowers during the day. Birthdays had always been a major event in her family, grandly celebrated with loved ones and friends. And this year, living far from her family, she had hoped Bill would come through. Ingrid soothed herself by thinking that he probably had a surprise plan for the evening, perhaps a gourmet dinner at home or an evening out. She was so busy at work there was no time for lunch and she had to stay late. She felt starved and shaky when she got home.

When Ingrid walked into their house, Bill still did not acknowledge her birthday, even though he knew how important it was to her. She asked him what they were going to do for dinner, and he replied that he would make something as soon as the television show he was watching was over. She was surprised at his coolness but calmly said, "I'm hungry now," and went off to the kitchen to fix a cup of soup to stave off her hunger pangs.

Bill exploded unexpectedly at this remark. "That's just like you," he shouted. "You're so *selfish*. I've been here all day, and you're just going to cook something for yourself. When I come in, I fix something for both of us." She ignored his attacks, explaining that she needed a snack because of her hypoglycemia and that they could decide about dinner later. But that didn't satisfy him. "He kept saying I was selfish and ungrateful. But to me marriage was supposed to be about appreciate, admire, cherish—not about *gratefulness*," Ingrid added.

Finally, Bill got up and told her he would boil pasta and directed her to cut up vegetables. He ignored her birthday, made no gestures, chided her, and now was asking her to cook on her special day. His neglect hurt, shocked, and angered Ingrid, but she said nothing and followed his directions. After eating in silence, she politely thanked him and went upstairs. Her friends and family called with birthday greetings. She fought back tears and struggled not to reveal that she had been so ignored by her husband.

At bedtime Bill came up to their room, put a card under her pillow, and went back to the television in the den. Ingrid opened it to find a simple "Happy Birthday" wish. There was no signature with love, no gift; it could have come from a distant acquaintance. So she calmly went down to the den and, with tears in her eyes, said, "I can't believe you blew off my birthday."

That was it. Bill slammed her against the wall and choked her. Bewildered, Ingrid had no idea what had precipitated his rage. As she ran up the stairs to get away, he threw her down the steps, screaming that she was as selfish as his first wife. Back in the bedroom he continued to choke her. She gasped for breath, believing she was going to die. Finally he released her, saying, "I should kill you right now, but it would hurt my career." Then he left the room.

She immediately ruled out telling her family; they would be unsupportive, especially since they had never liked Bill. She had no money for a cab, no friends or family nearby. She thought of calling the police, but at that moment Bill came up to her, lightly apologized, and made it clear that what concerned him most was that other people shouldn't see her leave him or for the police to get involved. He asked her to stay.

Ingrid became quiet and went to bed. She had no way to make sense of what had just happened, and she never talked about it again. It was so far from what she had expected of a husband who had promised he would take care of her, and so similar to her father's beating of her mother (which she had tried hard to forget), that she made a conscious decision to bury the truth and excused Bill's behavior by labeling it a one-time event. But it did change her. "That one incident just knocked me into a whole different person," she explained, weeping. "I used to be an outspoken person—I wasn't afraid of anyone. But after that, I never talked back; I never got smart; I never said anything. I walked on eggshells *for years*. I felt like, 'Well, you're in it now. You made a commitment to this man; this is what marriage is all about!'"

THE SEXUAL ANGLE

Few of these marriages remained sexually vital. Most often the woman's lack of responsiveness was closely tied to the way her husband treated her. Indeed, for many of my research participants, sex became an obligation that brought little pleasure. Often the sexual aspect of their marriages mirrored abusive patterns that had already been established in other areas of interaction. And this is consistent with widely held clinical wisdom that the quality and frequency of sexual relations is usually a barometer for what is occurring emotionally within a marriage.

Bill would literally demand sex with Ingrid whenever he was in the mood, even if they hadn't been talking or getting along. And it was orchestrated without foreplay to please only him. If Ingrid refused or tried to put it off until another time, he insulted her, charging that something was "seriously wrong" with her.

Ray was cold and calculating about sex with Sally. He paid little attention to her satisfaction. In fact, she referred to their intercourse as "unilateral sex." Ray was the only man Sally had slept with, so she had no basis of comparison. "I didn't discuss sex with anyone; I didn't know what it was supposed to be. At first, I thought enjoyment was just for the male. Actually that's Victorian thinking. But I never really enjoyed sex." In Sally's mind sex fell into the category of "Ray's needs," and she passively complied. Ray called her frigid. "How could I get turned on?" she asked in her own defense. "It was so one-sided." And it followed the pattern established in the rest of their relationship. Everything went Ray's way, and Sally's response was to accede and withdraw. Sally chose to consciously go along with the good parts of the marriage and since she had not had other sexual partners, she believed that "this is as good as it gets."

Stuart had continually pressured Kathleen for their relationship to become sexual before they married. Although she was not a virgin, she was protecting herself from getting hurt. Leaning on her strict Catholic upbringing, she made up many excuses to keep Stuart at a sexual distance. But once they consummated their relationship, sex was not wonderful. She confessed that Stuart never thought she was passionate or interested enough in sex during their marriage. "According to him, I was 'frigid.' I didn't want to have sex as much as he did, so therefore there was something *wrong* with me. It never occurred to him that I was just different from him. But I really didn't know that I had permission to be different—I believed that there was something wrong." Kathleen pondered whether her lack of interest related to her husband's moods. Moreover, he would use sex to end an abusive incident. "I went along with that," Kathleen admitted. But when I asked if sex ended the episode for her, she replied vehemently, "God no!" In truth, she was afraid of the consequences if she refused.

Allison had a different problem: she found that her sexual overtures would go unheeded. "A month would go by," she explained, "and we hadn't had sex. I would be *begging* Robert to sleep with me, but he would refuse, usually from behind a newspaper. He'd say, 'I'm reading right now.' But this would be at 2:00 A.M. Saturday or Sunday morning. And I would think, 'The *Wall Street Journal* is better than me?' That made me feel very low, to the point where I became incapable of having an orgasm when we did sleep together. That had never happened to me before. I just shut down."

It is interesting to note that many women and their husbands used the word "frigid" to describe the woman's lack of sexual responsiveness. This word, now considered to be outdated and pejorative, was readily accepted and adopted by both partners. It became part of their shared and accepted meaning system, part of the story they told themselves about their marriage. For the men, their wives' "frigidity" could justify their criticizing and debasing her. The women most likely bought into the idea of frigidity because their self-esteem had already eroded dramatically. Indeed, out of self-protection they had shut down any remnant of warm feelings toward their abusive spouses.

Bailey was in her second marriage when she went to work for Peter. She depicted their marriage as "boring, though not mean in any way." Ironically, it was the tedium that motivated her to channel her energies toward her work. She cared for her husband, but in retrospect she realized that she applied the energy she withheld from their relationship to her career.

The quickly disappearing sex life in Bailey's marriage was a prelude to the increasing physical attraction toward Peter. "I would go into his office and feel tingly and excited by him, but I never let him know," she explained. When I asked her the basis for the attraction she replied, "His power was sexy, and he was sexy. I was good at my job right away, and he needed my energy—we became a team."

Peter started to come into her office to complain about his marriage. Bailey never talked about her own marital dissatisfactions, but she was supportive and advised him to leave his wife. To her surprise, he did just that. Concurrently and privately, she was desperately trying to end her marriage of nine years. Alarmed by the strength of her attraction to Peter, she felt as if she were cheating on her husband, which was something she could never do. Nobody knew what she was going through—she kept her passion and guilt to herself and felt lonely despite the fact that her career and industry popularity were now skyrocketing.

One night, after an office party, Peter seduced her. "He was the most powerful and persistent man I had ever been with," she said. "If his actions hadn't had some humor and flirtation attached, I could easily have seen the incident as date rape." Her ambivalence allowed her to feel the pleasure of being so desired while simultaneously feeling violated. This episode resulted in her decision to leave her marriage, no matter what. She also remained terrified about the implications of their sexual encounter. Would the power he exerted over her physically be echoed at work? Would he fire her? Would he act as if nothing had happened? Would she be just another in a list of conquests? She felt a combination of lust, fear, rage, excitement, and uncertainty.

The next day Peter called Bailey into his office and told her he was madly in love with her. Waves of relief washed over her. She knew it was inevitable that they would be together, but she pretended to be ambivalent. She needed to be convinced. She eventually left her marriage and married Peter. But his behavior changed over the course of that first year. "He started to show me who he was. His whole persona was frightening to me." And that fear and growing dislike of Peter eventually found its way into the bedroom, an arena that had been tremendously satisfying for the couple before. At some point Bailey stopped sleeping with her husband.

COPING STRATEGIES: SURVIVAL OR COLLUSION?

Coping with any type of abuse or attack begins with the first incident. How the woman makes sense of it and how she reacts sets the standard for what she will tolerate. It has been posited that the first time a woman stays with a batterer after an abusive event, she tacitly agrees to his behavior.[2] For the abused upscale wife, Benjamin Franklin's maxim "We teach people how to treat us" holds all too true.

In each of the cases I studied, it was clear that the woman understood and interpreted the first incident of abusive behavior in a way that allowed her to stay in the marriage. She was becoming a victim of a tyrannical and abusive husband. This picture didn't fit with her friends', family's, community's, society's, and even her own image of who she was, and this became alarming to her. While any woman might share this anxiety, the upscale woman's concerns become all the more palpable because she has no referents in her culture with which to compare herself—that is, "this doesn't happen to people like us." Because she feels isolated and without emotional support from others, she develops her own coping strategies to deal with the assaults as the husband progresses. Some of these strategies (many of which are similar to those adopted by abused women of all socioeconomic classes) are brought into play immediately after the first incident; others become most prominent toward the middle and later segments of the path:

- She denies what is happening, burying the reality deep below consciousness or distancing herself from it.
- She blames herself, buying into her husband's claims that her behavior causes his violent rage.
- She calms herself by thinking that this is what marriage is about.
- She chooses to believe he won't do it again (by her wish or by his words).
- She reminds herself of the solemnity of her marriage vows.
- She uses alcohol or drugs to soothe herself.
- She becomes very quiet, "plays possum".
- She watches vigilantly, scanning to predict or anticipate the abusive behaviors.

- She does not discuss the abusive episode with her spouse.
- She explains away his bad behavior—for example, "his rage at me is a reflection of his worry about work"—a practice I call *justification by explanation.*
- She clings to the idealized view of how the marriage could be.
- She secretly strategizes her escape from the marriage.

In the upscale marriages I examined, episodes of abusiveness were often intermingled with periods of calm, even pleasurable times. By providing the false hope that her situation would improve, this intermittent positive reinforcement—which I referred to in Chapter 3 as *slot machine love*—induced the woman to decide to stay. Variable or intermittent reinforcement, like playing the slots, is seductive and addictive. The woman never knows when it will pay off, and she stays longer since she has already invested so much. She would hate to walk away just when she believes her investment of time, energy, and pain is about to hit pay dirt! Seeming passivity, "playing possum," ignoring or going along with abusive behavior—these actions are quite different from learned helplessness, which results in inaction. These are conscious strategies to achieve the greater goal of making the marriage work. Paradoxically, these active coping responses are very typical of the upscale woman, who is used to being effective in the world; learned helplessness, on the other hand, arises in response to an uncontrollable environment.

Ingrid tried to forget about her husband's birthday assault. She wanted to honor her marriage commitment, and she especially did not want to be divorced like her mother. "Except for Bill's rages and sexual demands, I liked my life," she said. She thought of Bill as an intelligent and engaging man. What had occurred was so ugly that she wanted it to all disappear so she could continue the life she hoped she would have. "Time passes, you don't talk about it. It's under the rug," she explained.

The coping strategies also make the abuse seem survivable. Kathleen's initial response was to withdraw from her husband after his tennis court tirade. "I didn't do anything," she explained to me. "I would just go and do my 'quiet thing,' which is what I learned to do. I would be withdrawn for a few hours. That would last for a few days. I would play possum." Drinking also became part of Kathleen's defense. "Whenever I was angry with him, I would drink. In fact, I would drink a lot when we were alone. He made me nervous, and I was calmer and better able to deal with him after I had a few."

"The first time he hit me," Kathleen recalled, "a part of me said, 'This isn't supposed to happen when you get married, so I should *go now.*' But there was another part of me that said, 'No, you're married for better or for worse.'"

The very few upscale women who left after the first violent incident re-
united with their husband shortly thereafter in an effort to "make the marriage work." This is understandable. Many women want to salvage a
relationship they had pledged to be part of through good times and bad.

The ups and downs in Allison and Robert's marriage were typical of the
terrifying roller coaster ride in store for the battered woman who tries to
"make the marriage work." After their disastrous European honeymoon, the
negative aspects of their marital life did not abate. But at the same time Allison luxuriated in the glamorous and colorful lifestyle. She took wonderful vacations, received compliments on her spectacular engagement and wedding
rings, enjoyed membership in an exclusive country club where Robert played
golf, employed a maid for their new condominium, and was able to pursue
her doctorate without having to work. All of this led her to look away from
Robert's foul moods. She distracted herself by putting her mental energies
into writing her dissertation.

But a year into the marriage they had a fight that ended with Robert as-
saulting her. Someone had taken Allison's designated parking space. When
she asked Robert to talk to the garage managers, he became irate. She had
asked him to help her with something he believed she could handle on her
own. Instead of simply telling her to deal with it herself, he shoved and
mocked her. Then he took the car keys and house keys and locked her out of
their condo.

This was the first time Robert had laid hands on Allison during a fight, and
the first time his actions could have put her in physical jeopardy. She banged
on the door, begging him to let her back in. "I'm really sorry for anything I
did to make you so angry," she wept. Robert never opened the door. It was
winter, and Allison had been thrown out of the house without her coat or
purse. Freezing cold, she finally walked two miles to his sister's house. Blaming herself all the way, she wondered what she might have done to provoke
such behavior. Her sister-in-law welcomed her, and she stayed with her family for a week. This was the first time anyone outside the marriage learned of
the escalating domestic tyranny that Allison was enduring.

Robert and Allison got back together when she decided to give him another chance. She made excuses for his behavior, believing that maybe he was
depressed because of a reversal at work and was just taking it out on her. She
thought that he would never be so cruel again; after all, they were educated
and civilized people who didn't behave like this. Robert was glad that she returned but showed no remorse for his behavior. This pattern—Allison apologizing in order for their relationship to continue—had started before they
were married, but their reconciliation this time marked a significant turning

point—from this time on, physical abuse would become part of Robert's explosive style.

One night months later Allison complained that she resented his sexual indifference. If she didn't get more attention from him, she suggested, they would have to go to a marriage counselor. Robert became enraged at her suggestion that someone else become involved in their private lives. He threw her on the bed and tried to smother her with pillows. Unable to breathe or scream, she thought she would be murdered during these moments of terror. He finally released her, and punched her in the face, blackening an eye. She believed this was the last straw.

Unlike many upscale abused wives, Allison did not keep the horror of Robert's actions a secret. The next day she decided to share what had happened with a professor in her program. Her teacher was empathetic. She told Allison she didn't have to tolerate such treatment; a loving, marital relationship did not include violence. Allison also told her parents. They, too, were immediately helpful and protective. Rather than judging her as having failed at her marriage, as she had feared, they were outraged at her husband's behavior. They encouraged her to leave him and invited her to stay with them. She moved to her parents' home that night.

After a week Robert called and asked Allison to return, agreeing to go to counseling. He was more attentive during her first days back. She began to feel hopeful but was concerned that he was not more apologetic or interested in how they could make their marriage better. Allison made an appointment with a counselor. But the weekend before this meeting her hopes faded when Robert hit her again. "I just put it out of my head," she confessed about her state of denial. "I was in shock. I just didn't think it happened."

In thinking about Allison's situation, we must wonder whether her attempts to cope and adapt actually became her way of colluding with her abusive partner. As she sought the means to "make the marriage work," was she simply getting herself more deeply entrenched? It is the continued denial and perseverance in the face of abuse that sets the abused woman apart from other women who are unhappy in their marriages. Yet Allison, like the other women I studied, seemed to talk herself into staying.

THE DEEPER PSYCHOLOGICAL UNDERPINNINGS

The status of the abused woman's self plays a part in convincing herself to stay in an unhealthy marriage. A cohesive self would be sorely dissatisfied with and unwilling to tolerate an abuser's injuries and assaults.[3] The battered upscale wife is so in need of reassurance, however, that merely a kind word from her husband keeps her on the path. In an ironic twist, the very man who cuts down her self-esteem is the one to whom she turns to help her feel better about herself. If he isolates her from others, as so many abusers do to maintain control and loyalty, she is that much more dependent on his erratic nurturing to make her feel whole and unfragmented.

Life with the upscale abuser certainly has its particular ups and downs. The woman may be depressed and experience a keen sense of internal emptiness, which she tries to ward off. Even the randomness of her husband's explosions provides excitement that can distract her from her despair. The abuser partly attenuates the loss and insecurity his vulnerable wife has suffered. Their connection, while cruel and inconsistent, is filled with intensity and drama and provides additional stimuli (aside from the stimulation of the upscale lifestyle) to ward off her deadening feelings of emptiness. Consider Kathleen, lost and lonely in Europe. Her relationship with Stuart had a medicating effect and was one way she dealt with the pain of separation from her family.

These are misdirected connections, generated in the hope of feeling better by becoming attached to someone who provides special attention and seems to have so much to offer. But as her husband's "good" side is slowly overshadowed by his darker and abusive nature, the woman continues to hold fast to the belief that she can influence him to give her what she sorely needs. She hopes she can "make" her partner become a loving and protective caregiver, and this new challenge provides her with vigor and direction.

Heinz Kohut suggests that the need for admiration from another can become addictive. The self-esteem of a battered wife is compromised while she remains in the abusive situation. No doubt there are moments when her partner can connect with her and even provide her with a sense of *twinship*—the feeling of being exactly like her in thought, spirit, and mind, hence a feeling of deep connection.[4] Such moments are fleeting, of course, but they recur often enough to trigger the syndrome of slot machine love.[5]

From a self psychology perspective, in the beginning and middle phases of the path the abused upscale wife

- makes an unhealthy attempt to get her husband (a significant other who knows her well) to provide selfobject functions and complete her sense of self
- uses the drama of the relationship as a palliative against the emptiness within

- finds herself addicted to the intermittent positive feelings that her partner provides, causing her to remain ever hopeful for more
- focuses on the material benefits and status of the upscale marriage
- stays connected to an abusive partner to ward off the anxiety that losing him might evoke

But no matter what her reasons are, the woman is constructing a story she is living in, telling herself a story about her marriage to make it tolerable for her to remain in it.

HOW AN ABUSED UPSCALE WOMAN CONVINCES HERSELF TO STAY

The distinct impression that she is solitary in what is happening to her and that she is so different from her peers evokes in the upscale abused woman feelings of inadequacy and embarrassment. She tries to comprehend the behavior of her bright, successful, and allegedly loving husband while striving to maintain her grasp on her sense of self and identity. But these two realities do not mesh. Sally's sad joke about Martha Stewart frowning upon a husband beating his wife after a dinner party poignantly reflects this dissonance.

Accustomed to success and achievements, the upscale woman initially reacts to her husband's abuse by turning to her own abilities for answers (although in the end she forgets she has resources that would allow her to leave). This is known as self-blame. If a woman convinces herself that she caused the problem, then she can believe it to be within her control to find a solution. She uses her skills to try to predict the next outburst so that she can avoid it or soothe it away. The goal-oriented woman may cling to the ideal view of marriage, believing it to be something she can attain if she works at it hard enough.

Moreover, in her attempts to flee the embarrassment of being so different from the people around her, she embellishes rationalizations for why the abuse occurs. She justifies the assaults with elaborate psychological explanations about her husband's childhood. Or she soothes herself by buying into the notion that staying is a conscious choice that will help her reap financial benefits for herself and her children. The tendency toward such rationalization was pronounced in all the women I met. Sally explained: "I had two children, and I had high expectations for them. They were very bright, and I wanted them to reach their full potential. I realized I could never provide for them myself. Ray always told me, 'If you ever leave me, I'd never give you a cent. You'd be out on the street selling pencils.' How could I do that to my kids? I made a choice to stick it out for their sake."

It is remarkable that Sally, like the others, rejected her own powers of reasoning. If she left Ray, she could probably receive alimony—and most likely handsome alimony and child support at that. Why did she buy into his threats? It is apparent that during this stretch of the path, the woman's reasoning becomes attenuated as her self-esteem plummets and her isolation increases.

By believing that she has made her bed and must now sleep in it, the abused woman rallies her inner resources to be tough and rise to a difficult occasion. The more highly educated she is, the more likely she is to fall into this way of thinking. The self-justification of making one's bed is defensive in that it diverts a woman's attention from the heart of the problem—she is being abused and doesn't deserve such treatment—and reinforces the belief that she should have known better. It implies that the she has the fortitude to "make do" and "stick with" her original decision, which she made based on what she knew about her future husband at the time. For an educated woman to abandon such an important decision would be an embarrassment and an admission of failure.

Having used this rationalization, the woman looks at the upscale neighborhood in which she has made her bed and tells herself that she should cope with her situation because the benefits of the marriage and its lifestyle greatly compensate for the periodic abuse. As Sally explained, "I felt I was taking whatever I had to in order for my children to be raised in the type of environment they should be."

Besides, she believes she must be able to endure because she is smart enough to do so. Ironically, the upscale abused woman may become a victim of her positive self-image: the ever-successful, resourceful woman who can do or fix anything. Such a demanding self-perception may give her strength and self-confidence, but it may also lead to a perfectionistic perseverance that renders it difficult to expose a personal failure—her marriage—even though it is her husband's abuses that have brought it about. It is ironic that she doesn't readily use this self-image to propel herself into creating a new life.

THE NARRATIVE APPROACH TO ONE'S LIFE

No matter how a woman justifies or adapts to abuse, she spins some kind of story to make sense of it, a narrative to soothe her crippled sense of power. Like all of us, the battered upscale woman creates a story to give meaning to the events in her life. Our personal meaning system is paramount in our experience of our identity and our sense of self in the world.[6] The postmodern constructionist view posits that there is no absolute reality. We each bring our own meanings, twists, and interpretations to it.[7] If there is no objective "real" world but rather an infinite variety of unique mental creations, then a person's self-narrative determines what is possible for her.[8] Joseph Palombo, a psychotherapist and founding dean of the Institute of Clinical Social Work in Chicago, has suggested that one's mental health is relative to "the degree to which the narrative integrates not only personal meanings derived from experiences but also shared meanings created in interaction with others."[9]

External voices contribute to the narrative. Women, more than men, rely on others (often authority figures) for the information that makes up what they know about the world.[10] Society, religious institutions, and significant others may tell a woman that she ought to be patient, supportive, tolerant, understanding, and other-oriented. It is important for a person's sense of meaning to feel "part of the human community,"[11] and many women feel compelled to go along with what society indicates are appropriate thoughts, feelings, and actions. Unfortunately, these messages may cause an abused woman to disregard her inner voice and may reinforce her attempts to explain her partner's unacceptable behavior. They also may increase her sense of shame. In a community where "such things never happen," the abused woman may obey the imperative of silence, expecting no support.

It is therefore possible that a woman who stays in an abusive relationship has become so identified with her problem that it has become the dominant narrative around which she constructs her life story. It is this story that may keep her on the path.[12] If society tells a woman that what she is experiencing at home does not exist in our world, she must construct a narrative that conforms with her culture. She becomes *emplotted* in the story that our culture has assigned her: "Abuse doesn't happen to people like us, so make the best of your life, which is pretty good anyway if you compare it to everyone else's."[13] She may be so wrapped up in this narrative that she loses all sense of volition—hence the justifications by explanation, the excuses, and the self-blame. She may buy her husband's line that she is a bad wife, sharing his meaning system. The abused woman's story may be incohesive—out of sync with what she knows to be true—yet she sticks with it because it guides her in directions that she thinks are in her best interest. But they may not be.

Ingrid was determined to tell no one about what had happened to her. She was embarrassed that she was scared of her husband and ashamed that she was unable to make him happy—the explanation she gave herself for his battering. In addition to feeling responsible, she also thought that no one would believe her. Bill had such a cadre of admirers in the state government, the university system, and the community that people would think she was insane or lying. She rationalized to herself that being married to Bill could provide her with the best of worlds as a politician's wife, a graduate student, and a mother. She felt a sense of control over his behavior as she tried to modify her actions in order to mollify his moods. She clung to the idea that it could be a reasonable marriage.

Although women of all classes may rationalize and try to make an abusive marriage last, when an upscale woman identifies with and becomes part of the myth that "this doesn't happen to people like us," the need for a self-narrative is even more profound. She is alone and feels like a shamed misfit who endures in isolation. Believing that no one else in her social circle is also experiencing such abuse (since no one talks about it), she feels separate and uniquely secluded. She is caught between blaming herself, leaving, or calling the police. Her coping skills reinforce her decision to stay in a marital situation that only worsens, slowly destroying her sense of self.

This again leads to the question: Is the upscale abused wife adapting to her situation or is she implicitly collaborating by partaking in her husband's abusive behaviors? I believe that when this woman makes the usually conscious choice to stay, she takes on an active role in perpetuating the abusive marriage. This concept is not blaming in nature. *If the abused upscale woman can recognize her role in colluding in her husband's behavior, she can more quickly find a way to exit the marriage.* She can build a new narrative—one that fosters her sense of self, power, and ultimately well-being—as a foundation for creating an abuse-free world for herself and her children.

SECRET STRATEGIZING: HOPE FOR A WAY OUT

Of all the coping mechanisms I have seen, the one strategy that can become a woman's ticket out of an abusive marriage and a key to her psychological survival is what I call *secret strategizing*—that is, her plan to survive while she stays as well as her plan to leave.

Bailey, for instance, went into psychotherapy with her husband, Peter, hoping her lot could improve. But after three sessions the psychiatrist spoke to her separately and, breaking with professional tradition, told her, "I don't know how you can stay with him. He is impossible and will not change. You must get out!" On one level this admonition was a relief, since it was the first direct validation Bailey had received about Peter's actions toward her.

She pondered what to do next. Rather than leave or confront him, she slowly started to set money aside, money that was hers alone. She also found ways not to go to bed. Peter's arms felt like a straitjacket around her and caused her to hyperventilate. So she would sneak out in the middle of the night, although two out of three times he would awaken and scream at her to return. Despite his bullying behavior, she didn't give in. When he discovered that she was saving money and confronted her, asking if she was planning to leave him, she denied it. But it was her secret strategizing that kept her sanity intact for the next year.

Allison, too, made long-term escape plans, after Robert punched her. She decided to finish her Ph.D. with his financial support and then leave him once she had a job. She figured she would find a way to tolerate his abuses and try to stay out of his way. But during this planning phase she became pregnant. Her decision to keep the baby forced her to stay in the marriage for two more years. But she remained true to her original plan—she would stay only as long as it took for her to become able to support herself (and now her baby, too) as a single parent.

Although Allison continued to believe that domestic abuse occurred only among lower-income groups, and that she was just in a bad marriage with serious communication problems, she was ashamed that she put up with being struck and embarrassed that she had married someone who would hit her. She resurrected a shield of secrecy and never again told anyone about her home life. As the "star" student, she could not be seen as living in an oppressive marriage. She lied to her parents when she told them that things had gotten better between her and Robert. She did not want them to worry. And she learned to read his moods. When she saw a certain look on his face, she went to the library to work. She avoided talking to him about his behavior since that would inevitably lead to a fight. She tried to accommodate to his refusal to help with chores.

Why would she do this? Her baby was coming, and Allison still harbored a slim hope that Robert's gentler nurturing side would emerge after their child was born. She still wished that the marriage could become more peaceful, even if not idyllic. Unfortunately for Allison and her new baby, this did not occur. Robert continued to hit her sporadically during the pregnancy and thereafter, until the day he tried again to smother her and she locked herself and their seven-week-old child in the closet. It was then that she made her final plans to leave him.

Bailey and Allison were not victims as they began their plans to escape. Like prisoners of war, such women find it soothing and emotionally sustaining to envision ways to escape. But the overall policy of keeping the domestic abuse a secret is a choice determined in part by the culture within which the upscale abused wife lives.

SECRECY AS A SUSTAINING FACTOR

Although there may be some early secrecy among abused wives of other income levels, it is the intensity of isolation and secret-keeping that is emblematic of upscale violence. Indeed, I have found that what distinguishes upscale violence is that this wife isolates herself and keeps the abuse hidden as a direct result of her social class and the environment in which she has been raised and currently resides.

Typically we keep a confidence when we have pledged silence or when something occurs that we feel should be hidden. Intimacy requires that lovers keep secret the words they speak to each other in bed or the way they share their love for one another. But when the reason for hiding an action is unrelated to such private matters, our motivation is usually based in our anticipation of the negative consequences of exposing what we perceive to be a shameful or embarrassing situation.

In Chapter 2, I discussed the many reasons why an upscale woman would conceal the violence in her marriage. In addition to the shame and her concern that no one would believe it could happen to "people like us," this woman also fears that others will not believe the true character of their abusive husbands. Unfortunately, in all too many cases the persona that the charming, successful, well-respected upscale man projects is seriously at odds with who he is as a husband. Remember that Ray's friends saw him as "Gentle Ben." Unlike Bailey's Peter, whose rage was part of his "killer" reputation, many of these men appeared to be wise, kind, and loving; those who knew them held them in high esteem. As one of my patients said, "Everybody loves Joe. He's real sweet. No one could ever buy that he beat me. I think that's the reason I never told anybody. They would have laughed at me!"

And in fact all too often, important people in the lives of these women—people whose belief in their complaints might have helped them leave their abusers earlier—never believed them. This reinforced the wives' decisions to keep their terrible secrets. When Irene mentioned Carl's abusive humiliations to her mother-in-law, she was sternly reminded of what a great provider he was and told that, compared to most women, she "had a good deal." But most of these women felt they had a bad deal, and often they felt responsible for it.

"Failure" in an upscale marriage could also result in material and financial losses, even for women like Bailey, who were doing well on their own professionally. Many feared they would be forced to leave their home, their neighborhood, and their lifestyle if they revealed what was happening. Some were aware that if they brought the abuse to light, as Irene did by publicly exposing Carl's behavior, the negative impact on their husband's reputation could hurt them as well. They also feared retaliation. One woman told me, with a sigh, "If I talked about the abuse, his wealthy family would have warned me. . . . How do I say this? I would have been punished financially, and I probably would have had to move from this community."

Indeed, another very potent reason for keeping the abuse a secret is the woman's fear of inciting her husband's rage and vindictiveness. Some women fear for their own and their children's well-being. As we will see in the Chapters 6 and 8, the husband's slightest attempt to harm the children tended to be a final straw for the wife. Far more often, however, her concerns were financial. And even though despite their fears most women who ultimately divorced were able to continue living in homes and neighborhoods of comparable economic status (Appendix A), they had no way of knowing that outcome in advance.

What becomes increasingly clear is that, owing to her abundant educational and financial resources and her access to friends and helping professionals, the upscale abused woman is not a victim of her marriage. Rather, she actually makes conscious decisions to stay, utilizing coping strategies to make her life bearable. What she is up against, however, is society's lack of belief in upscale abuse and lack of support and help for her need or efforts to exit the marriage. She is part of a community that clings to the myth that abuse only occurs among the lower classes—a myth that serves to invalidate the upscale abused woman's experiences, leaving her on a downward spiral of isolation, self-doubt, and in some cases depression.

Secrecy protects the highly valued intimate bond the woman has forged with her husband, however badly he has broken his vow to love, honor, and cherish her. And yet it is breaking through this isolation and talking to others that ultimately help the upscale abused wife to free herself and start life anew. Indeed, most of the women I studied found this to be true. The upscale woman needs to "come out" (and to more than just one person or her parents, as in Allison's case) in order to learn that spousal abuse is happening not just to her but also perhaps to her neighbor in the eight-bedroom home across the cul-de-sac. The secrecy that she believes is protecting her is actually condemning her, in some cases sentencing her to physical injuries and even death.

One woman vividly recalled her feelings when she finally opened up to her attorney. "It was unbelievable," she told me. "It was like I was stepping toward the light." And Sally recommended that other upscale abused wives put an end to the silence. "You should talk to others," she said, "so that you understand that what you're living through isn't normal."

STAYING THE COURSE

Over time, single incidents turn into a chronic pattern of abuse. The hardening of an abusive upscale marriage is marked by the following signposts:

- *Emotional and physical abuses:* The husband's emotionally and physically abusive behaviors increase and even worsen.
- *Coping strategies:* The woman's coping strategies change and intensify to keep up with the husband's worsening behavior. Her narrative reflects her justifications for staying in her abusive marriage.
- *Adapting to the situation:* The woman's denial and rationalizing increases. She uses justification by explanation. She may secretly begin to strategize to leave.
- *Man's behaviors that she adapts to:* Entitlement, insistence on strict domestic roles, abuse in front of the children or threats to children's well-being, inadequate or minimal apologies after abusiveness, sexual entitlement and attack on woman's sexuality.
- *Secrecy and isolation:* The woman's need for secrecy increases because there is more to hide and more that she feels would probably be disbelieved.
- *Into the fray:* The woman's choices, and her ways of enduring in an abusive marriage and keeping it going, push her that much further into her role as an upscale abused wife.

It is the upscale abused woman's increased coping, her expanding tolerance for her husband's heinous behavior, and her intensifying secrecy and isolation that entrench her in an untenable situation. Through these accommodations to domestic and marital horrors she becomes habituated to her new role as recipient of abuse within her upscale marriage. She is in effect making choices and taking steps further along the path of an upscale abused wife.

The Path of the Upscale Abused Wife: Staying In

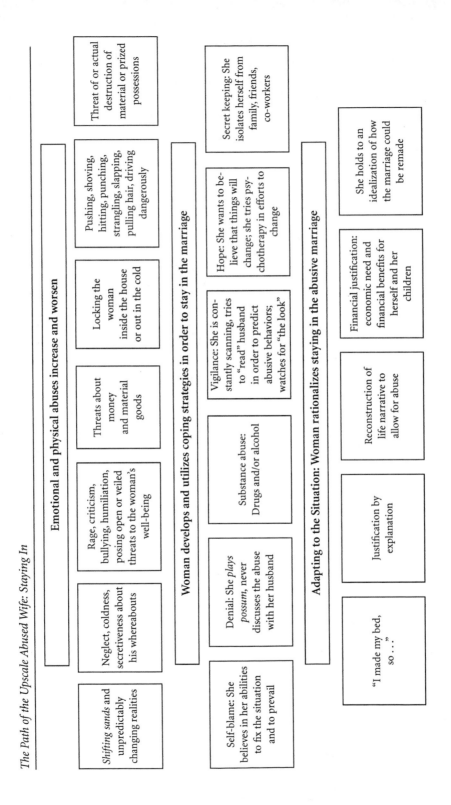

Emotional and physical abuses increase and worsen

Shifting sands and unpredictably changing realities

Neglect, coldness, secretiveness about his whereabouts

Rage, criticism, bullying, humiliation, posing open or veiled threats to the woman's well-being

Threats about money and material goods

Locking the woman inside the house or out in the cold

Pushing, shoving, hitting, punching, strangling, slapping, pulling hair, driving dangerously

Threat of or actual destruction of material or prized possessions

Woman develops and utilizes coping strategies in order to stay in the marriage

Self-blame: She believes in her abilities to fix the situation and to prevail

Denial: She *plays possum*, never discusses the abuse with her husband

Substance abuse: Drugs and/or alcohol

Vigilance: She is constantly scanning, tries to "read" husband in order to predict abusive behaviors; watches for "the look"

Hope: She wants to believe that things will change; she tries psychotherapy in efforts to change

Secret keeping: She isolates herself from family, friends, co-workers

Adapting to the Situation: Woman rationalizes staying in the abusive marriage

"I made my bed, so . . ."

Justification by explanation

Reconstruction of life narrative to allow for abuse

Financial justification: economic need and financial benefits for herself and her children

She holds to an idealization of how the marriage could be remade

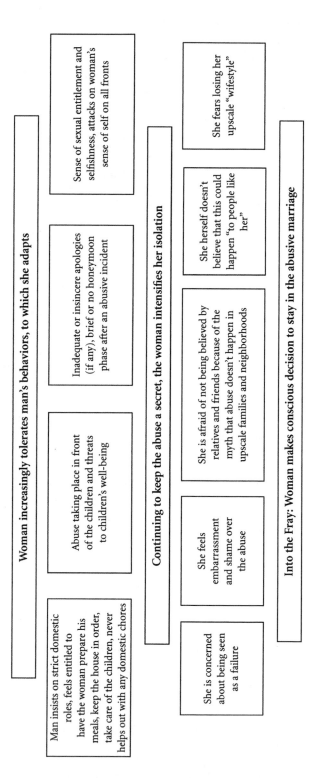

Woman increasingly tolerates man's behaviors, to which she adapts

Man insists on strict domestic roles, feels entitled to have the woman prepare his meals, keep the house in order, take care of the children, never helps out with any domestic chores

Abuse taking place in front of the children and threats to children's well-being

Inadequate or insincere apologies (if any), brief or no honeymoon phase after an abusive incident

Sense of sexual entitlement and selfishness, attacks on woman's sense of self on all fronts

Continuing to keep the abuse a secret, the woman intensifies her isolation

She is concerned about being seen as a failure

She feels embarrassment and shame over the abuse

She is afraid of not being believed by relatives and friends because of the myth that abuse doesn't happen in upscale families and neighborhoods

She herself doesn't believe that this could happen "to people like her"

She fears losing her upscale "wifestyle"

Into the Fray: Woman makes conscious decision to stay in the abusive marriage

6

Going Public and Getting Going: "I'm Outta Here . . ."

SALLY TOLD ME SHE FELT AS IF SHE WERE TRAPPED and hunted in a "Chippendale prison" during the years she was married to her violent husband. Held hostage by her fear of retribution and loss, she concluded that she could not leave Ray until her children were launched and on their own. Sally was ensnared within the elegant confines of their home and told no one about Ray's worsening attacks. But the silence with which she enshrouded herself only stiffened her sentence. Like many other battered upscale women, she lived in a torture chamber. It was well cushioned and beautifully decorated, but she suffered unimaginable emotional and physical torments there nonetheless.

Bailey also reported feeling trapped within the silence she had created. Because she was determined to keep the private image of her marriage as shiny as the public one—both were under scrutiny—she relegated her moments of agony to a secret dwelling within. Although Bailey would easily have garnered support and credibility in revealing Peter's obnoxious behavior and violent moods to those who knew him, she kept silent, maintaining the facade of their marital partnership.

In the face of Bailey's obligingness, Peter's public tirades against her increased and even became routine. She grew weary of defending him to others and patching the rifts he created. She longed for the day when she would leave him. And yet, within the gates of their beautiful vacation retreats along the eastern seaboard, Bailey's *secret strategizing*—saving money and making plans to leave—did not result in immediate change. She still hung in, hoping against hope that a business failure might humble Peter a bit. Unfortunately, corporate setbacks merely increased his defensive arrogance and his hostility toward her and the rest of his world. For the patient and gracious Bailey,

Peter's behavior had to escalate beyond his "normal hideousness" before she could finally tell others and walk out.

Yet Sally and Bailey, like the hundreds of other women with whom I have worked, did manage to break free. How did they cut through invisible bars and smash a hole in the polished walls to escape their abusive husband's tyrannies? What are the obstacles these women must negotiate as they try to leave the path? Let us be clear at this point that not all upscale abused women get off the path by leaving their partner. Some opt to remain in the marriage but step off the path by setting and enforcing limits with a husband who is motivated to save his marriage and able to modify his behavior (see Chapter 9). Either choice requires courage, for the risks can be great.

SEPARATION VIOLENCE

The battered upscale woman must consider many impediments to leaving. Typically a woman leaves several times before finally quitting the abusive marriage for good. Often an abuser uses threats about money, the children, and further violence to compel her to stay. He is in a financial position to thwart her legally with numerous proceedings, even if frivolous, and can also wage a custody battle, obstructing her efforts to keep the children. According to Deborah Tucker, executive director of the National Training Center on Domestic and Sexual Violence, upscale husbands have even used their power and influence to put their wives in psychiatric hospitals. "If a batterer is smooth and well heeled and says, 'Doctor, my wife is a danger to herself and our children—she is hysterical,' it is very difficult for the woman to be believed," she told me.[1]

And while remaining in the marriage may not be the answer, the most dangerous time for a woman is precisely when she decides to leave. In a *Psychology Today* article about Sarah Buel, clinical professor at the University of Texas School of Law and codirector of the university's Domestic Violence Clinic, the former Massachusetts assistant district attorney explained that "one of the biggest reasons women stay [. . .] is that they are most vulnerable when they leave. That's when abusers desperately escalate tactics of control. More domestic abuse victims are killed when fleeing than at any other time."[2] The following statistics tell the tale:

- In 1991 the Bureau of Justice Statistics reported that separated and divorced women were fourteen times more likely to report having been a victim of domestic violence than married women.[3]

- In 1995 the same agency found that women separated from their husband were three times more likely to be victimized by their spouse than divorced women, and twenty-five times more likely to be victimized by their spouse than married women.[4]
- A 1997 report from the Florida Governor's Task Force on Domestic and Sexual Violence found that 65 percent of intimate homicide victims physically separated from the perpetrator prior to their death.[5]
- Research published in the 1980s revealed that 73 percent of abused women seeking emergency medical services sustained injuries after leaving the batterer.[6]
- Other studies have found that women are most likely to be murdered when attempting to report abuse or to leave an abusive relationship.[7]

Why the upswing in violence at this time? When the woman threatens to leave she challenges her husband's control over her, takes action on her own behalf that may interfere with his interests, and signals that she is contemplating life without him.[8] Perhaps the escalation of violence is retaliatory, or maybe the husband is seeking to coerce or intimidate his wife into staying. As we will see in Chapter 7, leaving is the ultimate betrayal for the narcissistic batterer, and his rage can engender murderous impulses as the woman he believed to be a part of him appears to be separating from him. Many a batterer murders his wife when she admits that she no longer loves or trusts him.[9] These dangers are heightened if the woman is isolated and gets no support. This can also be an especially treacherous time because the courts and police are limited in their ability to protect her (see Chapter 10). Her husband's renewed threats and violence often convince her to return to the domestic prison.

Nevertheless, although leaving an abuser may pose additional hazards, ultimately a battered woman is best able to achieve safety and freedom apart from him.[10] Strategic planning and legal intervention are required to dodge separation violence. Enforcement advocates and battered women must work in partnership to ensure that the separation process is safeguarded against batterer violence.[11]

EMOTIONAL DIFFICULTIES IN BREAKING FREE

Aside from the threat of continued or worsening violence, battered upscale women may have unconscious emotional barriers to contend with when they contemplate leaving. In most abusive upscale relationships, the women do not stay because they are masochists. Good times and luxurious perks often intersperse with violent episodes. Their lifestyle becomes part of their identity. And many women point to their need to stay the course for the sake of their children or their commitment to their marriage.

However, there may be a deeper psychological motivation. If the woman experiences her husband as a selfobject—a person whose presence lessens her anxiety about herself and her place in the world—the prospect of losing him can stir up primitive anxiety akin to what a child might feel if her environment is uncertain or marked by change. The woman not only anticipates losing her husband, who provides some form of financial and emotional security, but dreads the disintegration of her sense of self.[12] In truth, she can be less afraid of losing her husband than she is of losing the sense of connectedness he provides.

There is a need for selfobject functions in all relationships.[13] When two people attach to one another, both must open their semipermeable boundaries to let the energy flow between them. In creating this emotional connection, they feel enlarged and made more whole than when each was single. This is especially true when we fall in love.[14] If divorce or death splits a couple, grieving is natural as the boundaries slowly mend. Some withering of the original boundaries reflects the loss and the impact of the other person. However, the anxiety surrounding the loss of selfobject connectedness is heightened in abusive marriages. If a woman starts off with somewhat deteriorated boundaries, owing to either a chronic deficit or an acute depleted state, she feels the absence of her spouse that much more keenly.

For the wife who is shakily related to an abusive husband, the thought of terminating the relationship can cause anxiety. She fears missing the wholeness she attributes to her connection with her mate, especially if he has isolated her from friends and family. The end of the marriage is filled with despair and emptiness. This also helps us to understand why coming out and making new connections are so vital for the upscale abused woman who has shrouded her drama for so long. These new relationships help to fill her internal void.

THROUGH THE EYES AND EARS OF OTHERS

A woman cannot escape an abusive marriage unless she first realizes that she is being battered and puts a name to her situation. Often this insight comes through others. As psychiatrist Jean Baker Miller of the Stone Center of Wellesley College[15] has aptly observed of women in unequal relationships:

One can know oneself only through action and interaction. To the extent that their range of action or interaction is limited, subordinates will lack a realistic evaluation of their capacities and problems. Unfortunately, this difficulty in gaining self-knowledge is even further compounded. Tragic confusion arises because subordinates absorb a large part of the untruths created by the dominants. . . . This internalization of dominant beliefs is more likely to occur if there are few alternative concepts at hand.[16]

Upscale abused women have internalized their husband's and society's scripts for them. And because of their shame and isolation, they have limited interaction with others outside the home who might offer them alternative viewpoints. Yet these women retain a glimmer of their own truths and reality—no matter what the accepted cultural myth, no matter what their husbands tell them, and no matter how strong their denial. This disparity creates an inner tension. Interacting with others brings the inner truth to the surface, simply by acknowledgment and validation. Most women report that it was input from *external sources*—friends, relatives, therapists, lawyers, even strangers—that ultimately helped them recognize they were in an abusive marriage and gave them the courage and permission to get out. But this is not simply another example of a "talking cure." For these women, talking and sharing breathed life back into their own perceptions, desires, and standards; it revitalized their moribund sense of themselves and their self-worth. After gaining this confirmation, over time they were able to reconnect with their own power and competencies.

One woman told me that a friend's physician—not her own—had helped her conclude that she was married to a batterer. She had visited her obstetrician for a one-year postnatal checkup. "The doctor was just checking off overall health history," Marsha explained, "and he said, 'Of course, no abuse or violence in the home. . . .' I started to say, 'But . . . ,' and he was just so confident in how he had ticked that off as a 'No' that I didn't speak up."

I asked Marsha why she thought the obstetrician was so sure there was no domestic violence in her home. She replied, "Because I have an image of being you know, I live on the North Shore. I'm *educated*. I have a medical background. We had more of a professional relationship than a patient-doctor relationship. I talked to him about all sorts of things."

The opportunity was missed. But a few months later Marsha was talking to a friend's doctor, a woman she knew socially. "She asked me why I looked so worried and what had happened to cause the bruise on my arm. Her kind questions caused a mixture of relief and terror in me. When I turned pale and hesitated, she added, 'Are you OK?' She was so warm and accepting, I just blurted out what was going on at home. She looked at me and said, 'I suspected years ago that you had it tough, that you were taking on *everything*, that you had to be concerned about everyone's needs, and that there was no one doing that for you.' Then I told her about my husband's violence. She didn't flinch or act like I was crazy. And I was *amazed* that in two minutes she had a grip on the situation. 'I'm so sorry. I always had an uncomfortable feeling around your husband but couldn't put my finger on it. Is your husband from a family with an alcoholic? Was his father abusive to his mother?'

"'When his father drank, all hell broke loose in the house,' I said.

"'That's the same cycle he was probably put through and learned,' the doctor explained, 'and then he puts the other people in his life through it too.' That's when I started to recognize a pattern of abuse. Not that a lightbulb went off, but I thought, 'Phew, now I have a reason.'" The feedback from an outsider helped Marsha begin to crystallize her thoughts about what was happening in her marriage. Her husband's outbursts weren't just disconnected incidents; they were part of an ongoing pattern of abuse.

As she breaks the silence, the upscale abused wife begins to feel affirmed and validated. The rationalizations she once relied on to sustain her within the marriage and to maintain the marital relationship begin to break down. Soon they become useless and obsolete. She slowly rejects them as she confronts the *cognitive dissonance*—the contradiction between her own knowledge and what she sees going on. It is remarkable yet not surprising that battered women have the highest tolerance for cognitive dissonance and can square two disparate realities that will never match—hatred and violence in a "loving marriage."[17] At this point the woman is relieved to step away from her self-deception.

For Ingrid, the mere fact that someone important to her had overheard an abusive incident was enough to awaken her to reality. "Jeffrey was three weeks old when Bill's mother came to stay with us," she told me. "Bill and I were in our bedroom, talking. He was getting ready to go on a trip, and I was nursing the baby. Actually, we were arguing about something. And at one point, he walked up to me and said, 'You know what? Shut the fuck up!' and slapped me in the face right there, in our room, with this tiny baby in my arms. I was caught totally off-guard. I started crying, and the baby began to scream. But Bill's mother was in the next room, and I *know* she heard what went on. I was so embarrassed and humiliated. That's when I realized the abuse was not just an incident. But I didn't say anything. Bill slept on the couch that night and left on his trip the next day." His mother never said a word.

When others witness or comment on abusive behaviors, the little voice that the upscale abused wife once heard inside her and ignored or muffled becomes amplified. Slowly she starts to recognize that she must stop enduring the abuse. Although this incident awakened Ingrid to the pattern of Bill's abuse, her turning point came several years later; each woman comes to grips with her situation at her own pace. However, talking to others is key to her growing capacity to recognize and label her experiences, reclaim her self, target important turning points, and ultimately leave her tormentor.

THE POWER OF THE STORY

What is it about a sympathetic ear that motivates an abused wife to step away from the difficult path she has been treading for so many years? As I noted in Chapter 2, a woman learns about the world through reflections of herself and her universe as viewed through the eyes of those whom she connects with and respects.[18] She learns within relationships and incorporates others' perceptions into her own to confirm her experiences and to be better able to see how she fits with the rest of humanity.[19] When others validate her reality by listening to her story and taking it seriously, she gains the strength she needs to take action.

Moreover, as the abused woman talks to others, she is forced to construct, often for the first time, her own terrible story from beginning to end. She has concealed the truth from others for so long, and on some level she may have been keeping it secret from herself as well.

It is as if the woman has endured experiences that remain disjointed in her consciousness. They don't make sense to her. There is no place to put them in her mind, so she distances herself from them by using denial and rationalizations. But in telling her story to others, these disconnected pieces suddenly coalesce into a horrifying whole—she sees the pattern of abuse and understands her situation. The support and input of empathetic others guides her toward a more realistic view of her circumstances.

As she speaks out, she begins to realize that her rationalizations and justifications have led her in directions that are not in her best interest. Previous theories of domestic abuse suggest that insight—independent of others—promotes shifts in behavior. But I have found that for these women piercing the veil of secrecy, *telling the story,* sets them on the path toward freedom. The abused upscale wife slowly comprehends what it means to acknowledge that her husband is a batterer—to admit that her reality is different from what society supports and considers normal. In speaking her truth, she feels relief and a sense that her world has expanded, that she has options. And this allows others to help her.

Once Bailey began breaking the silence, her family was accepting and supportive. Her parents and sisters reassured her that they were there for her, and they did stand by her during drawn-out court battles. They frequently restated their less than kindly view of Peter, which was only reinforced as they learned about his physically violent side.

When a woman talks with someone who acknowledges her dilemma, her inner voice and abilities enlarge. She sees that she was correct in her initial impression that her husband's behavior was wrong, even if she believed no one else in her community was undergoing the same assaults. Her previously squelched feelings of fear now reemerge and become dominant, and over time she begins to listen to herself.

Coming out of the closet, breaking the isolation, and freeing herself of the burden of keeping the abuse secret provide many benefits for the upscale battered woman:

- Her thoughts and experiences are affirmed.
- She begins to trust herself again.
- She reclaims her sense of self (especially if she feels she lost herself within the tyranny of the abusive marriage) and slowly begins to strengthen it.
- She leans on external supports, which bolster her self-esteem and resolve.
- She begins to remember or acknowledge her inner and material resources.
- She is able to plan actions to leave in ways that foster her own best interest as well as that of her children.

The issues of upscale women may differ from those of lower-income abused women, who probably don't feel as great a need to shroud their situation in secrecy because they have not lived with the same socially endorsed silence and shame regarding their husband's violence. Although sharing stories is healing for those who have undergone trauma,[20] for the lower-income abused woman that process may not represent quite as significant a turning point. She may not struggle with being believed since she is not shattering a popular myth. In fact, I have seen lower-income women who stay with their battering mates bond with one another over the respective abuse. They more easily get support from each other because they are more forthcoming in sharing similar experiences. Moreover, external supports such as shelters and domestic violence hotlines may be more accessible to these women and better attuned to their needs, because their outreach efforts are geared to the disadvantaged.

However beneficial it is for the woman to tell her story and for her complaints to be taken seriously, it can set her back if she attempts to share her reality but is rejected by the professionals or friends from whom she seeks help, or if her story is minimized or marginalized. When Sally first broached the subject of Ray's behavior with her mother, her mother responded, "But he's such a good provider. Where would you go? How would you manage without him?" This response only isolated Sally further—she believed she could find no solace from anyone outside her marriage—and she became increasingly dependent on the man who was bent on destroying her. Allison told me that when she started telling Robert's parents and others in her community about his behavior, they ignored her and worse. "They would treat me as if I were *urine*," she recalled bitterly. "It was like, 'Stay away from me!' Everybody else seemed to have perfect marriages. Everything seemed so whitewashed."

THE "FINAL STRAWS"

The battered upscale woman goes through a series of phases before she is ready to leave the relationship. As the assaults and abusive behaviors accumulate and escalate over time, her coping strategies begin to wear thin. She realizes that she is married to a batterer, and she recognizes her situation. It will not get better. Any hope she might have harbored for happiness in the marriage finally dwindles. Eventually she starts to secretly strategize a way out—saving money on the side, planning her escape, looking for an opening, preparing herself emotionally. One woman even decided to have a longed-for second child before she left her abusive marriage. She reasoned that divorce and dating to find a suitable father would take more time and effort than she could muster, so she rationalized completing her family before fleeing her abuser. Although this is an extreme example of secret strategizing, it is not untypical of the kind of energy the abused upscale woman puts into the leaving phase. However, even as the woman secretly makes plans to reach certain personal goals before leaving the path, she holds to the very end a wish that the marriage will become healthier.

Still, this is one of the biggest turning points on this stretch of the path. It is common to hear a woman in any troubled relationship say, "I wish we could just go back to normal, to the way we were, back to the beginning, when everything was so new and shiny." In this stage it finally becomes apparent that *that was then, and this is now.* What the woman is enduring—an abusive, emotionally destructive, fear-laden, and often violent marriage—*has become normal for her.* In this last phase she must recognize, often with a deep sense of defeat and resignation, that this is as "normal" as her marriage is going to get. None of her capacities to fix situations, save the day, win at work, or talk problems away ("make them nice") will be effective.

An event or a set of circumstances triggers her feeling that a critical mass has been reached. The silence is now broken and usually with a vengeance; she shares her terrible secrets with family members, therapists, police, attorneys, and coworkers. Her hope-against-hope attitude evaporates, and she starts looking at how she can save herself, her children, her self-respect, and possibly even her life.

In this final trajectory of the path, the woman reaches a point at which she can no longer participate in the abusive marriage. Her husband is no longer Prince Charming, and the glass slipper pinches and rubs in ways she could never have predicted. For some women it has even shattered, and its shards have become painfully apparent to others. A single incident or "final straw" often precipitates the woman's escape from the relationship. The decisive turning points and precipitating events that emerged for the women I studied or counseled fell into one of the following categories:

- The husband's threats to his wife or children's well-being have become increasingly severe (and may include death threats).
- There has been yet another episode of public humiliation.
- The husband's abuses and infidelities—in some cases including having children with other women—have accumulated and worsened.
- There has been a violent incident requiring medical attention.
- The woman's sense of support from her family, friends, or coworkers has increased.
- The woman's reasons for staying have been satisfied, as when the last planned child has been born or the youngest child has left for or graduated from college.
- The woman has an extramarital affair, which reminds her that she is desirable and that not all men are abusive.

Bailey's last stand was simple but powerful. After Peter forbade her for the umpteenth time to use his steam shower in their country estate ("and if you do, you'd better replace the settings *exactly* as I set them if you know what's good for you"), he pushed and kicked her to the ground while they and their neighbors were walking their dogs together. Although Bailey barely remembers what comment prompted Peter's attack, she was ragefully and tearfully humiliated. She somehow managed to pick herself up, take the dog, and, without any keys, contact her mother and sister. That was it. She left Peter, never to return. This was her first step toward reclaiming her life, but she spent most of their twelve-year divorce process continuing to reassemble the pieces of her former self.

As she walked away from her violent husband for the last time, many thoughts filled her head. "How did I ever get into this? Who am I? What happened to the 'me' I once knew?" And on an ironic and almost girlishly innocent note for an advertising executive so well versed in image management, she kept repeating like a mantra to keep herself emotionally afloat, "If I can just get the right haircut I'll be all right."

Sally's turning point was when she found herself in the hospital and learned that the damage to her hearing and jaw would be permanent and scarring. Now that her children had graduated from college, her concerns for herself came to the fore. She realized that she had wasted good years of her life, and that time was becoming more precious. Her husband was threatening to kill her. She began to shift internally. Sally talked with her parents right after the doctor's visit, and this time she received their support. They were shocked that Ray had beaten her and remorseful that they had not been more protective of her.

Kathleen's final straw did not come as a result of a beating or a long, heartfelt confession to another person. Rather, after learning of several of her husband's multiple affairs, she began one herself. Her involvement in a sweet but short-lived romance with the architect who had remodeled their house reminded Kathleen of how men should treat women. When she realized that her vicious and violent mate was not treating her the way she deserved and wanted, she knew it was time to escape his grasp.

Irene split after the final public humiliation at the industry luncheon; her grown sons convinced her that her husband's behavior was no longer tolerable. When they cut off contact with their father for what would be several years because of their profound anger at him for his mistreatment of her, she was impelled to take action on her own behalf. "I learned that I don't need to put up with this sort of treatment from a man who supposedly loves me and has been my mate for more than thirty years."

For Ingrid the last straw came with Bill's threat to their child. "Bill didn't respect me at all," she admitted. "And you know, I had no backbone after that birthday incident. I was no longer the woman he had married. But when I gave birth to Jeffrey, the old Ingrid came back. I had a clear-cut idea of how I wanted my son to be raised. I knew how I wanted him to be bathed and how I wanted him dressed—little stupid things. I always put the diaper on him to make sure he was okay because if it was on low, the tape would slice his skin. So I would make a fuss about that. The only time Bill wanted to be bothered with him was in front of a camera or in front of a crowd. He was the perfect show dad."

After a change of administration, Bill was out of politics. He took a job in a different state halfway across the country and moved his young family away from their longtime home. "I had no friends or family here," Ingrid recalled. "So Jeffrey became my whole world. I had finished my degree and was not working. I stayed home with the baby. I nursed Jeffrey for thirteen months. I just knew how I wanted things to be.

"And soon after Jeffrey was born, I think Bill had a nervous breakdown," Ingrid continued. "Jeffrey never went to bed, and of course I didn't know then what I know now about schedules, and putting the baby down, and that you don't have to hold him twenty-four hours a day and rock him and pat his bottom. One night he was up till eleven, twelve o'clock as usual. Bill was drinking his Jack Daniels on the rocks, and he started changing right before my eyes. He got really upset, and he said, 'I gotta get out of here.' He walked out the door, but then he came back in and started talking to me about how he never thought another man would come between us. He was talking about Jeffrey! He saw that my life was not revolving around him anymore, and he didn't like it.

"That's when I realized I couldn't pretend everything was fine, everything was great. I had finally made it to where I didn't have to work, and I could have this great life, but it really wasn't great at all. It looked like I lived this, 'wonderful life' but really it was a 'wonderful lie.'"

A final incident caused Ingrid to make the break. "Jeffrey was not quite two," she explained tearfully. "It was Mother's Day, and we were going out to brunch. Jeffrey was very strong-willed, and he was in that "terrible twos" stage. If he didn't want me to put on some piece of clothing, he would hold his body really rigid. I was in his room, trying to get him dressed. I said, 'Honey, we're going to brunch. Let's get this on you.' But he didn't really understand what was going on. He threw a tantrum. So finally I just said, 'Look, if you don't want to put this on, fine.' And I just left him crying in the crib and went to get dressed myself.

"Bill came in and started to intervene. He yelled to me, 'Jeffrey's mutilating himself,' because he was having a tantrum. So Bill went to restrain the baby from kicking and flailing. I was in the master bathroom, and I heard this. But now Jeffrey was calling for me, because he didn't want to be held anymore. He was crying, 'Mommy, Mommy.' I ran to his room to get him, but Bill yelled at me, 'Back the fuck up, or I'm going to kick your ass.'

"Now I was caught. This was my child being held and restrained by somebody I was afraid of. This was the *breaking point* for me, the point at which I knew I had to go. I was in the doorway, and Bill was telling me to back up. I backed up, but Jeffrey was crying for me. I thought, 'Whatever is going to happen is going to happen.' So I said to Bill, 'This is my child, and I'm going to get him.' I grabbed him from Bill, and he just backed off and went downstairs. I said to myself, 'Maybe you're getting tougher now. Maybe this is a good thing.'

"Finally, I came downstairs with Jeffrey all dressed, and Bill said, 'I'm going to the office.'

"'I guess we're blowing off brunch,' I commented, and that just set him off. He knocked everything off the countertop and started throwing stuff. He picked up a chair and threw it into the family room. Furniture and lamps were flying all over the place. I was sitting in a chair, holding Jeffrey's head while he was crying, 'Mommy, Mommy.' I looked at him," Ingrid continued, sobbing, "and all of a sudden I saw my whole childhood all over again. And I said to myself, 'I am *not* going to raise another generation of this. I'm *outta here.*'

"I didn't know what to do at this point, because I didn't have a job; I was a full-time mother. I wasn't anywhere near my friends or family. While Bill was carrying on, I kept asking myself, 'How can I stay here? How can I stay here with my baby? I'll leave,' I told myself. After a week or so I finally got up the courage to ask a neighbor, 'Do you know anybody who can help me?' That's when I decided to call the lawyer, and it saved my life.'"

Although these incidents may have been the final straw for these abused women, what was more important was that something changed *within* them that made their marriage intolerable.

REWRITING THE STORY

The wisdom among workers at domestic violence shelters suggests that it takes a woman several attempts at leaving before she finally quits the abusive relationship for good. Sarah Buel explains: "We go back because we think we'll figure out a way to stop the violence, the magic secret everybody else seems to know. We don't want to believe that our marriage or relationship failed because we weren't willing to try just a little harder."[21] This was especially apparent in Allison and Robert's seesaw marriage. She threw him out of the house on several occasions but then decided to let him back in. He hit her, so she moved out and stayed with her parents. She came back, and they tried marital therapy. He slapped her in front of friends, and she moved out again. She filed for divorce, but he convinced her to try a new marriage counselor. They experienced a truce, but then his violence worsened during her pregnancy and the early weeks of their baby's life. And finally, cowering in a locked closet with her infant while her husband raged around the house, Allison made the decision to end the marriage. Still, it took her several more months of planning and strategizing before she could walk out.

The woman's initial attempts at leaving are similar to rehearsals: she is feeling out what life would be like without the batterer. She envisions freeing herself, supporting herself and her children financially, and finding a new and more peaceful existence. She may fantasize about future work opportunities and imagine her life as a divorced woman. These scenarios prepare her for what is to come and may even build her self-confidence. Sometimes, however, the rehearsals can result in false starts, especially when the woman clings to false hope that her marriage can be salvaged. At these times she may forgive her abuser and "give him another chance," postponing her exit and prolonging her agony.

What finally propels the upscale abused wife out of her marriage? Over time she reconstructs and revises her story. No longer does she see herself as a victim of a hurtful marriage, accusing herself of ingratitude for all that her husband has provided. Rather, she begins to perceive herself as a person who does not deserve such mistreatment from anyone—especially not a spouse—and who can go forward and create a new life without the abuse. As she slowly makes a plan to leave, she may experience myriad emotions, ranging from sorrowful mourning to explosive rage, but she realizes that she has strengths that allow her to manage.

In her book *Uncoupling,* Diane Vaughan traces how one's story changes during different phases of the divorce process.[22] Although a woman may start off as a victim, she may finish by recounting a different narrative of her marriage. It is as if she tries on various versions of her story as her reality changes. The women in my study started out believing that their husband had a lot to offer them and they were better off tolerating their violent marriage. By the time they left their spouse they had realized that they had their own strengths and abilities, they did not cause their husband's assaults, and they could make it on their own, abandoning the abusive husband (now correctly so labeled).

However, gaining these insights is not easy. Learning of alternative descriptions of her life experiences can make a woman sad and furious as she realizes that her story might have been different and that she need not have been subjected to her husband's brutality. As one sorrowful woman told me, "I can never get back what was taken from me. I feel I had a wasted life. I sacrificed my life for all of this?" For women of all classes, new representations of life events challenge their meaning system and threaten their view of the world and their identity.

Most of us would rather live with a meaning we don't like than with no meaning at all. It is not unusual for us to look for the best in a current situation rather than be terrifyingly propelled onto a blank canvas to start anew. Starting over is especially daunting for battered upscale women if they believe they had all they could ask for in terms of status and material means. How and why would they leave that known reality to launch themselves into an unknown void, especially if there are children involved whose well-being must also be considered?

It takes time to change this mind-set, through rehearsals and successive attempts to find freedom. However, a woman can more easily change her attitude if she speaks to other women who have endured similar abuse. Feminist theorist Joan Laird, also of the Stone Center, says that "stories help a woman make sense of her life, especially when she has experienced unexplainable, shameful, or deviant events."[23] When she learns that others of a similar socioeconomic background have been terrorized and beaten, a woman can incorporate this information into her narrative. This helps her feel less isolated and stops her from believing that she has provoked the abuse. Sharing stories can also help her think about other types of relationships—for instance, with a man who is caring, supportive, and nonabusive—and allows her to begin imagining herself capable of participating in such a safe union. Support groups or group therapy accomplish these goals and have been found to be useful treatment for abused women.[24]

THE GLASS SLIPPER NO LONGER FITS

As she listened to the doctor describe the surgery she would need to repair her injured jaw, Sally began to recognize that this was not how she wanted to live out the rest of her life. "I started to feel so sad for my old self," she said, crying. "I was a young and pretty woman who had gone into a marriage with so much hope and love." She saw that she had been sorely punished for no known or predictable reasons. The doctor's words, the critical culmination of all the physical and emotional injuries she had sustained within her thirty-year marriage to Ray, were enough—if not too much. She decided she would take no more of it. And so she planned to leave.

Sally asked a divorced friend to refer her to her attorney. Fortunately, this lawyer had walked many a battered upscale woman through divorce, and he was sensitive to the steps that Sally would have to go through. More important, he definitively labeled Ray's actions abusive and criminal. Sally knew she was making the right decision to leave, and working with this attorney was the prelude to her final exit strategy.

As a woman challenges her old narrative and begins to construct a new one, she may seek out alternative ways to act. What has occurred cannot be changed, but the upscale battered woman can be helped to make sense of her life experiences, create new meaning, and deal with the consequences of her past. The role of therapy—which she usually turns to after the fact—is to help the woman understand what the abuse and the abusive relationship meant to her, its effects, and what she wants to do about it. I explore these issues more fully in Chapter 9.

A SAFETY PLAN: BLUEPRINT FOR ESCAPE

A safety plan is essential for anyone living in an abusive marriage, and it must be established prior to an episode. It includes how the woman will escape each room in her home, and how she will get out of the house and away from the residence. She must also have an idea of where she can go, twenty-four hours a day, seven days a week. She should familiarize herself with the location of the closest hospital and police station and warn friends and family that she may need to call on them in case of emergency. Some women arrange a code word when they call their safe friend to indicate they are in imminent danger or need to leave the house and the abuser is present. At that point the friend should contact the police. Other women have the means to arrange for a private safe house, as Bailey did when she secretly rented a place in town.

A safety plan also means having everything ready for a quick getaway. In the movie *Sleeping with the Enemy,* which depicted upscale violence, Julia Roberts's character planned her escape for months, saving money in a plastic bag hidden in the toilet tank and gathering important documents. Similarly, the woman should pack a small suitcase with originals or duplicates of the following items:

- driver's license and registration
- ATM card, checkbook, bank account number(s), credit cards, cash
- identification papers, including birth certificate(s), passports, work permits, green cards, insurance policies, and her husband's social security number
- police records or evidence of past violence such as photographs and any other important legal documents
- children's school and immunization records
- address book or list of important phone numbers, including those of domestic violence hotlines or coalitions, the hospital, and the police domestic violence unit
- medication(s), keys, about a week's worth of clothes for her and her children, and anything of great sentimental value

This last point is crucial: the woman should have enough materials in hand that she need not return to the home right away. If she already has an order of protection (OOP), she should keep it with her at all times. It is good if she can arrange a place to stay, such as a friend's or relative's home or a hotel—somewhere she will not be isolated but can feel some sense of protection from her abuser. Children should be taught to dial 911 if they witness a violent incident. If they are aware of such violence between their parents, they should be told in advance where to go (to a neighbor's home, for instance) so that they can remain safe.

During a violent episode the woman should strongly consider police involvement, if merely to have on record accounts of her husband's behavior. This documentation can go a long way in circumventing trouble in a future custody case, when each parent's suitability may be in question. But even if the woman doesn't call the police, she should learn about her rights through an attorney well versed in the issues associated with divorce, custody, and spousal violence. She may find such a lawyer through a battered women's shelter, hotline, or coalition (see Appendix E), the state bar association, or a friend's referral.

There are many reasons to call an attorney. For instance, the woman should be aware that if she chooses to leave with her children and prevents her husband from seeing them, that is considered a federal offense. She may be charged with child abduction unless she first files either an emergency custody order or obtains custody provisions within an order of protection. Fear of and confusion about legal complications prevent many women from leaving.

A victim of domestic violence should not tell the batterer she is leaving or thinking about leaving in advance of making her move. She needs to plan the initiation of the divorce and her departure from her marital residence carefully, especially if her husband continues to be a threat. Attorney David H. Hopkins, capital partner at the Illinois law firm Schiller, DuCanto, & Fleck, is an advocate for legal reforms for victims of domestic violence. Specializing in upscale couples (25 percent of the two hundred divorces he has settled in the last ten years have included conduct that justified filing a petition under the Domestic Violence Act), Hopkins advises these women on how to proceed.[25] "An appropriate order under the Domestic Violence Act needs to be obtained on an ex parte basis (on one's own behalf without a lawyer) that provides for adequate protection for the woman and any minor children. It should specifically delineate personal items that she can take, and she also needs to organize herself.

"Let's say she is leaving the suburban home she formerly lived in. She must arrange the departure so that the police are informed and present, a process server is present, and a moving van and movers are present, all informed in advance of what's going on. They need to move in like a military convoy: police vehicle, vehicle with victim and supporters, vehicle with a process server, movers, moving van, process server (at the office) to alert the husband as to what is going on. You have to give him notice as to the order against him."

Why is such protection necessary? Hopkins explains that if a woman starts moving out while her husband is at work, a concerned neighbor, seeing the commotion, might call him to ask what's going on. He then could come flying in, while belongings are being moved out, and create a dangerous scene. "It helps if at the very time he gets served with papers (orders of protection and divorce), the police are right there. The objective is to get the woman out of the house with what is essential. That will minimize her need to come back."

Hopkins also urges departing women to think about what type of temporary residence they should be going to with the kids. "The upscale woman will probably not be a shelter candidate. There are more factors to be dealt with than can be handled by a typical shelter, and she will be coming with more than a suitcase. And if the marriage has been really terrible, for longer or more permanent relocations she may have to think about living in a high-rise with twenty-four-hour security. In a home there is far more risk of the husband coming during the night." Hopkins points out that terms of temporary financial support also need to be worked out. All of this takes careful planning.

GETTING GOING, GETTING OUT

The upscale abused woman follows a certain path as she decides to leave her abuser and make a new life for herself. The markers of this last phase include:

- *Accumulation:* Assaults and abuse build over time.
- *Wearing down:* Coping strategies wear thin as abusive behaviors increase.
- *Secret strategizing:* The woman starts to secretly strategize a way out.
- *The final straws:* She experiences the final humiliation, discovers the final affair, witnesses an assault on the well-being of her children, or suffers excessive injury to herself.
- *The silence is broken:* She tells family members, a therapist, police, an attorney, or coworkers and comes out of her isolation. She begins to lean on this external support, which validates her assessments, bolsters her resolve, and fosters her self-confidence.
- *The burden is shed:* By coming out of the closet and breaking the isolation, she sheds the burden of keeping the abuse secret and the happy-family facade intact. Others play the role of selfobjects for her, serve as support systems, and coauthor the rewriting of her narrative and the reframing of her life situation.
- *The glass slipper no longer fits:* She starts to integrate these internal shifts. Her new narrative and external supports ameliorate some of her fears of loss and disintegration of the self.
- *Rehearsals and plans:* She makes plans to leave (with or without rehearsals) in a way that will serve her own and her children's best interest. She addresses the dangers of leaving by creating a safety plan and getting legal advice. The woman who stays married leaves the path by creating firm boundaries and making demands of her husband who is equally invested in change.
- *Finally out:* She makes careful plans and leaves the abusive marriage permanently, securing an attorney, as needed. Alternatively, she monitors changes in her husband's behavior and evaluates her decision to stay.

The Path of the Upscale Abused Wife: Getting Out

Accumulation: Assaults and abuse build over time

Wearing Down: Woman's coping strategies wear thin and lose their effectiveness

Secret Strategizing: Woman looks with intention—is there a way out?

The "Final Straws": Critical mass is reached

Secret strategizing reaches fruition: Last planned child is born, money is saved, last child leaves for college, escape route is readied

Incident of abuse requires medical attention

Wife has extramarital affair, learns that men can be kind, non-abusive

Husband's extramarital affairs are discovered

Public humiliation

Well-being of children or wife is severely threatened

Silence Is Broken: Woman comes out of isolation and turns to outside support sources such as friends, family, co-workers, police, psychotherapists, attorneys

Her self-confidence increases

She gets support and marshals internal fortitude to leave

Her concerns and assessment about the abusive marriage are validated

Burden Is Shed: Woman uses external support to rewrite her narrative

Woman no longer keeps the abuse secret and no longer maintains a facade

The glass slipper no longer fits: External support is validating

She creates a safety plan or new boundaries within the marriage

She rehearses leaving the marriage and casting off the role of the abused wife

She begins to integrate her internal shift

Woman makes conscious decision to leave abusive husband and concrete plans to get out of the marriage or monitors boundaries and changes in husband's behaviors

Woman steps off the path of the upscale abused wife

PART THREE

People Along the Path: Those Who Help or Hurt

7

The Men:
Arrogance and Insecurity,
Grandiosity and Self-Doubt

WHO IS AN UPSCALE BATTERER? What qualities do these educated, high-income husbands have in common? Although I learned about these men primarily through their wives' tearful stories, commonalties among them did emerge. Sally's initial impressions of Ray were typical of how the majority of the women described their prospective mate.

When Sally first met her future husband, his handsome good looks and air of sophistication impressed her. She was immediately attracted to Ray and, as she put it, "took great comfort in the fact that he was substantially older" than she was. She attributed many of his positive traits to his "maturity." As she explained at the very start of our interview, "Ray was worldly and treated me with more sophistication than men who were younger." In Kathleen's mind, society's accepted image of the violent husband was totally at odds with her husband Stuart. No redneck he, Stuart lobbied for gun control, abhorred tattoos, and sported Armani suits. He was vastly unlike the Stanley Kowalski archetype she associated with violence—a tattooed, undershirt-clad beer swiller who points a gun in his wife's mouth. But Stuart did do more than his fair share of whamming Kathleen around their estate.

Are these rich but vicious husbands anomalies? Or are they prototypically violent wolves in sheep's clothing? I believe the answer is more the latter, but in fact there is no charade involved. We are simply using an adjusted lens when we examine the upscale abusive husband, one that forces us to rethink our assumptions and stereotypes. Just as the picture of these wives differs from the one society typically has of the battered woman, so the image of the abusive husband revealed here diverges from the expected norm. Although I acknowledge that I run the danger of creating a new stereotype, my aim is to identify a previously unrecognized category of violent men who can be just as brutal and just as dangerous as their lower-income counterparts.

One caveat: In this chapter I seek to identify and describe the emotional and behavioral patterns of the upscale abusive husband with the understanding that further research examining these men should be undertaken to gain a better understanding of their internal dynamics. I do not claim that my hypotheses are absolute, but rather they are a synthesis of my observations.

HISTORICAL UNDERSTANDINGS OF THE BATTERER

In studying men who batter, researchers have examined sociological factors, family history, and psychological dynamics to understand why these husbands lash out at their wives.

Sociological Factors

Studies have found that domestic violence is more prevalent in families that

- conserve traditional sex roles[1]
- come from lower socioeconomic classes[2]
- have an unemployed male[3] and
- have lower education levels[4]

In a 1977 study representative of many other investigations, Maria Roy, founder of many battered women's shelters, identified nine factors that, in descending order of frequency, are common agents of domestic violence: arguments over money, jealousy, sexual problems, the husband's alcohol and/or drug abuse, disputes about the children, the husband's unemployment, the wife's desire to work, pregnancy, and the wife's use of alcohol and/or drugs.[5]

In a 1983 study that included upper- as well as lower-income couples, Lenore Walker found that violent men were less educated than their wives and came from a lower socioeconomic class or a different ethnic, racial, or religious group.[6] The couple's early sexual intimacy was often a factor in these abusive relationships. Men who tended to become abusive were insecure, overly in need of nurturing, highly possessive of the woman's time, and extremely jealous. The women perceived that their husbands initiated the violence and were unable to control their behavior when angry. The men had learned in the past how to lash out, and they had been rewarded for doing so. Walker found no specific personality traits to suggest a victim-prone personality for women, although she did speculate on the possibility of a male violence-prone personality.

Findings published in December 1999 in the *New England Journal of Medicine,* and based on a study of women who had been seen in the emergency departments of eight large, university-affiliated hospitals, suggest that the top five domestic-violence predictors in men are alcohol use, drug use, intermittent unemployment, low educational attainment (not having completed high school), and a previous divorce or estrangement.[7] However, these researchers cautioned that their findings might not apply to domestic-violence victims as a whole. They focused only on women who acknowledged their domestic violence injuries and sought medical care for them in emergency rooms. Women who denied being abused or who shunned medical attention were underrepresented.[8]

Three frequently mentioned factors in studies during the past three decades—low socioeconomic status, low income, and low educational level— are irrelevant to the upscale batterer. Based on the hidden nature of the population of upscale abused women, they rarely present themselves in emergency rooms and shelters. With the exception of Walker's study, which fairly representatively cuts across all demographic domains including class and race, the upscale were little seen and undercounted. Moreover, from what I know of the upscale batterers with whom I have been acquainted, the trouble is rarely rooted in unemployment and only occasionally in financial reversals.

However, some of the men I have encountered were engaged in some sort of addictive behavior, which often affected their moods. Ingrid found that Bill became more belligerent when he took to his bottle of Jack Daniels. Kathleen's husband Stuart snorted cocaine with his partying crowd. He also seemed to suffer from some type of sexual addiction—he was constantly looking for new sexual partners, then boasting about them—as well as an impulse to gamble. He made and lost millions of dollars in his high-profile real estate dealings and was fired from many agencies because of the unwarranted risks he took with other people's money.

Substance abuse and other addictive behavior can be symptomatic of deeper problems. For some people addictions are ways to medicate themselves so they feel less pain. However, at the same time they are behavioral disinhibitors. Although alcohol and drugs do not cause domestic abuse, they may make people less likely to check their violent impulses.

Family History

Studies have suggested that a history of violence in the batterer's family of origin is a contributing factor to his future abusiveness. Murray Straus, Richard Gelles, and Suzanne Steinmetz at the University of Delaware, in their groundbreaking 1981 study of 2,143 intact couples who were representative of the overall population of the United States, found that one out of ten boys who witness abuse between their parents become wife beaters, which "is a 600 percent greater rate of wife beating than . . . for the husbands who came from non-violent homes."[9] Similarly, 10 percent of men who had witnessed abuse and experienced it themselves (known as the "double whammy" effect) battered their wife, compared to 3.8 percent of the study's entire population of husbands, which included nonabusers. "Men with parents who were violent in both ways have an annual incidence rate for conjugal violence of over 25 percent, compared to a mean sample rate of 12 percent for men [who witnessed it], and to a 6 percent rate for men whose parents were non-violent in both respects."[10]

In his research of populations of men who were known to batter, Lewis Okun found much higher rates of what may be termed *intergenerational transmission of family violence.* According to Okun's findings, published in 1986, 71 percent of the male batterers had been abused as children, and 66 percent had been exposed to domestic abuse between parents. In addition, 79.8 percent of his sample population had been exposed to some combination of family violence, compared to the remaining 20.2 percent of population of batterers whom he interviewed.[11] In 1992 Dan Saunders, a psychologist from the University of Michigan, identified a linkage between the severity of the abuse a man endured while growing up and the degree of abuse to which he subjected his spouse.[12]

Although several women in my study had observed abusive interactions between their in-laws (in one case it was the mother-in-law who was the feared attacker), it is still unclear to what degree a family history of domestic violence influences the upscale abusive husband. Further study is required to confirm the relevance of this theory to an upscale population.

Psychological Dynamics

Researchers have tried to describe the typical personality traits and behavioral style of the abusive husband. Lewis Okun, who extensively surveyed the literature on wife abuse, found that batterers "generally suffer from poor self-esteem and negative self-images," are possessive and jealous, and try to control their wife and foster her dependency.[13] Batterers also commonly project blame onto their wife, placing the onus for the violence on the victim.

Some researchers have probed the motivations, intentions, and driving forces behind behavior that physically and emotionally hurts one's partner. Neil S. Jacobson and John M. Gottman, both at the University of Washington, skillfully incorporated fluctuations in male heart rates during abusive incidents into the development of a typology of batterer personalities.[14] They suggest that abusive men can be divided into two groups—"Cobras" and "Pit Bulls." Men from both camps are violent toward their wife, but their physiological responses are different. The Cobra's heartbeat slows prior to his attack; he becomes calm and deliberate before striking, just as a snake seems to. This gives his prey little advance warning of the venom that is to come.

In his earlier work Jacobson identified this type of man as a "vagal reactor."[15] (Vagal refers to the vagus nerve, which communicates with the autonomic nervous system.) Cobras comprise 20 percent of batterers. In fact, 50 percent of all antisocial personalities are vagal reactors and usually report violence in their families of origin. These men were the most vicious toward their mate.[16]

The Pit Bull, on the other hand, shows his rage incrementally. As with the growling and snarling of an attack dog before it lunges at its victim, this batterer's heartbeat accelerates prior to the assault. His physiology matches his demeanor—he becomes excited and agitated, his eyes widen, his face flushes with rage. There is some warning to the woman who will be the object of his temper.[17] My experience to date has been that upscale batterers fall into both categories.

After examining batterers for more than twenty years, Donald Dutton, director of the Assaultive Husbands Program in Vancouver, British Columbia, and author of The Batterer, suggests that there are several types of batterers, and he offers explanations for their behavior. One type (40 percent of his population, he claims) is what he calls the "psychopathic wife assaulter."[18] These men meet the diagnostic criteria for antisocial personality disorder. They show no remorse, exhibit little conscience, much less empathy for others, and usually have a criminal history. Even their brain scans show flat brain stem activity, which is different from normal men.

Dutton refers to another 30 percent as the "overcontrolled wife assaulters." These men are either dominating or distancing from their spouses. They tend to abuse their wives emotionally and can erupt with physical violence after a long period of built-up rage, which may have been acted out through passive-aggressive behaviors before the explosive assault.[19]

A third group, the "cyclical/emotionally volatile wife abusers," have a deep need to control the level of intimacy in a relationship and are unable to express their feelings. Their rages build and discharge in cycles that include a confusing and unpredictable remorseful period after an attack. When they aren't violent, they can be wonderful, and their wives claim that they seem to have "dual personalities."[20] Dutton concluded that the majority of batterers from this cyclical group probably suffer from post-traumatic stress disorder (PTSD), which contributes greatly to their anger and mood swings. Themselves abused growing up and shamed by the rejection they felt as children, these men feel ambivalent about their ability and desire to attach to others. They are fearful of attachment and may bring anger to relationships.

Dutton eloquently argues that, given this cluster of symptoms—fear and rage, repetitive self-destructive thoughts, an overriding preoccupation with securing affection, and alternating feelings of fury, love, and guilt toward others—the batterer can be diagnosed with borderline personality disorder (BPD), one of a number of personality disorders that can emerge from an abuse-laden and traumatic childhood.[21] And in clinical practice it is probably often the case that the abusive husband exhibits these and other BPD traits, such as impulsivity, affective instability, and "inappropriate, intense anger or difficulty controlling anger (e.g., frequent displays of temper, constant anger, recurrent physical fights)."[22]

Dutton's conceptualization has much to recommend it. But does it apply to the highly educated and upper-income husbands? For the most part I agree with his theory in that the upscale batterer is suffering from a personality disorder and is not just a victim of substance abuse or his societal environment. According to the *Diagnostic and Statistical Manual of the American Psychiatric Association* (*DSM-IV*), used by psychiatrists, psychologists, and social workers when making diagnoses and assessments, a person with a personality disorder demonstrates an enduring and inflexible pattern "of inner experience and behavior that deviates markedly from the expectations of the individual's culture. . . . [The pattern is] pervasive across a broad range of personal and social situations . . . [and leads to] clinically significant distress or impairment in social, occupational, or other important areas of functioning." This stable and long-standing pattern has its onset in late adolescence or young adulthood. It is unrelated to any other significant mental disorder or to the physiological effects of drug abuse or medication of a general medical condition (such as a head trauma).[23]

What we know about people with a borderline personality disorder is that they have great difficulty in relationships and often in holding down a job and being successful. These problems are especially acute for people suffering from PTSD. They come into their therapist's office complaining that life after trauma makes it difficult to follow through on career challenges. Those who endure PTSD and simultaneously achieve great success in their chosen field are extremely rare. Although some upscale batterers may well be borderline personalities, we must wonder about the extent to which Dutton's group included this socioeconomic class. We can easily find examples that fit his thesis in the general population, and even, in some cases, among the highly educated and economically advantaged. However, when we specifically examine batterers from this group, a diagnosis of borderline personality disorder would be difficult to justify because *these men are highly successful in their work lives.*

Besides, if the upscale batterer were truly borderline, he would impulsively lose his ability to control his rage at all times, not simply with his spouse.[24] Although some of the men described by the women in my study did vent their rage with others (Peter and Robert), for the most part upscale batterers show a charming and composed face to everyone else; they reveal their true nature only to the person upon whom they most rely for the maintenance of their sense of self. It is my contention that the upscale batterer has a personality disorder, but one that is slightly different from, although not totally unrelated to, the borderline. Its hallmarks are disturbances of the self and erosions of self-esteem that cause him to act as if he feels eminently entitled. This contributes to his ability to mete out humiliation, beatings, and death threats to the woman he supposedly loves. I believe that the diagnostic category *narcissistic personality disorder* (NPD) is far more useful for describing and understanding the upscale batterer's behavior than that of borderline personality disorder or any of the other categories researchers have suggested.

NARCISSUS: A VIEW INTO THE LAKE

In Greek mythology, Narcissus was a handsome young lad who broke the hearts of the most beautiful girls, for he would love none of them. One maiden whom he had scorned prayed to the gods that Narcissus would be cursed by falling in love with himself. Nemesis, the goddess of anger, was enraged that the young man had wounded so many hearts and granted this wish. When Narcissus bent over a pool of water to drink, he caught sight of his own reflection and immediately fell deeply in love, suddenly understanding why so many women had yearned for him. Forever after he was doomed to pine for his own reflection, burning with self-love and a desire to reach a likeness in the water that he could neither possess nor abandon.[25]

Building on this myth, the diagnostic category of narcissistic personality disorder describes someone who is stricken with a deep yearning for others to reflect and mirror his self. According to the *DSM-IV*, a person with narcissistic personality disorder manifests "a pervasive pattern of grandiosity (in fantasy or behavior), need for admiration, and lack of empathy."[26] The narcissistic personality is a collage of arrogance and insecurity, grandiosity and self-doubt. But at first blush, being adored and feeling superior to others is vitally important to such a man's sense of self. To be diagnosed with this disorder a person must exhibit at least five of the following traits. He or she

- has a grandiose sense of self-importance
- is preoccupied with fantasies of unlimited success, power, brilliance, beauty, or ideal love
- believes that he or she is 'special' and unique and can only be understood by, or should associate with, other special or high-status people (or institutions)
- requires excessive admiration
- has a sense of entitlement (unreasonable expectations of especially favorable treatment or automatic compliance with his or her expectations)
- is interpersonally exploitative (takes advantage of others to achieve his or her own ends)
- lacks empathy: is unwilling to recognize or identify with the feelings and needs of others
- is often envious of others or believes that others are envious of him or her
- shows arrogant, haughty behavior or attitudes[27]

(Appendix C includes a full listing of the traits of the abusive husband, which my patients have found tremendously helpful.)

This cluster of traits and behaviors applies to most of the upscale abusers I have heard about or met. And in truth, the proposition that NPD is the upscale batterer's primary character disorder does not totally contradict Dutton's assertion that batterers suffer from borderline personality disorder. Most clinicians agree that personality disorders seem to have diffuse and overlapping boundaries. A person can float along the continuum of personality disorders. What distinguishes one diagnosis from another is the individual's level of functioning. A person with narcissistic personality disorder would generally function better than someone with borderline personality disorder.

The line between a high-functioning person with borderline personality disorder and a low-functioning person with narcissistic personality disorder is blurred. The distinction lies in the ability to react to responses from others.[28] Although people suffering from either disorder have deep-seated needs for recognition in order to feel integrated and whole, someone with NPD, after a perceived injury or disconnection, is more resilient and better able to restore his sense of inner balance in the face of the empathic understanding of another. He can more readily regain a sense of inner cohesion. Compared to someone with BPD, who typically lacks the psychic structure to respond to another's selfobject functions, the person with NPD can momentarily perceive that his needs are being met and at those moments be soothed, regulated, and feel less fragmented.[29]

As we shall see, however, the ability of someone with NPD to feel soothed and to experience the effects of having another person completely in accord with him does not jive with the actions and motivations of the people who populate his daily world. Unlike a therapist, who is exclusively available to attune empathically to the patient, others are not so altruistic. They have their own needs, and often there is hell to pay.

NARCISSISTIC RAGE

The one question I constantly asked myself as I heard story after story of upscale violence was, Why does this man stay if he disdains his wife so much? If he is so unhappy, and the woman clearly cannot meet his psychological and emotional needs, why doesn't he just get a divorce instead of hanging on and tormenting her?

I have come to see that the answer to this question is twofold. First, the narcissistic batterer is empowered by remaining in the relationship. When the woman remains steadfastly on the path with her husband despite the abuse, she provides him with constant confirmation of her devotion that reinforces his inflated sense of self-worth. After all, he would have to be great for a woman to be willing to put up with the neglect, infidelity, mood swings, humiliation, and beatings he sends her way.

Second, because of his damaged sense of self, the narcissistic husband has deep-seated needs for recognition and validation in order to feel whole. Unfortunately, these are needs that no one human can ever fully meet, in part because the narcissistic individual is usually incapable of viewing significant others as anything but extensions of himself. In fact, he may view his wife as if she were an arm or a leg, and when she does not respond to him in the hoped-for way, he reacts with all the indignation one would feel toward a limb that disobeys one's commands. I once heard about a man who killed his wife and then, when questioned about his motivations, exclaimed in protest and justification, "I'm a sick old man—and she was going to leave me!" His wife existed simply as a function of his own needs.

If responses to a child's psychological needs have been inconsistent, or if the child's psyche has been threatened or injured, the child often reacts with narcissistic rage. This rage reaction is derived from terror and a threatened and vulnerable self; the child feels fragmented because he perceives that he is unseen and abandoned. This type of reaction to such deficits continues into adulthood as his sense of being the entitled victim grows. Usually the rage is directed at people to whom the individual has turned for selfobject experiences but who, at the moment, have failed to fulfill that need. Venting the anger offers a temporary solution and perceived sense of self-cohesion.

As Miriam Elson, lecturer emeritus of the University of Chicago's School of Social Service Administration and the foremost conservator of Heinz Kohut's works, has observed, "These people have no conception of others as individuals with needs and wishes of their own." One student she worked with, distraught when his wife (also a graduate student at the time) left him, reacted in a way typical of this mind-set. "Before she left me, it was perfect," he declared. "She had my breakfast ready, my lunch, my clothes were taken care of. At night she would keep the house quiet so I could study—and she had to break it all up!"[30]

According to Elson, this was an excellent example of a person possessing "a sense of absolute unawareness of the other as other." This man was completely oblivious to the fact that his wife was a graduate student with needs of her own. Such profound blindness to the other as a living, breathing human being is the expression of the narcissistic husband's sense of entitlement that is so integral to his emotional makeup. Everything is coming to him, and others exist only as part of a movie in which he is the writer, director, producer, and star. This student wife would never have been able to please her husband, no matter how empathically attuned she tried to be. The person with a narcissistic personality disorder will forever have needs that "shift in accordance to anything that threatens his stability or diminishes his stature."[31]

This issue of stature is of great significance. Bailey described Peter in terms of his need for prestige and recognition. "He can't travel anywhere without people knowing who he is," she told me. "We usually flew by private plane, but if we couldn't, he made sure the travel department called ahead and told the airline he was coming and to have the VIP people meet him and greet him at the other end. If we arrived in a country where nobody met us, we would have to go through customs alone, and he would go crazy, screaming, calling his secretary and waking her up in the middle of the night. He had to be recognized at all times. He was terrified to be nobody again. He fought his way to the top, and he was uncomfortable just being anonymous."

TERROR BENEATH THE ARROGANCE

Peter, like most narcissistic people, may appear arrogant, entitled, and overly self-confident. The women in my study described their husbands as self-assured and sophisticated men who later revealed themselves to be self-centered brutes with a desire to control and punish, to destroy their wives psychologically and physically. In truth, the abuser's psychological landscape may be at odds with the suave image he projects to others. Bailey's insight that Peter was terrified of being "nobody" again gives us a clue to his internal dynamics.

On the surface the narcissist's abusive actions don't seem like a way of dependently turning to his wife to help him feel better about himself. In fact, the situation looks quite the opposite. And yet, there is a part of him that is far more fragile and far less assured than he wants others to believe. His self-esteem is so brittle that his very sense of self is easily jeopardized by real or perceived narcissistic threats such as

- the fear that he will be abandoned
- the perception that his wife is not responding to him quickly or in a way he desires
- the realization that he is not the "greatest" or the "best" in any field of endeavor
- some accidental or inadvertent slight that no one but he perceives

It is at these moments that the narcissist lashes out uncontrollably.

Consider Ray, who wanted his favorite birthday cake all for himself as he turned forty. When Sally innocently gave away the leftover slices, Ray interpreted this to mean she didn't think he was special. Or take Robert's rage when Allison wandered away from the camp. He probably felt that she had abandoned him at a time when he wanted to prove to his family that he had won her absolute devotion. His rage was also a controlling act.

When a narcissistic man perceives that he has been injured like this, his sense of self is imperiled, and he starts to feel emotionally fragmented. In that moment the lessening of his internal cohesion and vigor can feel terrifying and overwhelming. The fear may be so severe that he can think of no action sufficient to help him recover equilibrium. As a result, he experiences a tidal wave of rage that knows no bounds, and violence seems the only outlet. As Mike Gunther, a psychoanalyst at Chicago's Institute for Psychoanalysis explained, "Narcissistic rage is characterized by the persistence of the goal of *physical destruction* of the object beyond the goal of simple competitive victory or the elicitation of an apology or some other form of redress. Feelings of humiliation, overt or concealed, usually accompany such an outrage. Such outrage and humiliation express the overt regression from the adult to an infantile level of relating."[32]

Gunther's description of the narcissist's abusive patterns of relating mirrors the upscale abusive husband's behavior toward his wife. The narcissist, says Gunther,

- expects absolute control over the other's behavior
- expects the other to respond perfectly
- has an utter incapacity for empathy with the other, the other's behavior, or the other's motives
- is unable to distinguish his own issue or problem from the other as a separate entity[33]

The fragmented individual's attempt to restore cohesion and reestablish his self-esteem, even if it means exploding in rage, has been called *self-righting.*[34] The intensity of this act of self-righting, coupled with the above four traits, allows the narcissistic husband to externalize his terrifying internal conflict. He blames and ultimately projects his rage onto the person closest to him— his wife—who in his mind has become an extension of himself. His hapless wife then infuriates him further by responding imperfectly to his internal injury of the moment—an injury caused by the normal slings and arrows all of us face in daily life. But he feels irreparably injured; he is wronged, and no expression of regret or act of contrition on his wife's part will ever repair the damage.

But if he is angry at the world for doing him harm, why does he take it out on his loving partner? Couldn't he just as readily express his rage by playing racquetball or pounding pillows? His ideas about her role seem paradoxical. On the one hand, the narcissistic husband has vested his wife with tremendous power. She is necessary for his self-repair, but instead of valuing her and seeking comfort in her arms, he beats and humiliates her. Because he sees her as available to meet any and all of his needs, he releases his rage and any self hate at her; such an act helps him ultimately feel powerful again, making him realize he is not weak and shattered.

When the narcissistic man feels the terror and rage associated with his own internal fragmentation, his outburst restores his sense of power and control. He turns the anger expanding within him away from himself, toward his wife. He insists that she's the defective one, she's to blame, because she has not met his needs. Such acts of externalization are key to the NPD batterer. His violent behavior restores his self-esteem. He believes that his actions are not his fault; he is just trying to take care of himself.[35]

THE ENTITLED HUSBAND:
INSATIABLE DEMANDS AND IMPOSSIBLE BEHAVIORS

The rage of the upscale husband is closely linked to his strong sense of entitlement, marked by untenable expectations that can never be fully satisfied. Sally told me about a situation at Christmas that typifies the difficult dynamics of her husband's overblown sense of entitlement and need for recognition. "Ray didn't like the gift I gave him one Christmas," she explained. "He felt that he deserved something much grander than the cashmere sweater I had given him, and he didn't like it. When he opened his gift, he was in such turmoil. 'This is *all* I got?' he screamed. 'I don't believe it!' And then he beat me. He beat me on Christmas morning in front of our children."

All the husbands I have heard about in my research and at my office, as well as those whom I have actually met, possess this sense of narcissistic entitlement that often seems to trigger their abusive behavior. In general, they express little gratitude toward their wives; there's an absence of give-and-take in the marriage. Sally described her husband's refusal to help out in the home. "I was always subservient to him," she explained. "I was always *waiting on* him." As the women in my study became more firmly entrenched in their marriages, their husband's controlling demands and threats became more frequent and disturbing. These patterns were extensions of the early warning signs that the women had ignored or denied. Such behaviors, which can be viewed as various aspects of narcissistic entitlement, take any and all of the following forms:

- Demands that are not necessarily clear, discrete, or consistent about how the wife should look or behave
- Enforcement of specific requirements as to meal preparation
- Expectations about and imposition of strict domestic roles, especially refusal to help out with childrearing
- Refusal to apologize, even after brutal attacks
- Blaming the wife for any household mishap, whatever the cause
- Creating shifting sands—unpredictable changes in expectations, conflicting and contradictory messages that throw the wife off balance
- Demeaning attacks on the wife's femininity, sexuality, appearance, and maternal behavior
- Absence of the honeymoon phase after violent episodes or emotionally abusive tirades (or short-lived post-abuse honeymoons)
- Feeling of impunity regarding his behavior
- Interest only in his own sexual gratification and disregard for the wife's needs, leading sometimes to multiple extramarital affairs, to which he feels entitled
- Violent reactions to pregnancies; belief that the child is an interloper who threatens his power
- Using money and power as leverage or threat
- Isolating the wife from her friends and family
- Possessiveness and/or jealousy

HOW SOCIETY CONTRIBUTES

Although the husbands of the women I have studied exhibited many of the psychological traits characteristic of narcissistic personality disorder, we may also attribute some of their self-indulgence and smugness directly to their status, accomplishments, prestige, and the very real power that came with their money and influence. Often society sanctions and reinforces the abusive behavior of such men. As Kathleen protested, "My husband's success made him *worse*, because it affirmed his narcissism and his arrogance. He had these adoring *fans*, these other commercial real estate brokers who wanted to be like him and make killer deals. One month he grossed more than $3 million. And after that he just got more *joy* out of humiliating me in front of other people."

The narcissist's insatiable demands and expectations seem justified by a society that gives the upscale, educated husband so many benefits. In addition to whatever material rewards he garners, he accumulates adoration from his professional associates and from his community. In our society, wealthy, powerful men are held in higher esteem than other men.

The prosperous often reap the benefit of others' admiration of their financial achievements. Success and rewards breed more success and rewards. These advantages increase with each success, sometimes exponentially. Consider Kathleen's husband, Stuart, who made $3 million in one month, or Irene's husband, Carl, who almost ran for mayor of the town in which he bought land and built his business. Consider Peter, buoyed by his entourage, his chauffeur, his staff of ten, his VIP service, his private jet. Society reinforces these men's feelings of entitlement. The powerful modern-day business mogul is supposed to stop at nothing and to have little regard for those he steps on to get what he wants. The upscale batterer who beats his wife and is condemned by neither the courts nor society is thus in some ways acting in accordance with our social values.

In all fairness, I should add that some of the women enjoyed the perks their entitled husband received. Bailey never said that she liked the staff of ten and the private jets, but when I interviewed her she did indicate that she was only willing to be with a man of means. Indicative of the high standard of living to which she has become accustomed was her comment that even though she preferred to be with a highly successful man, she did know some couples who were "getting by" comfortably on $150,000 to $200,000 a year. Similarly, when I once asked a patient who was thinking of leaving her emotionally abusive mate, "What if you could find happiness with a man who loved you deeply and was passionate about his work but who made $50,000 a year?" her face nearly curdled as she replied, "Oh, I could *never do that!*"

Some of these women collude with their mate's sense of entitlement and reinforce society's esteem for the wealthy husband.

OUTRAGEOUS EXPECTATIONS

The narcissistic upscale batterer brings a set of expectations to the marriage about what a wife should do and how she should act.[36] Allison, worrying about which fork to use, sensed such unspoken rules of decorum at her first lunch with Robert. Bailey's husband was constantly criticizing her, shouting expletives and crying, "How could you have done that?" or, "You idiot! You said what to which competitor?" Sally never knew what her husband might want at any given time. He demanded that she prepare meals even when she was too sick to leave her bed. Ingrid was amazed that her husband thought her novice mothering skills were faulty. And he humiliated her in front of others at a restaurant, calling her the "Burger Queen" because she wasn't sophisticated enough to order lobster. (In fact, she didn't like seafood.)

Wives of upscale abusers, like abused women of any class, often hope that learning and fulfilling their husband's expectations may be key to survival. Her rationale is that if she can anticipate what her man wants and give it to him, she may avoid punishment. But often her efforts fail dismally, especially if vagueness or inconsistency compounds the unreasonableness of the husband's demands. For the person with narcissistic personality disorder, an insult to the ego can come at any time and from any source. "You're kind of walking on eggshells all the time," Kathleen explained. "I know this sounds naive now, but I believed in marriage, and I loved this guy. I can remember still living in our first apartment and *praying* that I would be a better wife so that he wouldn't do this. I thought there was some failure in me that I wasn't doing my wifely duties properly. I worked, I cooked, I did the laundry, and I cleaned the house—I did everything I thought a wife was supposed to do, but somehow I failed to please him."

Later on in an abusive marriage some women employ the opposite strategy. Julia, Sally, and others reported that after a while they began triggering attacks because they couldn't bear the unpredictability.[37] They just wanted to "get it over with." Kathleen, for instance, gradually became aware of a pattern in Stuart's behavior. "It was just about an eight-week buildup to me thinking, 'I know it's going to happen; I know it's going to happen,'" she explained. "It was as inevitable as the full moon. So if it hadn't happened yet, I knew it was coming. I didn't realize until later how regular it was on the calendar, to the point where there'd almost be a *relief* when it did come." Then, rather than making efforts to forestall her husband's explosions, Kathleen eventually began provoking them. "I would become quieter when I knew it was coming," she explained, "and he couldn't tolerate quiet. I provoked him because I was scared, and I knew it was coming anyway!"

Some husbands are specific in their demands, but the demands are so unrealistic that they become an emotional torture for the woman. Attorney Sarah Buel, herself a survivor of domestic violence, told of a case she prosecuted in which the husband, a lawyer, exhibited one of the most brazen displays of entitled expectations I've ever heard about. The husband gave his wife, who was a dentist, an extensive list of acceptable behaviors with which she was to comply. She called the list "Reasons He Feels Justified to Hit Me / What I Need to Do to Be a Good Wife." Some of the absurdly controlling items included:

- Don't open the window or door if I tell you not to.
- Don't scream and wake the neighbors.
- Do not make comments to anyone when in my presence insinuating that you are unhappy, fed up, or having any marital problems. Do not make me look stupid or embarrass me in front of others.
- Don't flirt with other men or have an affair.
- If I decide that we sleep together, you will humbly comply without a fight.
- Don't go for a walk without first asking me if you can.
- Don't talk about the past in any manner.
- Don't physically resist me.

The list went on for four pages. In court Sarah asked the husband, "Why did you feel you had to write such a list?" He replied, "Because my wife is so stupid I had no choice."[38] When she didn't comply, he punished her with beatings and threatened divorce.

Similarly unrealistic expectations were imposed on Sherry, an attorney, by her Stanford graduate husband, who was obsessed with her weight. Every night after dinner he made her get on the scale under his critical gaze. If she had not lost a few pounds, or at the very least maintained her current weight, he would assault her verbally, shouting, "How could anybody love you like this? A perfect woman should be petite and weigh one hundred pounds no matter what!" Sherry's five-foot-eight athletic build would never conform to such an unrealistic ideal. Although she understood this at some level, she would nevertheless try to fast all day or take diuretics prior to her weigh-ins to avoid feeling rejected and unlovable.

A WOMAN'S PLACE . . .

Despite their affluence, many of the women in my research said their husbands insisted that they, not a domestic servant, do all the housekeeping, cooking, and childrearing. These strict domestic role structures, like other demands made on the wife, represent the husband's narcissism. No matter what the woman was dealing with in her life and daily activities, the typical husband in the study expected his wife to keep house, entertain, and raise the children in a certain way. This aspect of marriage among the upscale—the husband's expectations of maintaining a lifestyle, or at least the image of a lifestyle, consistent with upper socioeconomic values and mores, possibly supportive of his professional advancement or the couple's social advance-ment—may be in contrast to lower-income marriages.[39]

Meal preparation was a particularly sore issue. Many of these upscale hus-bands had specific demands as to what, how, and when they were served; the wives indicated that numerous abusive incidents were triggered by com-plaints related to meals and housekeeping.[40] Ray's demand to be fed on schedule despite his wife's severe illness is indicative of how narcissistic these behaviors become. Julia's husband Marc justified his after-hours affair with his graduate assistant on the grounds that the younger woman, unlike Julia, took the time to prepare elaborate meals for him.

Because I have not interviewed the husbands, I can merely speculate as to the meaning of their expectations regarding food and its preparation. They may have learned from their mothers—as many of us have—that food repre-sents comfort and affection. The old Pillsbury Foods jingle "Nothin' says lovin' like somethin' from the oven" may be overly important to the man who believes he can and should "have it all." Perhaps he feels that he should be catered to, that his home is truly his castle. Or perhaps his need for demon-strations of love and warmth from his woman have coalesced in his mind into her taking care of him and nurturing him with meals.

But the husbands' expectations of their wife's domestic performance usually go beyond food service and culinary customs. Regardless of their ages or the current socially accepted view of women's roles, these men enforced domestic role structures in their homes. All of my respondents said their husbands did nothing to help with domestic chores or with the children. This was true even when a child was seriously ill for a period of time or the wife was incapacitated, whether owing to childbirth, illness, or her husband's abuse.

As Irene, an older woman, described her relationship with Carl, it became clear that his needs were always paramount. "He has a very controlling power," she explained, "and because I'd become so *passive* in the relationship, there were times that I felt like a paid servant. I was there just for his needs when he was at home and to take care of the family. I really didn't count; my feelings or opinions didn't matter. It almost became like a business arrange-ment. I had a job; he had a job; we had a family together. I was to take care of the family. That's what I *did*."

Many of the women felt abandoned, as if they were raising their families alone. For instance, Lynne said, "I got pregnant, I had my daughter, and he was gone even more. So I would work, and I found the day care. I did everything. Looking back, it's sort of embarrassing." And when Irene's husband left her alone for weeks and then months at a time, she bent over backward to accommodate him. "He'd come home on a Friday night, and then he would leave again on Sunday night. I always saw to it that I had all the chores done. I did everything I could possibly do around the house so that he wouldn't have to. I shoveled snow, I mowed the lawn, so that we would have more time *together,* as a family and just as a couple, when he was home, because he rarely was."

Sometimes the child was a source of friction and even violence. Bill became jealous of the attention Ingrid lavished on their baby son. And as another woman explained to me, "God help me if the baby cried in the middle of the night and it woke him up, because *he* had to get up to go trade in the morning. In fact, I used to sleep with the baby most of the time—more than with him—for fear that it would wake him up."

THE POWER OF ELEGANT PURSE STRINGS

With strictly enforced role structures, often the wife is the one who keeps house and raises the children, while the husband is the breadwinner. The husband tends to use money (and lifestyle) as a threat or leverage to control her. This is the case whether or not the woman earns money. Peter had arranged his and Bailey's combined upscale finances so that Bailey's money would go for services (such as staff and housekeepers) that she would never get returns on monetarily while Peter's funds went toward the principal on their home, which he could later claim he had paid for single-handedly. In other situations the husband uses money as a weapon to keep his financially dependent wife in line. Ingrid explained, for example, that "when Bill would get mad, he would take the credit cards away. That was my *punishment* for whatever he was pissed at. I had student loan bills . . . and he would use my debts against me." Kathleen told me that the biggest mistake a woman can ever make when she's married to an emotional abuser is not to have a job. When I asked her why, she replied, "Because you don't have any other frame of reference. You don't have a boss giving you a review telling you you're okay. Or actually, *he's* your boss when you're a housewife, right? From that point on, what self-esteem I had left went steadily downhill. I was a wife and mother, and that's all I was."

The men often exploited their wife's fear of poverty. When a woman threatened to seek a divorce, her husband warned that he would cut her off without a cent—or as Ray had put it to Sally, "out on the street selling pencils." Although many men ultimately don't or can't follow through on their financial threats, the prospect of poverty made some upscale wives, already weakened in their resolve and sense of power, back down. However, sometimes the men actually do make good on these promises—or at least try to. Irene described going to her safe deposit box after she discovered her husband was having an affair. "When I called the attorney, he told me to get all of my financial records together. So I went into the safety deposit box. There was no reason before this for me to go into the safety deposit box. Carl took care of everything. He sent me a check for enough money to pay the bills for the month. I'd never been in there alone. I took the box, went into that little room, and opened it up, but there was nothing in there. It was *empty.* I knew we had stocks and bonds and other things that were of some value, but nothing was in there. I sat in that little room in a state of shock. There was only $900 in the savings account and whatever monies for the month that he would put into the checking account to take care of the bills. Everything else was gone. He had just taken it all out and put it someplace else."

When Irene confronted Carl, he said, "I took them out because I knew that you would probably go to an attorney."

AT THE VERY CORE: SEX AND POWER

Most of the abused upscale women in my study had turned off sexually to their violent husband. Often this was a response not only to his abusive behavior in general but also to his lack of regard for her sexuality. The wives consistently reported that their husband was sexually selfish. Indeed, one wife was so unaccustomed to receiving pleasure that she couldn't remember the word *foreplay* during our interview, calling it *pre-sex* by mistake. For the majority of these couples, the bedroom became one more area in which the narcissistic husband felt utterly entitled and blamed his misdeeds on his wife.

The upscale abuser consistently said things that made his wife doubt her abilities and her self-worth. Demeaning her sexuality by calling her "frigid" and "inadequate" cut to the core of her being as a woman. Ingrid's sexual encounters with Bill were typical of many wives' experiences. "I was supposed to be ready at the drop of a hat," she explained with a snap of her fingers. "There was no foreplay, no nothing. I started to feel, 'What do you want from my life?' And I told him, 'If I'm not thinking about having sex, then *help* me think about it.' But for him it was always, 'What is *your* problem?' After months and months of 'What is your problem?' I really thought I had a problem."

Many of the husbands had extramarital affairs, which served several purposes. Some used infidelity as a way to further humiliate and punish their wives. Others simply felt entitled to do as they wish, regardless of the pain it caused. One man had the audacity to offer his wife what he thought was "a good deal" after she caught him *in flagrante delicto*. "It's not a big problem," he told her the very next day when she confronted him. "I will keep sleeping with other women, but we can stay married."

Some of the husbands boasted openly about their desirability. Ellen told me that her husband "liked to flaunt the fact that he could attract any woman. He was always a cocky guy who said, 'I can have any girl I want.'" The behavior of Kathleen's husband Stuart—the man who had sex in the swimming pool with a girlfriend while Kathleen was upstairs delivering their baby—was particularly egregious. He bragged about his affairs and sexual peccadilloes in front of his wife, their friends, and even her family. "This one woman practically *lived* with us," Kathleen said. "She was a real estate attorney in his office, and they partied together. I was being a *mom*, so I was no fun and boring, and I didn't like to go out, and I couldn't stay out all night. So it was my fault that he needed these other people to be with. He didn't admit that he was having a sexual relationship with this person. But he would brag about picking up a hooker and having a blow job driving down the street. He would say that in a room with other people in it, including *my family*, and I was just supposed to sit there as he talked about it."

These sexual insults found physical expression when a husband attacked his wife's genitals (as Marc did to Julia) or beat her while she was pregnant or nursing. In fact, according to Lewis Okun, studies conducted in the 1970s found that "pregnancy tends to increase the frequency of woman abuse. Richard Gelles reported that 23 percent of the assaulted wives in his sample were attacked while pregnant."[41] This is a particularly dangerous time for an abused wife: if her husband is anticipating the feeling of being displaced, she is exceptionally vulnerable physically and emotionally.

Their husband's lack of concern about birth control was another source of torment for some wives. "Maybe a month after he started this new business I found out I was pregnant," Ellen told me. "And I remember thinking, everyone's going to blame me. Everyone will say, 'How could she get pregnant at such a tough time for him?' But then I remembered he never once offered from day one in our relationship to be responsible for birth control. It was always my responsibility. So instead of being happy that we're going to have a baby, I felt guilty about getting pregnant a month after he started this business."

Painful emotional wounds such as these don't heal quickly, for they cut to the core of a woman's sexual identity.

LOVE WITHOUT APOLOGIES

A person with narcissistic personality disorder rarely apologizes after lashing out because he is convinced that he himself has been mistreated. Why should he apologize when he believes with every fiber of his psychological and emotional being that he is the one who has been wronged and injured? This is why he not only refuses to take responsibility for his abusive acts but also blames his wife for the violent episode.

Ray had hurled a heavy table at Sally, severely bruising her leg. When I asked what happened after he threw the table, she replied, "The same as before. Nothing." And when I asked whether her husband cared whether he had hurt her, she reacted angrily, "Oh, no! I showed him what had happened to my leg a few days afterward, and he said, 'It's your own fault.'" After Stuart's first physical assault on Kathleen, he ignored the situation entirely. As Kathleen described it, Stuart stormed out of the house but "came back at three o'clock in the morning. I was in bed, pretending I was asleep. He got in bed and never said a word. He never said a word for fifteen years about it. It wasn't like *Sleeping with the Enemy* or those other movies where the men bring their wives flowers and chocolates and try to make up. He never said anything."

Such patterns were typical of the upscale batterers in my study, as well as of my clinical population—reportedly the husbands make no amends after abusive incidents throughout the relationship. Many of the men act as if nothing at all had occurred. This lack of remorse is in keeping with the strong sense of narcissistic entitlement these upscale men have. It is certainly a distinctly different pattern from the alternating cycle of violence and remorse that lower-income abused couples often go through.

And despite the wealth, power, and resources of these upscale husbands, many of the wives reported that their husband never attempted to make up after an abusive episode with gifts or other forms of material indulgence. As Lynne told me, "Sometimes if a man is really abusive he apologizes afterward, and he buys you nice stuff. Well, he didn't even do that. He'd just say, 'Oh, you know it's all right,' or something dumb like that."

I am not claiming that the upscale narcissistic batterer is totally lacking in empathy. Although he may be so thoroughly self-absorbed that he is oblivious to any pain he inflicts on others, he can also be amazingly tuned in to his wife in ways that are key to his ability to hurt her deeply. Narcissistic personalities can have exquisite empathy in that they can read their victims and fine-tune their behaviors so as to inflict the most hurt. As Heinz Kohut has shown, empathy does not necessarily lead to kindness; people skilled in manipulation and coercion are also making use of their empathic ability. The person who can hurt you the most is the one who truly knows you the best and therefore is empathically attuned to you.

Kohut's oft-cited example of empathy put to cruel use was the Nazis' decision to precede their bombing of England with whistles indicating that the planes were coming. The Germans understood that the sound would cause terror long before the bombs arrived. It was their way of going for the jugular. The Nazis were empathically attuned to the British but used their empathy for negative ends.[42] And so it is with domestic violence. The abuser is often empathically attuned to the vulnerabilities of his partner. He knows which of his actions will hurt her the most, and rather than use this insight as a guide to being kind to her, he uses it against her.

Unfortunately, this empathy, even put to cruel ends, can foster in an abused woman a sense of connection with her abuser and some fulfillment from her relationship with him. Sometimes he mirrors her feelings; he can be adoring and seductive in his nontoxic state. At other times she believes he protects her. She views him as bigger and stronger, satisfying her need to idealize his powerfulness. She may even feel a twinship with him: they are both peas in the same pod of the toxic relationship, and only *they* truly understand each other and how they tick. As one of my patients told me, in defending her abusive husband, "He may be a jerk, but he's *my jerk*."

This unusual feeling of attachment to an abuser may be similar to the Stockholm syndrome, in which hostages become attached to, even protective of, their captors. It is a feeling that grows out of a mix of terror, dependence, and gratitude.

TURNING THE TABLES

Many of the men justified their actions by blaming their wife for the abuse. Although their husband's reasoning was flawed, the women often seemed invested in accepting it. Kathleen told me, "The night he threw me across the room, he was very mad at me. So he went to a bar, and he picked up this woman and had sex with her. And it was my fault, because, according to Stuart, I had caused this fight."

"How did you cause it?" I asked, truly interested in how she had bought into his accusation.

"I wanted to go to Seattle for the Fourth of July. That's where my family was, and my first cousin was getting married. He didn't want to go. There were so few times that I would assert myself, and this particular time I really wanted to go to," Kathleen replied. In other words, she expressed her own needs, which were different from her husband's, and in so doing made him aware that she was not an extension of himself.

Irene, sensing that her husband was having an affair during his many absences—as indeed he was—brought up to him how neglected she was feeling. But still she found no satisfaction. "If I would make an attempt to discuss it with him," she explained, "he would turn things around. He would say, 'You're lucky. I'm working so hard all the time, and all you do is complain about this. You know this is the way it's going to be.' So I figured this is the way it's going to be, and I'd bite the bullet."

Over a period of time, blaming the victim becomes the routine to which the couple is accustomed, the way they relate to each other. As the woman's self-esteem withers, she becomes increasingly vulnerable to attacks on her personality and readily believes and integrates her husband's accusations that she has caused his insults, rages, and assaults. Paradoxically, in so doing she retains the hope that she can change a situation in which she really has very little power.

The shifting of blame is also integral to the way these couples develop shared meaning systems.[43] Just as couples adopt and develop particular terms of endearment, so they develop shared ways of viewing themselves, their relationship, and the world. They tacitly, if not explicitly, agree on their own customs, on what is unique and acceptable to them. The shared meaning systems in the marriage of most abused women include an agreement that when the husband acts badly, they both concur that she was the provocateur. In this way couples in abusive relationships legitimate the battering.

Like any unfamiliar family culture or code, the shared meaning systems of such couples can seem bizarre to those outside the pair. For instance, a researcher in Sweden studying couples who had reported domestic assault during their marriage found that even when the man and woman believed that woman beating was an immoral wrong, they agreed that wife beating as an act within the social context of marriage was perfectly acceptable and understandable![44] It was the personal social context that contributed to the mutual meaning the couple assigned to domestic violence.

If a batterer does not believe that he has committed a wrong, why should he apologize or be required to make amends? The narcissistic upscale abusive husband buys into his fabricated externalizations and revisionist history, which dictate that his wife is at fault for inciting his actions, and he is blameless. This logic justifies his feeling that he needs mollifying and excuses any emotional or physical abuses he inflicts.

ABOVE THE LAW?

The narcissistic person often feels that society's rules do not apply to him. Take the nonchalance with which Peter could alter Bailey's life by offering her a job and then capriciously withdrawing the offer with no remorse whatsoever. Sarah Buel told me about a noteworthy instance in which an upscale batterer was treated like everyone else. This case came to court in Seattle in the 1980s after a mandatory arrest policy had been instituted. A dentist had smashed his wife's jaw. When the judge ordered him to jail, the husband's shocked response was, "Sentence, your honor? You must be confused. I am a dentist. I would be willing to pay a fine, but you can't give me a criminal sentence!" Fortunately, the judge had been trained in issues of domestic violence. He picked up one of his law books and said to the offender, "Show me in the statutes where it says dentists are exempt from the law!"[45] This man simply couldn't fathom that he had committed a crime and was going to jail for it.

The narcissistic upscale abuser's strong sense that he could get away with murder was a recurrent theme in my research. Indeed, the richer the abuser, the more he seemed to feel that he was above the law. More than half of the women in the study reported fearing for their lives; significantly, the mean income of this group of women was greater than the mean income of all the other women in the study. In fact, the two women in marriages with the highest income (greater than $500,000 per annum) both reported serious concerns about their husbands having the means, the intention, and the capacity to murder them.

The upscale husband's belief that he can commit the crime but not do the time is at the heart of upscale abuse and indicative of what distinguishes this population from others. Because they assume they will not be punished, men with financial means may be more likely to threaten to murder their wives. Outcomes from recent celebrity trials might seem to justify this assumption. Though the juries of public opinion and the civil courts deemed O. J. Simpson guilty of double homicide, he was wealthy enough to employ a team of high-profile attorneys and was found innocent at his criminal trial. He is a free man today.

The upscale batterer probably also knows that most people would doubt the charge that he is physically abusive. Maybe he has carefully groomed his public image, hiding his true nature. He instinctively relies on the cultural myth that abuse rarely occurs among the highly educated or upper-income populations. "Abusers feel they have the leverage to force their wives to capitulate," attorney David H. Hopkins told me. "It isn't so much they feel above the law as they tell themselves, 'I am too smart to not beat this—I will figure out a way around it.'" Some upscale abusive husbands pull the children into the situation. They threaten adult children who could testify on behalf of their mother with disinheritance. This puts the victimized wife in a terrible position. If she seeks appropriate relief under the Domestic Violence Act, to what extent is she putting her children in jeopardy economically? And in families with small children, we get into phony custody battles and false accusations that the mother is unfit."[46]

One woman told me how her husband used the system to intimidate her. The police came in and separated them during a physical attack. "Paul became belligerent to the officer, saying, 'What are you going to do? Why do you believe her? Why aren't you listening to me?'

"They asked me, 'Do you want to press charges?' and I said, 'Yes, I do.' He had my arms and was shaking me and then threw me. I was all scratched up and bruised. That's the first thing they saw, so they assumed he had hurt me. They took him to the station in a squad car. I stayed home, and they helped me find my glasses. Then they asked, 'Would you come to the station to give your statement?' I went in and gave a statement, which I signed. The paramedics took photographs and asked if I needed to go to the hospital. I said, 'No, I don't think so.'

"About an hour after I had been there the officers came in and said, 'You're not going to believe this. He just talked to his attorney, and he now wants to press charges against you for domestic battery.' So I had my fingerprints and my mug shot taken. He was in a holding cell, a room right next to the processing room, and I had to stand against the mug shot background, looking through a window at him. He was snickering at me. I was devastated, and he was saying 'Ha, ha, you think you can do something to me? I'm going to make it just as bad for you.' And ever since then he has used every financial and emotional ploy against me."

Above all, the upscale man suffering from narcissistic personality disorder truly believes he is blameless and has not committed a crime. It's easy for him to hurt others because he has no sense of their pain and no consciousness that they are individuals independent of himself. Perhaps that is why domestic abuse escalates, often to the point of murder attempts just as the woman is about to leave. The prospect of her departure proves that she is a separate being, and this so shakes the narcissistic abuser's equilibrium that he becomes murderously enraged.

ENTITLED AND *MEAN,* TOO!

If many of the emotionally and physically brutal acts these upscale husbands commit stem from their sense of entitlement, other abuses reflect a more general kind of mean-spiritedness and desire for control. These sorts of abuses have been documented among lower- and middle-class abusers and are often associated with them, but they are just as prevalent among the wealthy men described by the wives in my study.[47]

Many of the husbands sought to isolate their wife from friends and family. Marc locked Julia in their home, imprisoning her and their children. The spouses of Ingrid, Kathleen, and Allison made sure they moved far from their nuclear families after the wedding. The distance allowed the husbands to set the agenda and deprived the women of support or validation from outside sources. Isolating his wife enhances an abuser's control. She becomes more dependent on him and less able to judge her options. Judith Herman, associate clinical professor of psychiatry at the Harvard Medical School and director of training at the Victims of Violence Program at Cambridge Hospital, has observed, "As the victim is isolated, she becomes increasingly dependent on the perpetrator, not only for survival and basic bodily needs but also for information and even for emotional sustenance."[48]

The upscale abusers were possessive and jealous. Paula recalled her future husband's response to a European trip she was planning with sorority sisters: "I remember my boyfriend didn't want me to go. He had become . . . I guess *possessive* would be the only word I can think of." Peter was always accusing Bailey of cheating on him if she so much as looked at another man or had business meetings with male clients. And Irene's husband, always away yet secretive about his whereabouts, expected her to be home awaiting his return. This type of possessiveness is also a product of the husband's need to control his wife's every movement.

It is important to understand that the upscale batterer is not always horrible. That he can be charming, gentle, and loving simply makes the woman's involvement with him all the more addictive. Today might be the day that her investment of time and energy pays off; today might be the day he will be nice to her—at least, that is her fondest hope.

8

What About the Children?

THE CHILDREN OF AN UPSCALE ABUSIVE MARRIAGE become victims in the family drama of abuse because they have no choice about their participation. Like their mother, they are trapped in a family situation that sanctions abuse. Ironically, often it is fear for her children that keeps the abused wife from leaving the marriage. Sometimes, however, the children become her main reason for escaping the trap of dependency and abuse. The same little hands that hold the abused upscale wife on the path and keep her with her mate can ultimately tug her toward freedom.

HOW CHILDREN INDUCE THE WOMAN TO STAY

Many of the upscale abused wives I have known say that the financial benefits for the children justified their decision to remain in their marriage. They believed the children needed the husband's financial support to maintain an acceptable lifestyle, and that he would cut off this support if the marriage ended. The women's secret strategizing often included waiting to file for divorce until the children were grown up and well provided for. This was especially common thinking among older women, who matured before the women's movement.

Sometimes the women viewed their decision to stay as an act of self-sacrifice. Irene told me, "I had no great educational background to provide for my four children. There were times that I wanted to get out of the relationship. I'd think about it, and then I would back off, asking myself, 'How am I going to take care of four kids?' My fear of not being able to provide for them stopped me—the family commitment and those children. I was responsible for them. I had brought them into this world, and no matter what I was to do, I had to take care of them."

Family members reinforced this reasoning. "I would get a little angry and say to my mother-in-law, 'I can't believe how Carl is treating me,'" Irene recalled. "One day she walked over to the refrigerator, opened the door, and said, 'You have a refrigerator full of food. That is very important. He provides well for you and the children.' That was like saying to me, 'Stop and think about it. You're fortunate. There are a lot of people who are starving in this world. You have four children. You have food enough to feed them, and you have a roof over your head.' So you grin and bear it."

Sally also opted to put her children's needs above her own. To this day she feels that her sacrifice was justified. "I was on a mission," she told me, shaking her head. "I was going to raise my children, and Ray had thoroughly convinced me that there was no way I could survive financially without him. I was in it for the long term. I've gone through all this suffering, true, but it was worth it because I did what was best for my kids. Everyone tells me that they could have gotten student loans. They were bright, and they could have gotten scholarships, but this was the best way."

Ingrid was afraid of becoming a statistic. "My fear was that I would become a stereotype," she told me. "Black female, head of household." For Ingrid this didn't seem a viable option. "I didn't know how I would make it. How would I support this child? I thought, 'My God, aside from the abuse, you're taking him away from the type of life you would have loved to have grown up in. Jeffrey wanted for nothing. Whatever Jeffrey wanted, Jeffrey got."

Like Ingrid, Sally, and Irene, nearly half the women in my research group claimed they stayed in their marriages because of the financial benefit to their children. The combined marital incomes of wife and husband were over $100,000 per annum, and two couples had an annual income of more than $500,000. The women in my study gave birth to up to four children. Of the five who claimed they stayed married because of the advantages their socioeconomic status afforded their youngsters, two had two children, two had three, and one had four. The mean was 2.8 children, markedly higher than the group mean (1.9). The women with larger families were more likely to stay in their abusive marriage because they believed it was essential for their children's financial support. Except for Ingrid, none of the women who had only one child reported staying for this reason. And in my clinical practice the women who reported staying "for the sake of the children" also had two or more youngsters. We may speculate that the more children a woman has, the more she worries about how she would support them on her own. And the greater the family income level, the more valid the woman's concerns about being able to maintain the lifestyle as a single parent.

For others, staying "for the sake of the children" reflected a desire to safeguard the ideal of the family. Julia endured Marc's mistreatment because she had been raised with the belief—as many of us have—that an intact two-parent family, even a dysfunctional one, is better for children than a single-parent household. Another woman told me, "I had such a devotion and commitment to *family*. That's why I stayed in the relationship for so long. It's because of that *bond*. There was nothing more important to me than family."

Women typically pride themselves on their ability to cultivate relationships. They also reinforce their feminine identity by nurturing others, especially their children. These efforts, however, can mislead the abused woman into believing that the best way to fulfill her role as wife, mother, and woman is to remain married.

HOW CHILDREN INDUCE THE WOMAN TO LEAVE

Although many of the women stayed married "for the sake of the children," once the husband's aggression directly threatened the children's safety women decided they could no longer tolerate the marriage. Allison explained that Robert's behavior around their child pushed her into leaving him. "Everyday there was something going on. I would be breast-feeding Jason, and Robert would come in and punch me in the arm, arguing, 'Why don't you give him a pacifier?'

"Usually when the baby cried in the middle of the night it would set Robert off too," she told me. "I was breast-feeding, so I was the one who got up with Jason all the time. Robert refused. One evening I got sick, and I asked him to help me. He screamed that I wasn't taking responsibility. I was in the bathroom, throwing up. He came in, hit me on the back, and dragged me out of the bathroom by the hair to Jason's nursery. 'You take care of him, he's your son,' he yelled. I tried to breast-feed the baby, but I was so tired and ill that I put him in the bassinet and took him over to Robert, who was lying in our bed. I said, 'Robert, he's your son too. You need to take care of him too. I'm too sick.' And then I went into the guest room, locked the door, and lay down."

Jason continued to scream. Robert just put him on the floor in the portable bassinet outside the door of the guest room and walked away. "I couldn't stand it," Allison continued. "I went down the hall and said to him, 'You need to take care of the baby.' He turned around, grabbed me by the neck, backed me up into the guest room onto the bed, and started to strangle me. I remember lots of pillows and feeling like I was being smothered. Then he smashed my face into the pillow, calling me 'bitch' and 'asshole.' I was scared and shocked. I couldn't believe what was happening. He ended up taking Jason and going downstairs. I could hear him fumbling in the kitchen, trying to get a bottle. He came up the steps, but there were no lights because the house was being renovated. He dropped Jason in the stairwell on the way up."

As soon as Allison heard the thud and her infant's renewed screams, she ran out of her room, scooped him up, took him to the nursery, and locked the door. "I called the doctor to check if the baby was all right. He told me what to look for, and it seemed that Jason was okay. Now I was putting on clothes, getting ready to escape. I was going to take the baby and leave, except it was three in the morning and I didn't know where to go. And it was below zero outside. He was only seven weeks old. I remember at that point knowing that I would leave. I didn't know how. I had no job, and Robert had taken away all my money, but that was it.

"I was seeing a therapist at the time, but I hadn't told him what was going on with me and Robert. Finally, the next week, I made an appointment and went in to see him. I told him the whole story, and he said, 'Get out. Get out now. He's going to hurt you. If you can't get out for your own sake, get out for your child.'"

That was the turning point for Allison. She left the therapist's office, went home, and made plane reservations. "I called my mother and said, 'I don't know how I'm doing this, but I'm coming home.' I packed a suitcase and took a laptop computer because somehow I was going to do freelance writing. The nanny drove me to the airport. I called Robert before the plane took off and said, 'I'm leaving.' He didn't think I was serious, but I went home and never came back."

Other upscale battered wives described similarly dramatic scenes. Ingrid decided to leave when Bill became violent while she was nursing their baby. Another woman realized that her children were in danger when her husband, in a fit of rage, smashed their toys and threw them around the house.

Some women are motivated to leave when the children show protectiveness toward them or witness them being abused. Although Irene didn't leave for the children's sake, it was their concern and validation that got her out. She believed their perceptions and protests as to the wrongfulness of Carl's behaviors toward her.

There is an essential question here: Why would the mothers leave for their children's sake but not their own? I believe their identification with the role of mother exerted a much stronger force in these women's psyches than self-compassion. Perhaps their diminished self-esteem limited the amount of protectiveness they could muster on their own behalf. In addition, perhaps the helpless innocence of their children triggered an unconscious recognition of their own need to trust and receive love and security—and thus of their vulnerability to the dangers of abuse.

THE PERILS OF SECRECY

The upscale abused wife takes great pains to conceal the abuse, not only from her friends, family, and community but also from her children. She leads a double life, striving to keep the household as normal as possible for her children. But she is often unsuccessful.

Sally thought silence could protect her children from her husband's rages. On a night when Ray had choked and beaten her, the children had been playing with her friend's kids. When the friend called, announcing that she was about to bring the children back for the evening, Sally put on her best face. "Once again I had to choke back the tears," she told me. "I splashed my face with cold water and powdered my red nose. We couldn't even discuss the incident; I never would in front of the children."

Sally was determined that her children would neither see nor learn about Ray's abuse of her. However, her attempts at shielding them were ineffectual. Following one of Ray's early attacks, which sent Sally to the emergency room with a broken arm, her four-year-old son called his grandmother to let her know. And once Ray beat her in front of the children at Christmas. Still, Sally continued to hope that the children would forget these early incidents. "My son was very young," she insisted. "After that, he didn't see anything until he was fifteen."

When I commented, "You seem proud that you could keep much of the abuse away from your kids," at first Sally replied with some enthusiasm. "Yes, I am! But it was also wrong," she continued, suddenly rueful as she realized the full impact of her behavior. "My daughter had seen very little of it. There was a time when I had actually called the police. I was about to press charges when my husband said to me, 'Ashley is coming home in five minutes. You're not going to let her see this, are you? Don't do this to Ashley.' That was enough to make me back off. So when we separated Ashley really went into trauma because she couldn't believe it was happening. She never thought we had problems, so I did her a disservice." Sally began to weep as she reflected on the trap she had created for herself and her family. "What's worse?" she asked me with tears streaming down her cheeks, "a child growing up seeing her father abuse her mother or not knowing that he abuses her and then waking up one day to find he's gone?"

Although Sally was certain that she had succeeded in keeping the truth from her daughter, I found it hard to believe that Ashley was oblivious to what was happening. Despite any parent's best efforts at subterfuge, children are radar devices for every nuance of emotion at home. If parents are angry or violent with each other the children sense it, whether or not they actually witness it or their parents discuss it openly. However hard a battered mother tries to shield her children, they become victims too.

Sometimes even the best attempts at hiding the abuse are futile. This was the distressing discovery made by my patient Norma. She and her husband, Alan, had been fighting in their bedroom. Much like Ray, Alan was disappointed in a gift Norma had given him for his special birthday. He proceeded to beat her, just before the family was to leave for his brother's home for a birthday bash. Unnoticed by either of them, their five-year-old daughter, Chelsea, drawn by the commotion, had witnessed the violence from behind a door that had been left ajar.

After the incident the family packed up and went off to the party—Norma putting on "a good front because it was Alan's birthday, the family would be there, that sort of thing." Chelsea brought along her favorite doll, which she dragged into the room where her cousins were playing. When Norma peeked in to see how the children were faring, she was horrified to find Chelsea hitting her doll quite roughly, saying, "I am spanking you because you are bad—like Daddy spanks Mommy. Bad dolly. Bad." Norma knelt down next to her daughter and quietly tried to explain the situation, but her explanation only served to lock the family more firmly into its abusive pattern. She defended Alan's behavior, thinking it was important to make him look good in his child's eyes. "Daddy was just angry, and he was tired," she whispered to Chelsea. "He's never going to do it again. Don't do that to your dolly. Spanking is not good; we don't hit anyone—that's unacceptable!"

When domestic violence is hidden from the children, the effect on them is similar to that on youngsters growing up in an alcoholic family. The kids may pick up cues that something is wrong with their parents, but they are coaxed (or brainwashed) into believing that they are perceiving the situation inaccurately or attributing incorrect meanings to the event. This sort of denial throws their reasoning abilities into question. For instance, in an alcoholic household the child may be sitting at the dinner table when Mommy passes out drunk, slumping to the floor. Alarmed, the child rushes to help, but her father sternly tells her, "Sit down and finish your supper. Mommy is fine!" In upscale families, among whom denial of domestic abuse is rampant, children are often presented with such confusing explanations.

Unfortunately, concealment of domestic abuse is a no-win situation, for once the children do learn of it and perceive the silence with which their parents handle it, they too feel that they must hide the family secret. Like their mothers, they believe, "This is happening only to me. None of my friends are talking about it. And if my mother has kept it quiet it must really be a deep dark secret." The need for secrecy leads to feelings of isolation and shame for the children, who may now believe that the imperative to silence inhibits them from talking with others or seeking assistance for their mother and themselves.

EFFECTS ON CHILDREN
OF WITNESSING DOMESTIC ABUSE

Women whose husbands abuse them have to deal not only with the emotional and physical hurts but also the terrible sense of being trapped and helpless. Children in abusive homes suffer in the same way. But while the mother, as an adult, at least has language skills, reasoning abilities, and insight to help her make sense of her difficult situation and perhaps escape it, children unfortunately often lack these tools.[1] Instead, they are often overwhelmed by their exposure to spousal abuse.[2] People commonly believe that infants and young children are too young to understand domestic violence, but witnessing abuse or living in a violent home can have a lasting impact on youngsters, who learn many unconscious lessons from what they have observed or sensed.

Because so many upscale battered wives claim they stayed in the relationship "for the sake of their children," I believe it is vital to examine the consequences their decisions have for their children. Children depend on their parents to take care of their physical needs, such as food, shelter, and clothing, as well as their emotional needs—safety, warmth, love, and nurturing of their self-esteem. It is in the home environment that children learn to deal with and integrate a range of emotions—some of them intense, many of them complicated. All children use their parents as role models, so it is not surprising that youngsters in an upscale violent home learn to deny and ignore reality as they mimic their parents' attitudes. Although the same can be said of all socioeconomic classes, a parent's privileged status can drive home the lesson in particular ways. When Daddy gets away with bad behavior, his young son learns to feel a sense of entitlement, which can be doubly reinforced if the father is wealthy.[3] Daddy *really* slips by unscathed, doesn't he? He plays golf with judges, including the one who dismissed his case the other day. I guess I can get away with stuff too! A young daughter, meanwhile, sees Mommy enduring abuse within a relationship and learns it is okay to tolerate it. Mommy has a doctoral degree and a job; with her money and authority she could get by without Daddy. So why does she stay even though he is hurting her? It must be how relationships work.

To date no longitudinal studies have been conducted on children from upscale violent families, following them from childhood into maturity, so we know very little about the impact of growing up in such an environment. But we can hypothesize the effects. Miriam Berkman, a lawyer and social worker for the Child Development Clinic at Yale University's Child Study Center and clinical coordinator of the Child Development Community Policing Program[4] and the Domestic Violence Intervention Program, told me, "It is striking how complicated domestic violence situations are for the children."[5]

One of the complexities is that abusive husbands are not necessarily abusive fathers, Berkman explained.[6] "These aggressive guys can also be loving, fun, warm, good fathers and providers." If this is the case, the children will have trouble distinguishing the good guys from the bad. In fact, there may be no identifiable "bad guys," especially since children have an equally strong desire to bond with Mom *and* Dad. "Because children usually have very strong and significant ties to both parents, they are not just traumatized in classic ways," Berkman continued. Relationships with battering fathers can be confusing to a young child, filled with a mixture of affection and resentment, pain and disappointment.[7] As the children grow older and are exposed to more abuse, their involvement in the marital dyad "may switch as they try to run for help, stop the violence, get in the middle, and often become injured themselves as they try to protect mother." Children also become overwhelmed. It is as if all of the models for psychological identification are at play here. The child can identify with the victim (Mom) or the aggressor (Dad). Berkman poignantly noted, "Of course, they certainly see the aggressor as the effective, more powerful one of the team."

All of this takes a psychological toll. Studies have found that boys witnessing domestic violence are more likely to externalize their experience and engage in hostile and antisocial behaviors. Refusing to see themselves as victims, they become aggressive and act out. Girls, on the other hand, are more likely to internalize their mother's behavior and become fearful, shy, inhibited, and depressed. They may also voice somatic complaints and perceive themselves as powerless.[8] Whichever parent children identify with, however, their experience at home can manifest as trouble at school. If they prefer to be an aggressor as a way to fend off their inner feelings of helplessness, they not only get into trouble but may think of themselves as bad, internalizing the negative aspects of both parents.

Berkman told me about a girl who was unusually articulate about her emotional predicament. "She felt a sense of power and mastery in her own aggression, but also saw it as monstrous and bad. It becomes a big internal dilemma for kids—they can be withdrawn and depressed or be big and tough and bad. But even this choice has complicated consequences, not just in their behaviors (getting in trouble for acting out in school) but also because they pay a price internally for being bad."[9]

Despite the fact that public awareness of domestic abuse has increased over the last few decades, relatively little research has been conducted into the effects on children (in any socioeconomic group) of witnessing violence in their homes.[10] In 1999 Jeffrey Edleson of the University of Minnesota analyzed eighty-four such studies conducted thus far and found that only thirty-one met rigorous research criteria.[11] Moreover, most were retrospective studies. Both batterers and nonbatterers were asked to reflect on their childhood and state whether they had witnessed conjugal abuse in their family of origin. Few researchers have interviewed young children while they were growing up in such families—and none has interviewed the upscale. Also, there are no standardized measures to address the various problems of children who witness violence. How do you gauge a child's perception of safety?

Still, what has been discovered is quite unsettling. Domestic violence has the following immediate and long-term detrimental effects on children:

- Boys who witness their father's abuse of their mother are more likely to inflict severe violence on intimates as adults than those who grow up in homes free of abuse.[12]
- In homes where partner abuse occurs, children are 1,500 times more likely to be abused.[13]
- 40–60 percent of men who abuse women also abuse children.[14]
- Fathers who batter mothers are twice as likely to seek sole physical custody of their children than are nonviolent fathers.[15]
- In one study 27 percent of domestic homicide victims were children.[16] When youngsters are killed during a domestic dispute, 90 percent are under age ten; 56 percent are under age two.[17]

Although research into the effects of domestic abuse on children is still in its infancy,[18] we do know that it is a widespread problem. An article in the July-August 1997 issue of *Children's Advocate* relates that "nationwide, it is estimated that between 3.3 million and 10 million children are at risk of witnessing domestic violence each year. In families where there is domestic violence, most children—some estimate as many as 90 percent—see and hear it."[19]

It is a fallacy that an intact family, no matter how dysfunctional, is better for the children than divorce. Whether children witness the abuse or merely sense it, they are hurt by it. We all experience aggressive, passionate, sad, and painful emotions. Parents help their children to accept, tolerate, and appropriately channel these unorganized and often frightening impulses. A child's developing sense of self—his trust in his own goodness and that of others—is fragile. When a home is filled with tension, conflict, fear, and pain, when a mother is constantly "walking on eggshells" even though there is no tangible evidence of domestic violence, the child's growth and emotional well-being can be jeopardized.[20]

Anna Freud, a pioneer in child psychoanalysis, believed that the inner lives of children are extremely complex. This is especially true if damage to their development is "caused and maintained by active, ongoing influences lodged in the environment."[21] When those "ongoing influences" include domestic violence, the impact of "the specific dangers that overwhelm the individual child" and the "aspects and meanings of the event [that] are experienced" can be traumatic.[22]

There are limits to our understanding, given how much we have yet to learn. To date the majority of research on the effects of violence on children has focused on what happens when they are exposed to it on television, in poor neighborhoods, or in their community (such as the mass shooting at Columbine High School in Littleton, Colorado). But since *upscale* families have not been studied before, let us start with what is known about the impact of domestic abuse on children in all socioeconomic classes.

Spousal abuse spans such a wide range of behaviors that it is difficult to discuss its impact on children in general terms. This is compounded by the personalities of each child and their developmental levels. Steven Marans and Anne Adelman of Yale University's Child Study Center explain the developmental issues we must consider:

Rather than viewing violence and its effects as uniform across ages and experiences, it is important to recognize that childhood exposure to violence occurs in the context of shifting modes of adaptation, which reflect the unfolding maturational process and developmental fluctuations in the nature and expression of children's impulses, wishes, and fears. Children's experience of violence is not only determined by the events they witness, but also by their own capacity to mediate both external and internal sources of danger, and to contend with the pressure of conflictual urges and longings that change according to phases of development. These factors are linked to emotional, cognitive, and physical capacities that shape children's responses to internal and external demands, expectations, and impingements.[23]

Still, we do know that living with violence can take a lasting toll on children. Those who have witnessed conjugal abuse often suffer symptoms similar to those who have been abused themselves. According to Edleson, the impact can be evident in the children's behavior and emotions, in their cognitive functioning and attitudes, and in their lives as adults.[24] They exhibit more anxiety, depression, anger, aggression, and self-esteem problems than youngsters who have not witnessed domestic violence.

Such a home environment can also diminish a child's ability to be empathic. According to some researchers, "children from homes where their mothers were being abused have shown less skill in understanding how others feel and examining situations from others' perspectives when compared to children from non-violent households. Peer relationships, autonomy, self-control, and overall competence were also reported significantly lower among boys who had experienced serious physical violence and been exposed to the use of weapons between adults living in their homes."[25] And in 1991 Bonnie Carlson, at the State University of New York in Albany, "found that boys who witnessed domestic abuse were significantly more likely to approve of violence than were girls who had also witnessed it."[26]

In fact, many youngsters suffer the "double whammy" of witnessing abuse *and* being abused. More than two decades of research has found that in 30 to 60 percent of the homes where women are abused, the children are maltreated as well.[27] According to a report from the California State Justice Institute, children of battered women are more likely than others to suffer physical or sexual abuse at the hands of their father or their mother's partner. Some researchers estimate that at least half the men who batter their partners also physically abuse the children. In addition, women who are being battered themselves are more likely to use physical discipline with their children.[28]

However accurate these overall figures are for lower socioeconomic groups (the sample populations for the studies cited were usually drawn from women in shelters), a high incidence of child abuse does not seem common among the upscale. To my knowledge none of the children of any of the up-scale abused wives in my study or in my practice had been abused or neg-lected. Any signs of maltreatment of the children stirred a fierce protectiveness in the mothers, some of whom even left the marriage at that point. Moreover, since the reports of child and wife abuse in the same family were either retrospective or drawn from the mother's point of view (rather than based on data gathered directly from the children), research results may be skewed. However, this does not mean that there has been no serious im-pact on children who have only witnessed abuse and not been beaten them-selves. Research evidence suggests that witnessing domestic violence may be as harmful to children as suffering physical abuse.[29]

A study conducted by H. M. Hughes investigated children ranging in age from three to twelve years who lived in temporary domestic violence shelters. Hughes is among the few researchers who have examined the differences be-tween those who witnessed domestic violence in their family but were not abused and those who witnessed their mother's torment and were abused themselves. He compared these two groups with children from a similar eco-nomic background whose family was nonviolent. Results showed significantly greater distress (behavior problems, anxiety, depressive symptoms) among the abused-witness children than in the comparison group. The nonabused-wit-ness children fell between the two groups.[30] This finding was echoed in similar studies and in retrospective evaluations from adults as well.[31] One investigation went so far as to say that the traumatic effects on children of witnessing do-mestic abuse are distinct and as harmful as the effects of child abuse.[32]

According to the Guidelines for Policy and Practice created from the recom-mendations of the Family Violence Department of the National Council of Ju-venile and Family Court Judges, "a wide range of studies has shown that some children who witness domestic violence suffer considerably [and on average] exhibit higher levels of childhood behavior, social, and emotional problems than children who have not witnessed such violence."[33] In 1985 Deborah Sin-clair looked at the reactions of children of various ages who had been exposed to violence within their homes. From a developmental perspective, it was evi-dent that children had markedly different responses depending on their age and level of development. Children under five years of age often exhibited symptoms such as bed-wetting, failure to thrive, and separation anxiety. Chil-dren between the ages of six and twelve exhibited seductive or manipulative be-havior, eating disturbances, fear of abandonment, and concerns with losing control. Teenagers tended to run away, become pregnant, use drugs or alcohol, or have homicidal or suicidal thoughts.[34]

There are warning signs to look for in children who are growing up with domestic abuse, even in neighborhoods where it "doesn't happen to people like us." Children who have witnessed domestic abuse can exhibit any or all of the following symptoms:

- Feelings of fear, anger, depression, grief, shame, despair, and distrust; anxieties around separation and loss
- Physical reactions such as stomach cramps, headaches, sleeping and eating difficulties, nightmares, and frequent illness
- Slowed developmental capacities, such as poor school performance, difficulty concentrating, low self-esteem, difficulty relating to peers
- Substance abuse
- Behavioral problems such as running away from home, aggressive language and behavior, acting out; various troubled responses to their own fear, anger, and sadness
- Use of violence to resolve conflicts or control a situation[35]
- Difficulty resolving conflicts with siblings and other children
- Hypervigilance (exaggerated, constant fears of impending danger)
- Indiscriminate, quickly formed attachments to unfamiliar adults
- Counterphobic behavior (a child's drive to re-create circumstances that in the past have elicited a violent response in order to experience himself as the cause—and thus as in control—of his own pain and terror)[36]

These children may experience a good deal of confusion regarding parental loyalties, including ambivalence about their fathers. Typically feelings of intense rage and longing exist side by side—a combination most children are not developmentally equipped to handle. This leaves them feeling torn and needing to disavow aspects of their own identity. They may also feel powerless and exhibit defensive responses to this, including identification with the aggressor. In terms of survival, they experience it better to be "big and bad" like Dad than weak and terrified like Mom. They may also feel an exaggerated sense of guilt and responsibility for protecting their mothers and younger siblings. This is related to the syndrome of the *parentified child*, in which the child, old beyond his years, feels that it is not acceptable or safe to feel, be, or behave like a child.[37]

All these behaviors are similar to the various ways in which children manifest anxiety at different ages and even border on symptoms of post-traumatic stress disorder. When we consider the particular trauma that children in violent households experience, this makes sense. Trauma specialist Judith Herman states that trauma occurs when "the victim is rendered helpless by overwhelming force" and when "the ordinary systems of care that give people a sense of control, connection, and meaning" are overwhelmed.[38] Young children depend on their caregivers for a sense of familial security, consistency, and emotional stability. Domestic violence undermines these important qualities. Children from upscale abusive marriages experience much the same sense of danger (although certainly not material worries) that any less affluent child might. The only difference may be that they feel the threat less directly, since the upscale mother is determined to hide the abuse.

In the face of these facts and observations, it remains puzzling that so many battered wives repeatedly claim that they remain in their marriage for the sake of their children's well-being. Their belief that their children do not know about the abuse and thus come away unscathed most likely is erroneous, does their youngsters a grave injustice, and serves to keep the women on the abusive path.

POTENTIAL IMPACT ON
THE CHILDREN AS ADULTS

What is experienced at an early age leaves lasting marks on developing minds and psyches. Children who witness domestic violence between their parents grow up believing that relationships are volatile and that the world is unpredictable and dangerous. Although long-term effects have either been reported only retrospectively or been gleaned from records in the legal and medical systems and from those of social service professionals, we know that these children often act out as teenagers and young adults. One 1995 study that investigated 550 undergraduates found that "witnessing violence as a child was associated with adult reports of depression, trauma-related symptoms and low self-esteem issues among women, trauma-related symptoms alone among men."[39] Such a childhood also can lead to intense ambivalence in adult relationships.

Irene, who adamantly stayed with her husband for the sake of her children, had many difficulties with them as they matured. "When our daughter was in high school," she reported, "she got heavily into drugs. There was a big problem between father and daughter because Carl was so strong-willed and Christine had a hard time living up to his expectations. Then Chris got into drugs and took off; she ran away. I would stay up pacing the floor at night, crying, and my husband just went on with his life. When the mother of one of the boys that she ran away with called and said, 'I think I know where they're at,' I told my husband. And he said, 'Well go and find her if you want. I don't want to bother.' There was abuse all the way around.

"Our older son married at the age of nineteen. Looking back on it, I think that was probably because he wanted to get out of this lifestyle, this home. He wanted to get away from it all."

Many retrospective studies have been conducted examining the heightened potential for boys growing up in violent homes to become batterers themselves (see Chapter 7). However, there is still much research to do on the effect that growing up in such a household may have on a girl once she reaches maturity.

HOW TO HELP THE CHILDREN

Although the impact of witnessing domestic violence on children has not been acknowledged as child abuse, youngsters who live in homes steeped in conjugal abuse grow up in a climate of fear. These youngsters need to express their feelings about their observations in an environment that is safe and supportive—one that assures them that wife beating does in fact happen to "people like us."

What can a woman from any socioeconomic status do once the spousal abuse becomes apparent to the children? There are several ways to intervene:

- Explain the situation in language that children can understand.
- Tell them that the violence is not their fault.
- Give them permission to talk about the violence.
- Help make a safety plan they can follow.
- Find them someone outside the family with whom they can share their feelings.
- Let them know that others have had similar experiences.
- Discuss the situation with domestic violence or protective services staff to find out how else you can help the children.[40]

Ultimately, the best lessons an abused woman can teach her children occur when she regains her grace, dignity, and self-esteem by either leaving her abusive husband or changing the tenor of the marriage so that she and her children are assured of safety.

THE ROAD AHEAD

Interventions can be helpful, but we need to learn more about the long-term aftermath of domestic violence on children. Several organizations and individuals are embarking on projects to create a training protocol for professionals who deal with children exposed to violence. Such a program would help sensitize professionals to the effects that violence at home has on children. Perhaps early intervention (even before age six) will dispel the denial and its consequences and offer the family useful strategies for curbing the violence and protecting the children.

Much has been written on the overlap of domestic abuse and child maltreatment and on consequential intervention methods, but much more research must be done on the emotional, psychological, and behavioral effects on the children growing up in such environments.

In addition, studies are needed to investigate the short- and long-term psychological consequences of domestic violence on children from all socioeconomic classes, with information derived directly from contact with the children. This is fertile ground for future study. I have a great interest in interviewing children from abusive homes (of all classes) to learn about what this environment has been like for them and how it continues to be over time. Of course, finding such groups, especially among the upscale, may once again be like searching for unicorns. Unfortunately, these children are probably as closeted about domestic violence as their mothers have been.

9

Who Can Help?
Therapeutic Interventions

T HE CHINESE CHARACTER THAT CONVEYS THE MEANING "CRISIS"
stands for two words: danger and opportunity. All crises in our lives
may be dangerous opportunities, bridges between our past and our future. So
it is when an abused upscale woman seeks help. Indeed, a pivotal moment in
psychotherapy occurs *before* therapy starts—when the woman in crisis determines that she can no longer cope on her own. All her hopes and fears are
packed into that initial phone call to the helping professional. It cannot be
easy for her to take charge of this moment of danger and opportunity.

Her course of treatment will not be linear. As the woman grows and
changes, she and her therapist may move in and out of the following therapeutic stages.

- The woman recognizes there is a problem, overcomes her reluctance
  to seek help, and contacts a therapist.
- The therapist ascertains whether the woman is in imminent danger
  and discusses a safety plan.
- The therapist uses empathic understanding, acceptance, and mirroring to gain the woman's trust and develop a therapeutic alliance.
- The woman learns the impact of her past, present, and future
  choices; she comes to understand how she has deceived herself and
  begins to reconstruct her narrative.
- The woman refocuses on herself, learns to trust her inner voice and
  perceptions, and reclaims her self.
- The woman mourns the relationship that was (even if she stays in
  the marriage).
- The woman learns to connect with others in a support network.

IMPEDIMENTS TO SEEKING HELP

The stakes, while always high during a crisis, feel that much greater for someone who has shrouded her problem in secrecy. The initial contact with a therapist may be the first time the abused upscale woman has broken her silence and constructed her story in its entirety. It is common for her to experience a mixture of emotions at this time: shame about needing help; self-loathing for being unable to cope with or fix her own problems; fear of being seen as stupid or crazy; and sadness that she must finally grapple with a long-standing problem—she can no longer deny it.

These feelings are intensified when our culture tells her, "This doesn't happen to people like you." Contradicting the myth heightens any guilt or shame the woman brings to her first contact with a therapist. The situation may feel surreal to her; she may find it painful to imagine herself as deviating so extremely from the norm. Even if this is an opportunity for her to change her life and free herself from trauma, breaking the isolation and reaching for help may feel dangerous. Moreover, she may find it unthinkable that she, a woman accustomed to achievement, is failing in her marriage or chose a man who abuses her. All of these issues conspire to make it difficult for an upscale abused woman to seek help or, if she does, to admit the scope of her problem.

Experienced psychologists, clinical social workers, and physicians to whom I have introduced the concept of upscale violence tell me they are shocked at how many female patients reveal some form of spousal abuse once they are specifically asked about it. Unfortunately, most therapists don't routinely ask upper-class women about domestic violence, but I believe that gently opening this line of discussion will give the client permission to address the issue.

THE DECISION TO REACH OUT

What triggers the upscale abused wife's decision to seek help? Her choice suggests that she has begun to grasp that the coping strategies she has used to adjust to her husband's abusive behaviors are maladaptive, unrewarding, and dangerous to her and her children. Perhaps she has begun to realize that her efforts to sleep in the bed she has made are impractical. She has not gained control of the situation, and the violence and threats are escalating. Maybe she has finally confided in a friend or coworker who listens; perhaps she is lucky enough to have spoken with someone who has had similar experiences and offers the validation she needs. In some cases, friends or family have witnessed the abuse and confronted her. One woman watched a television program that affirmed her reality and motivated her to seek help. Whatever the precipitating factor, some external validation shakes the woman's resolve to keep quiet, and she decides to consult a psychotherapist.

This is a vulnerable time. The dangerous opportunity to quit her life as an upscale abusive wife lies before her. She has decided to change her course of action, but she is unsure what this will mean for her life and for the lifestyle to which she and her children have become accustomed. Not all upscale abused women come into therapy with divorce in mind. Some want to discover what they can do to make life better at home; they tell the therapist, "We've been having some marital difficulties I need to fix." Others just want the violence to stop so that life can go back to the way it used to be. But some women already realize that their marriage is no longer viable and are seeking assistance in separating; they are at the point of no return.

"WE'VE BEEN HAVING SOME
MARITAL DIFFICULTIES . . ."

When Rhonda first came to my office, she was unenthusiastic about being there. Her speech was replete with adjectives meant to convey that her problem wasn't "that big a deal." After all, it was a friend who had referred her. I have come to learn, however, that when a client opens a dialogue with the disclaimer that what she is about to say is "unimportant" or "irrelevant," it is usually very significant—or at least contains some powerful clues to what's really going on. The minimizing is defensive: the client is trying to deny the extent of the problem. She still doesn't want to admit that she is a battered wife married to a mean-spirited man.

Petite and attractive, looking younger than her forty years, Rhonda was dressed in a charcoal Calvin Klein suit and carried an exquisite calf attaché case. Specializing in high-end real estate sales in the suburbs where she lived, she regularly closed deals on expensive properties. She showed me a photograph of her husband, Andrew, also forty, who looked boyishly handsome with the slim build of a runner; he was a technology consultant and did well financially. Their combined annual income was at least $250,000; separately, they could each have been living comfortably. In fact, Rhonda earned more than her mate.

Yet this woman with a thriving career, and the self-confidence to match it, seemed shaken and uncomfortable in my office. She fidgeted on my otherwise cushy, overstuffed couch, crossing and uncrossing her legs as if she were perched in a straight-backed chair. Her eyes darted around the room, and her hands fluttered as she groped for tissues, smoothed her hair, or straightened her skirt.

Like many patients in the beginning phases of therapy, Rhonda often contradicted or undid her own statements. "I feel so ashamed," she told me. "This is my problem, but I can't believe it's my problem." Her sentences often ended with a questioning inflection, indicative of the uncertainty that flooded her.

In a quivering voice, Rhonda told me that her concerns were "simple"— she was "having some marital difficulties." A friend who was a clinical social worker had referred her to me. This was the only person she had confided in so far. However, I knew from his initial call that the friend was familiar with my work, making his referral quite pointed. He had called me after his conversation with Rhonda and told me he thought I was "the best therapist for her"—a comment that told me that he believed there was violence in her home. Rhonda knew I had been tipped off about her situation, and although she did her best to present the details, she minimized the facts.

"I am having a little trouble in my marriage," she began. "My husband can be difficult. He sometimes loses his temper." She spoke quickly, though her revelations came slowly, and like so many other battered upscale women, she believed that the task of "fixing" the marriage was hers alone.[1] "We've been married for seven years and have two kids, a girl, two, and a boy, six. Life is pretty good overall. Maybe it's silly for me to be here." She turned her head to the side and averted her eyes from mine.

"There's nothing silly about it," I assured her. "If you're here, you must have concerns about what's happening at home. That's an understandable reason to seek help." I continued to listen intently, wondering how and whether she would broach the issue of abuse. I knew I would raise it myself if she did not—but she eventually did.

"For the most part Andrew and I have gotten along fine over the years, but it's just that sometimes his temper gets going."

I gently probed: "Tell me about his temper."

"Well, it's gotten worse over the years. He hit me once, but he never did it again."

"Could you describe that one incident?" I asked. I could sense her discomfort growing as she started to tell me the story.

"My daughter had banged her head by accident," she said, dabbing at her eyes. "And this upset my husband a lot. I guess it was hard for him to see his little girl have a huge lump on her forehead." Rhonda was subtly rationalizing her husband's anger, justifying by explaining.

"What's so unusual about that? Kids bang their heads all the time."

"It was an accident. It could have happened to anyone," she agreed, sounding now as if she were protesting her innocence to an imaginary jury. "He came home from work and got very upset about the accident. He thought I should have been more careful. And I guess I really should have been watching more closely. Michelle was trying to reach for her teddy bear, which I had put aside, as I was about to serve her breakfast. I went to the stove to get the oatmeal, and she got herself out of her seat and onto the floor looking for her toy. As she stood up, she hit her head pretty hard on the underside of the table. She cried, but I knew nothing horrible had happened. I put a cold compress on it, but the point of impact had swelled to the size of a robin's egg and looked like it had been much worse. My husband came home that evening and was livid when he saw the black and blue bump on Michelle's forehead."

I found it interesting that Rhonda rarely referred to Andrew by name but rather by his role—"my husband." This is common among battered upscale wives, perhaps because they want to remind themselves of their commitment to the marriage or because it is a way for them to feel a connection to a partner who is emotionally remote.

"And that's when he hit you?" I asked.

"Yes. He got furious and screamed, 'What kind of horrible mother are you?' He slapped me hard on the face and shoved me against the wall and then punched me. He didn't apologize later, but he hasn't ever done it again. And you know, Dr. Weitzman, I really don't believe this is happening—this doesn't happen here in Highland Park. How did I get here?"

I looked at her warmly and felt a great compassion welling inside of me. We both sensed that the incident Rhonda described was not her fault, and that she wanted to make it disappear so that she wouldn't have to deal with it. Yet we both knew that we were sitting together because the problem was bigger than just this one episode. "How you got here was little by little," I explained. "It happens gradually. Rarely does abuse start with a big bang—there are many small steps along the way. Maybe you've relied on feelings of hope to look away." I told her firmly that I understood her disbelief, but that actually such incidents happened in Highland Park and communities like it all the time. "You're not the first professional woman I've seen from the North Shore with such experiences. Perhaps part of your discomfort in sharing it comes from your feeling it doesn't happen to people like you. But years of experience and hundreds of patients have taught me otherwise."

Rhonda reacted to my remark with silence. She was unsure she could trust my data. I knew I would need to convey it again, and probably more than once—cultural myths are strongly rooted. But we moved on to discuss the marriage.

I was to learn in that first session that physical violence was the least of Rhonda's troubles. Andrew had gradually created such an aura of fear in her that she anticipated his responses to her every action and word. This other-wise powerful woman had been reduced to catering to her husband's vacil-lating moods and bullying behaviors. And yet *she* was the one feeling embarrassed, and *she* was the one seeking help. Like other women in her po-sition, she believed that the problem, as well as its solution, lay within her.

"Well," I said after a brief pause, "let's see if we can sort out the difficulties in your marriage and decide on the type of work that would be helpful." I chose my words carefully, positioning the problem squarely on the marriage, where it belonged (if not on Andrew), not solely on Rhonda's small shoulders. However, at that point I chose to hold off telling her about the escalating nature of spousal abuse, for I sensed that she was not yet willing or able to integrate this information. Nonetheless, I asked, "Do you believe that you or the children are in imminent danger at this time?" She assured me they were not.

I wanted to convey to Rhonda that it was safe to talk to me about what was happening. I was not judging her or her husband, and we could deal with the problem together. However, I did not align with her notion that she had come in to deal with a trivial issue, or that this was merely her problem to resolve. I also didn't offer false comfort that a few marital sessions would set every-thing right. From my response, I conveyed that I was concerned for her well-being—there was trouble. But together, I assured her, we would explore the nature and extent of it. Rhonda seemed relieved, and her face relaxed visibly. We then began the task of unpacking the story of her marriage.

During our initial sessions Rhonda was not yet ready to face the destructive impact that her husband's behaviors were having on her and the marriage. She was still trying to repair the relationship. Just beyond denial, she realized there was a serious problem and was willing to break her silence to begin talking about it. Nonetheless, the task of treatment was to help her assess exactly what was going on, to recognize what it means to live with an abusive partner, and to examine her role so she could make decisions about her next steps.

"JUST STOP THE VIOLENCE . . ."

When Melody, age twenty-nine, first sought help, she felt deadened when she thought about her four-year-old marriage. She said she had "checked out of it" but still believed that if the physical abuse could stop, perhaps life would "get back to normal." She wanted to bring the relationship back onto an emotionally even keel so that she could see what was left. Melody's assessment of the situation was more realistic than Rhonda's, whose denial was deeper, and who blamed herself. The battered wife who wants the violence to stop is clear that her husband is behaving badly, and that this must change.

Melody was a psychotherapist. She was pixie-like, warm, and engaging, with a quick sense of humor. "You know, I'm here for the same old problem you must hear a lot—my husband doesn't understand me!" she said with a big grin. She went on in a more serious vein, "Actually, I think I want to stay married, but it is getting rougher." Her face went flat, and she looked around the room, avoiding eye contact with me. Although Melody was explaining how difficult her marriage was in a general sense, her use of "rougher" also suggested the escalating physical roughness with which she was contending. She told me that her husband assaulted her whenever he had a bad day or when his moods shifted. She then tried to explain it.

Steve was a handsome, muscular, thirty-five-year-old man, intense and introspective, a successful architect who did not let much stand in his way. The episodic depression he had suffered for many years was one of the reasons the couple had put off having children. He had gone to many psychologists and psychiatrists and tried numerous medications, but nothing worked consistently. Melody often felt great pity and compassion for her husband, who really seemed to want to get well. This was the explanation that had sustained her. She also thought she could talk him into settling down when he "lost it," but her efforts weren't working.

Melody came to me after having attended a workshop I had given on fatal attractions and abusive relationships. With all of her professional training, she believed she "should have known better." But despite her feelings of shame, she knew she could no longer bear her husband's volatile behavior. Her attendance at my lecture confirmed her worst fears—the distress in her marriage was a result of her husband's behavior. So she took the next step and sought help.

My approach was to understand her experience and educate her about the damaging aspects of her marriage to Steve. I knew she was scared and ambivalent—she sat as far away from me as she could and interspersed her sweet jocularity with the narrative of her husband's tyranny. I was also aware that I was her only outlet; she had told no one else about Steve's behaviors. Ironically, it was partly because she was a psychotherapist that she kept silent—she felt too ashamed to admit that even as a therapist she could be trapped in an abusive marriage and not even recognize the extent of the problem.

First we assessed the extent of the danger. For the moment she seemed safe. Steve was "always able to stop himself before he got too violent," she said. Still,

I let her know I was worried. "We know clinically that abuse only worsens," I told her. "From what you're telling me, I am concerned for your safety. If he is so abusive with you, have you ever considered leaving him?"

She started to sob. "How can I leave him when I know he's a sick man? How can I abandon him like that? I'm a therapist, for God's sake!" Her rationalization was also the key to her prison. In those few sentences she revealed what was keeping her on the path. She felt she would be a bad person if she abandoned her husband. Her identity as a clinician, a person able to help others, was at stake. Because she had told no one about what was happening, the daily feedback she got from her friends and family about what a fine man and talented architect Steve was reinforced her internal conflict. Indeed, to all appearances things were going wonderfully. His last year had been particularly successful. Together he and Melody, who was also doing well professionally, were earning quadruple what they had earlier. They were both well respected in their professional and residential communities. She liked their lifestyle and the personas they conveyed to others.

"Besides, he's not a batterer," she added. "We're successful, we have graduate degrees, and we both come from good families!"

"And you think successful people with advanced degrees are never abusive?" I asked. After inquiring whether I could show her a checklist, I pulled from my files the list of traits of an abusive mate (see Appendix C). She studied the items quietly, looking as if she were reading a letter written to her. After a few moments she looked up, eyes brimming with tears, and said, "So what am I going to do?"

I replied, "The first thing we're going to do is talk about what it feels like at home, and if this marriage is where you want to be."

She started to cry again. "He *is* abusive, and his moods are amazing. One day he got angry as we were coming in from the car carrying groceries. He accidentally tripped on a door jamb, which he had never repaired, and turned on me and shoved me hard—as if I had placed the door jamb in his way. When he sits at his computer, I try to read his mood before I enter the room. Sometimes he will get so angry he calls me every name in the book for no apparent reason. I have even wondered if he has Tourette's Syndrome [an illness in which an individual has an uncontrollable impulse that sometimes comes out in explosive obscenities]. Maybe I keep diagnosing him to avoid admitting that he's cruel."

I was moved by Melody's last remark, which struck me as quite insightful for a first session. She had come to the stark realization of how bad her situation was. She was crying for herself, for Steve, and for the gloomy state of her marriage.

"I know how hard this must be for you to think about," I told her. "And yet it seems you have known all of this prior to coming here. It must have been hard to keep this bottled up."

She looked at me and said, "Yes. But what a relief even to have said that."

We talked about her options; leaving Steve was not the only one. But in order for change to occur in their marriage, he would have to finally acknowledge the violence he was perpetrating (which he had never mentioned to his many therapists), and he would have to get help for it. That would include talking about his rageful behaviors toward his wife, not just managing his medication.

When she decided to come to see me, Melody knew she wanted the violence to stop, but she didn't know what that would involve. In our first meeting I offered support nonjudgmentally as well as a sense that I understood the marital abuse and the range of emotions that occur in the victim. I even offered, "Perhaps the reason you have effectively 'checked out' of the marriage is not just because you resent the pain that Steve has caused. Perhaps it's your way of keeping yourself safe for now."

We seemed to have made a connection, and we made an appointment for our next session. Months later Melody told me that she didn't want to come back after the first session and even felt frightened of me. I had, after all, named something she didn't want to name, even though it was all there before her.[2] But she also sensed that together we might finally get some work accomplished. She had been to many therapists before who were smart and kind but ineffective. She liked that I was able to be so present with her, or as she phrased it, "to be right there." She returned and eventually joined my women's group.

"IT'S OVER!"

Jacqueline came to treatment shortly after the physical violence had begun in her marriage but following years of emotional strife with her husband. She was a statuesque thirty-seven-year-old painter with flowing blond hair, born and raised in France. She had met Brian, now a thirty-nine-year-old sculptor, in art school. Married for six years and childless, they bonded through their work, which often dictated how they spent their time and energies and shaped their orientation to the world. They had both come from families of means, both had advanced degrees, and together they earned $100,000 a year from their various day jobs, artistic production, and teaching.

Jacqueline came in for her first session after Brian had "lost it" worse than ever before. During the previous six months Brian had hit a creative wall. People didn't like his sullen manner, so he was rarely asked to return for teaching assignments. In contrast, Jacqueline's career was thriving; she had been asked to show her paintings at a well-respected gallery and was asked to teach regularly. They had been arguing incessantly about money and spending time together. What began for Brian as social drinking soon evolved into a nightly bender. He would get drunker each time. Occasionally he shoved Jacqueline or threw her on the bed, but she wrote that off to his artistic temperament and the frustration of a creative block or to his possible jealousy about her success. Intelligent and well read, Jacqueline was familiar with psychology and eager to examine why the marriage was failing.

The incident that brought her to treatment was a destructive fight. "I came home from teaching, and Brian asked me when I would finish making supper," she explained with a Parisian lilt. "He had already put on some potatoes to boil, which I had peeled in advance. But he was slurring his words. He was moody and more edgy than usual. I told him I needed to warm myself up first because I just came in from a long walk home in the cold. He exploded at me. 'That's just great,' he said. 'Just look out for yourself!' With that he threw the wineglass he was holding against one of my paintings—one that had been part of a series I'd been working on for many years."

The glass shattered and the red wine covered Jacqueline's treasured work. But Brian didn't stop there. With a shard of the glass, he slashed another of her major paintings—an enormous wall-size project she had devoted years to. He angrily ripped the canvas from its frame and destroyed it. Jacqueline stood there in disbelief. Brian then ran into the kitchen and reached for the pot of boiling potatoes. He was about to heave it at her when Jacqueline shouted, "I am leaving you. I can't take this anymore!"

She grabbed her purse and ran out the door. She came to see me after staying with friends for a week. Jacqueline had no doubt she wanted out of her marriage. But even so, she still had to experience the mourning that accompanies the death of a relationship.

HOW THE STORY UNFOLDS

No matter what the woman's understanding about her situation is when she starts therapy, it is important to listen carefully to how she constructs her story. When she seeks help, she is often mired in self-blame coupled with a driving need to control the situation and make it right again. Her first thoughts are: "This can't be happening to me because it doesn't happen to people like me." Such disbelief shapes the way she constructs the story she tells the therapist.

Rhonda demonstrated her disbelief with expressions that minimized her situation. She was eager to fix whatever she had done to cause the marital "difficulties." Her initial denial was an attempt to control what was fast spinning out of control—her life with her husband and her view of herself. This cycle of thinking was exactly what prevented Rhonda from viewing her situation objectively and seeking help earlier. She constructed her story to include excuses, but it lacked a realistic assessment of what was wrong and what could be done. Her husband had been battered as a child and watched his father beat his mother—but Rhonda, rather than viewing his history as a warning sign that Andrew might become abusive, understood it as an explanation for his anger and behavior.

Melody had to surrender to the reality that she could not fix her situation by herself. When a woman is convinced that she can stop the violence in her marriage, her stubborn determination feeds her sense of failure each time she sees that she can't regulate her husband's demands and abuses. In a perverse type of review, she may then ask herself how she could have been so stupid as to overlook the early warnings. This further diminishes her self-esteem.

The woman who knows she will leave is facing a different type of shame. Jacqueline walked away from her marriage after all of her efforts failed. Women in her situation mourn the dream of what their marriage could have been. They must also deal with the possibility that others will turn away from them and disbelieve them or offer no support. Jacqueline's decision to leave took a great deal of courage.

THE KEY QUESTION: "WHY NOW?"

It is the therapist's job to assess and intervene. The key question that must be posed during any intake is: "Why are you coming to see me now instead of last month or six months from now?" The woman's answer to this question holds the vortex of her energies, fears, and crushed hopes and helps get at the crux of the situation, the "what's wrong" that made her life feel awful and drove her to seek help. Within the answer the therapist can see the woman's strengths and potential as well as her understanding of the problem. The three women described in this chapter had different "why now" responses, each of which revealed different investments of their energy and different goals for treatment and for their future. Only when the woman can see what's wrong will she sense what could be right. The skilled therapist hooks onto that tiny glimmer of the positive and uses it in the healing process.

Usually the answer to the question involves a turning point. Telling this pivotal story is not only cathartic but also gives the woman a new way to perceive life (past, present, and future) with her abusive spouse. Asking "why now?" helps her focus and order her story in a way that makes sense.

Rhonda's response was no exception. "Your marriage has been difficult for some time. Why did you decide to come in *now?*" I asked. My question evoked the description of a recent incident that had bothered Rhonda, although she described it as "not too big a deal." Although she insisted that she was to blame and that the incident was minor, her narrative nevertheless suggested the desperate life she had been compelled to live in order to survive in her marriage. I sensed in her story her wish to change her situation, though this wish was buried under her protestations that there was nothing terribly wrong.

"It was actually over something small," Rhonda replied to my question, once more downgrading her story's import. "Andrew was out with a client when he called to check in. Our little boy had just scraped himself while roller-skating, and I knew my husband would have a fit. I thought about waiting until he got home for him to see what happened. On the other hand, if I broke the news to him while he was with someone else, he would be less likely to fly off the handle, and time would have passed before he came home. I thought it would give him a chance to cool down. So when he called, I decided to tell him."

"Sounds like you carefully weighed how to talk to him. What did you say?"

"I told him Jimmy had knocked into another child while skating and had cut his lip. It was a little swollen, but everything would be all right. He just said, 'Yeah, okay. See you later.' I spent the next four hours worrying about what would happen once he got home."

"What were you worrying about? That he would hit you again?"

Tears welled up. "Yes, that he might hit me. But I was more afraid he would scream about what a terrible mother I was that I could let such horrible things happen to our son."

"That must have been an awful few hours. What happened next?"

"That's the amazing part. He came home and asked me, 'Why did you feel you had to tell me about Jimmy while I was in the car with a client?' I said, 'I didn't want you to be too upset.' He was shocked that I would have worried about that at all. Can you imagine? After the way he responded to Michelle's bump, now he turns around and makes me feel like an obsessive worrier! At that moment I felt sick to my stomach, like I was living with way too much fear and I couldn't take it anymore. I decided to get some help so I could learn to communicate with my husband better. That's when I asked my friend for a referral."

My mind quickly flashed on the many women I'd seen who had constructed the story of their unreasonable spouses in much the same way. Rhonda had convinced herself that she had a problem in how she talked to her husband. It never occurred to her to ask why a person who can complete six-figure business deals with aplomb would suddenly have to watch her every word to the person who loves her. However, I was glad to hear that she felt sick to her stomach—a sign that her self-deception was getting to her viscerally. It was a symptom she was aware enough to heed and get help about.

I accepted that at this point Rhonda could view the problem as one of poor marital communication, at most. That she chose to come see me represented a turning point—a coalescing of her inner fear that her husband was abusive. The part of her that was capable of such recognition was the part to which I needed to connect. "Tell me your understanding of how 'communication' with Andrew has gotten this way," I suggested. "Was it always like this?" I knew that her story would teach me more about how Rhonda made meaning of what happened between them. In understanding her lived experience within her marriage, I would be able to empathically enter her internal world. She would feel less alone as together we probed what was occurring and how she could take better care of herself within or without the relationship.

EMPATHY: THE KEY FOR THERAPY

My biggest challenge as a clinician is to empower my client by helping her see that her (and not just her husband's) actions and choices have determined her fate while at the same time refraining from blaming her. On the one hand, it is fortifying for the woman to recognize the extent to which her own choices have kept her on the path—she is not necessarily a victim, and if she identifies how her decisions have contributed to her staying, she can also see ways to escape the abuse. On the other hand, she is demoralized and despairing when she first comes to me, and the last thing she needs to hear from her therapist is, "Boy, did you make some lousy choices!"

This dilemma is a clinical challenge and a clinical task for the therapist, who must be able to step into the shoes of the woman to see why she made the choices she did. Empathy is the best way to resolve this quandary. It is crucial to understand that many successful women would have made the same decisions under the same circumstances. When the woman feels that the therapist is understanding, not judgmental, she feels accepted, despite the contrary messages her husband, family, and society are sending.

For instance, it is important to keep in mind that although the questions she keeps asking herself may seem illogical, they in fact serve to deflect her attention from the difficult issue of her husband's culpability. Typically her self-talk includes statement such as:

- "Why doesn't he love me enough?"
- "Would he be different with someone else?"
- "It hurts so much to think he could replace me and not feel a loss."
- "He keeps telling me things would be okay if I were less demanding."

The clinician can address this self-talk by gently challenging these statements in a way that identifies the couple's choices. For instance, the therapist might respond to the first question by saying, "Even if he doesn't love you, he still has other ways of expressing his lack of affection than with violence, anger, and humiliation. And if you are right, why would you choose to be with a man who doesn't love you?"

Other self-talk revolves around catastrophic fears about the future:

- "I don't want to be back out there dating again!"
- "What will I tell my family and friends? What will people think?"
- "How will the children and I survive?"
- "Maybe being with him is better than being alone."

Such thoughts gnaw at the woman obsessively. This is one of the reasons there are so many aborted breakups for the abused woman and her partner. What's more, despite their abusive behavior, these men can be appealing in other ways; they are often calm, soft-spoken, and polished in public. Because of her fears and her husband's charms, the woman may express a great deal of ambivalence, so the therapist should tread lightly. Openness is better than force. As much as possible the woman must be helped to begin exercising the muscle of her own free will while also being encouraged to continue with the therapeutic task before her.

At the end of my first session with Rhonda she said, "I guess maybe I should make another appointment? Can I call you if I want to do that?" Sensing her hesitation, I suggested, "Why don't you set up your next appointment now? You can always call to cancel if you don't feel like coming in later." I believe that it's easier to cancel an appointment than to admit needing help. If Rhonda really wanted to opt out, she need leave only a thirty-second message on my voice mail. Otherwise, she would have to start over again. Calling me to set up an appointment could once more evoke shame at her inability to solve her problems. My words removed the chance of a possible though subtle act of revictimization.

As it turned out, Rhonda kept her second appointment. I discovered that in the intervening days she had already started to integrate our initial discussion. She felt proud of herself for returning; it was a turning point for her. "I feel relieved to talk to someone who is direct and honest," she told me. "I can trust you. And it feels really good to focus on myself for a change."

The therapist's initial task is to form an alliance with the client. This often begins during the first session; people in crisis are eager to perceive their therapist as benevolent. The early interventions should encompass empathic interpretations such as: "All your vigilance in anticipating what your husband might do must take a lot of energy," or, "You have been trying to save the marriage, but it's not safe for you," or, "It must be hard to love a man who beats you."

In such instances the clinician becomes a selfobject for the woman, mirroring the emotional experiences she has denied. The therapist is a safe audience as well as a mentor, providing guidance away from ineffective self-justifications and a life of abuse. The woman not only feels supported but is able to begin believing in herself again; she is fortified, and her paradoxical need to use her husband to bolster her self-esteem decreases. She turns away from focusing solely on him for solace. Ultimately the clinician's empathy, accompanied by the woman's new awareness regarding her situation, leads to true healing.

As the woman's self-confidence grows within the comforting security of the therapeutic relationship and she sees her marriage more clearly, she becomes more ready to confront her own participation in keeping on the path.[3]

BURSTING THE BUBBLE OF SELF-DECEPTION

It has been said that self-deception is the sinking feeling in the pit of one's stomach that cannot be denied. Perhaps the most important turning point for the woman as she leaves the path of abuse comes when she can no longer deny to herself what is real. But denial is a powerful source. Jean-Paul Sartre cites a scene in Simone de Beauvoir's novel *She Came to Stay* that offers an insightful analysis of denial:[4]

> A young woman with green and blue feathers in her hair was looking uncertainly at a man's huge hand that had just pounced on hers. . . . She had decided to leave her bare arm on the table and it lay there, forgotten, ignored; the man's hand was stroking a piece of flesh that no longer belonged to anyone.[5]

Sartre analyzes how the woman in this scene practices self-deception in order to maintain the calm of the "romantic" moment.[6] When the man touches her hand—an act that telegraphs his desire—the woman faces a choice. Consistent with her wish to postpone (or maybe never respond to) his sexual advance, she can act in good faith and withdraw her hand. But this would threaten to ruin the social grace of the situation, or as Sartre puts it, to "break the troubled and unstable harmony that makes for the charm of the hour."[7] Her other option is to allow her hand to remain, which indeed she does. In fact, to deal with the conflict she chooses to leave her hand but *ignore it,* to detach it from her consciousness and deaden it like a piece of meat. Sartre refers to this behavior as acting "in bad faith." With this choice, the woman vacates her self from her body. But it's a false transcendence, a self-deception about what is occurring between her and her escort.

The woman has become complicit in her own subjugation. She does not want the man's hand to rest on hers, because she knows that this small gesture portends future physical contact, about which she is ambivalent. Yet she wants to be nice and maintain the congeniality of the moment. She is aware of her own discomfort, but she justifies her inaction by reassuring herself that the man's touch is not carnal but rather an intellectual appreciation of her beauty. By rationalizing her predicament, she avoids breaking the mood or offending the gentleman. Her choice serves her ambivalence toward the gentleman and buys her time before having to make the ultimate sexual decision.[8] This choice, however, comes at great cost: the woman has denied her own truth in exchange for the promise of kindness and favor.

Although there is no violence in this hand-holding scenario, the woman's predicament bears a resemblance to that of a woman entering the path of the upscale abused wife. In the literature on domestic violence, it is uniformly posited that once a wife abides any physical or emotional abuse, she tacitly agrees to the violence to come.[9] From a learning theorist's perspective, we could say that, since we teach people how to treat us, the woman tolerating her husband's first violent episode teaches him an important lesson about how he can behave toward her. Initially going along with her suitor's approach despite her ambivalence or even disinterest, and then averting her eyes from early warning signs and explaining away the first assaults, the woman takes up the dance of subjugation to her future husband's needs.

The fact that many of the women I studied made such excuses suggests that they were aware of something being amiss. Denying the early warning signs in exchange for connection, glamour, a seemingly enchanted lifestyle, and love, they used self-talk and justification to still an inner voice they preferred not to heed. Women who choose to continue on the path eventually deaden that part of themselves (as Melody did) to keep the relationship intact, and it would have to remain deadened if they were to stay in their marriage. By helping the woman have empathy for herself and her choices, the therapist points out to the client that although she does not cause the violence, she is responsible for what she chooses to tolerate. She has been her own jailer, and ultimately she can release herself.

Once this bubble of self-deception is burst and the mask that shielded her and others from what she wished to ignore is lifted, it is difficult for the woman to return to her life as it was. It has been said that "the discovery of a deceiving principle, a lying activity within us, can furnish an absolutely new view of all conscious life."[10] This reawakened awareness changes the upscale abused woman's life forever. Suddenly new choices stand before her. This can be a frightening and sad phase in therapy, a moment when the woman is grappling with a kaleidoscope of loss and potential future gain. Some women experience this period as the dark night of the soul. It can be sickening to face the truths one has chosen to ignore in hopes of maintaining the status quo. Even if the woman wishes to stay married, she will never perceive her life in the same way again.

That is why it is imperative that the discussions about the client's choices and even her self-deception do not make her feel worse about herself. The woman must understand her role without feeling blamed. She should feel able to participate in the discussion from a position of strength; only then can the therapy illustrate the power she has over her life. As an empathic guide, the therapist must be respectful of the woman's timing and decisions and try to step into her experience as fully as possible so that she feels that her helper is allied with her. Strengthened and supported by that alliance, she can slowly begin to re-create her life narrative.

It is touching to watch the progression from the first ray of awareness to the full daylight of consciousness. *Madrugada* is the Portuguese word for the moment just at the verge of dawn, when the sky is the darkest. That's what I often experience when working with an upscale abused woman. I know the realization is coming, and the moments before are as important as the breaking of first light.

There can be mourning with full awareness, but also eventually a sense of calm. Empowered by the support of others, the woman marshals her own forces. She knows she is continuing with her life but in a new direction. She rediscovers hope. Whether or not love is in her future, at some point she realizes that any pain-free life she creates for herself now is far better than the one she had chosen to live, riddled with heartache and self-deception.

NEW NARRATIVES AND RESTORYING

Emmanuel Kant believed that pure observation does not exist; our minds constantly contribute to perceptions, shaping and determining what we see.[11] History is not absolute, but relative.[12] We supply our own meanings to events in our lives because that's how we remember and make sense of them.[13] That is, we never experience or remember in some kind of pure, unmediated way. Rather, we shape and reshape our experiences of past and present through narrative—the story we tell ourselves and others.

Researchers have explored personal narratives to understand how people make meaning in their lives, and how they arrive at their decisions and rationales for behavior and action.[14] According to narrative/constructionist theory, reality is a compilation open to interpretation and reinterpretation.[15] Therefore, what a person verbalizes and feels is relative to the context within which he or she places the experience. And since a narrative can be told only from its endpoint—today, now—and the endpoint is always changing, our construction of our story is constantly evolving.

We also have cultural narratives, which derive their meanings from society. Meanings can exist only within a larger sociological environment, with its own norms, mores, and customs. For the upscale battered woman who lives in a community that denies the existence of such abuse, cultural pressure would initially influence her ability to grasp the problem, make meaning of it, deal with the ambiguities of the situation, and take action. The same husband who batters his upscale wife may be warm and loving in public. The woman might be relatively satisfied with her life—until her husband hits her again. In such a situation, she stretches her narrative to contain these inconsistencies.

The upscale abused woman feels internal, peer-group, and societal pressure to maintain an external image substantially at odds with how she feels inside. Balancing life in the public sphere with the brutal reality of her private life exacts quite a toll.[16] The woman's life narrative is clearly incohesive. And she may feel unable to construct her narrative any differently if there are no structures in the culture supporting the fact that domestic violence happens "to people like us." Most people don't feel sympathy for a woman with financial resources. Her major source of emotional support, until she seeks out a therapist, may have been her partner. The couple has probably constructed a culture with shared meaning that includes violence and the taboo about discussing it outside the home.

Although research suggests that battered women have a greater tolerance for cognitive inconsistencies than other women,[17] that tolerance reaches a breaking point when trusted voices sensitively but firmly point out that she doesn't deserve the abuse she is living with. When they do, the dissonance grows louder, the woman's narrative feels glaringly incohesive, and in hopes of soothing the self, she may reach out for help.

The steadying voice of the therapist confirms and concretizes all the initial concerns and early warning signs the woman had swept away to little avail. With the darkness illuminated, enlightenment takes on a life of its own. The woman's truth multiplies on itself, and she is no longer able to justify the abuse or carry her partner's narcissistic baggage. And once she recognizes that her husband's mistreatment of her is abnormal, even as she learns that she is not the only woman in her social class to whom this happens, she begins to feel the love for herself that allows for self-nurturing. In solidifying her instinctive need for survival, her narrative alters to include the knowledge that the abusive aspects of her marriage were not her fault. She becomes able to experience herself with compassion, as a child whom she must protect from painful attacks. Her inner strength grows with the support of her therapist and others who remind her that she deserves to be loved, not battered emotionally or physically.

Her story of the marriage begins to take new shape. This is an empowering reconstruction, a narrative that fosters her sense of self, her strength, and ultimately her well-being. The therapist's dialogue, based on empathic understanding, helps the battered woman create this new story. As she explores alternative narratives in treatment, new emotions come forth, such as grief, rage, fear, courage, and relief. She has made choices, and her choices can set her free. This sense of volition is key in the healing process.

MOURNING THE RELATIONSHIP THAT WAS

However, the woman does not move easily into the light of awareness. After the initial shock of realization about her choices and self-deceptions, she may experience a deep sense of loss. All too often clinicians overlook this mourning phase. The woman grieves the absence of her husband because, abuse notwithstanding, this had been a primary, significant relationship, one that had lighter moments and happier times.[18] Clearly she doesn't mourn the loss of abuse. Rather, she misses the love, the dream, and the hopes she had harbored for the marriage.

Some women confuse these feelings with reasons to stay. They erroneously believe that if they can only change their husbands or themselves enough, it would help them to avoid the painful feelings of loss and the impending emptiness they catastrophically predict will overwhelm them if they leave. The clinician can help the patient examine her feelings and whether her fears would be substantiated. For example, the fear of being alone is always worse than the reality of it. The therapist can also help the client to imagine her worst fears and to weigh them against the reality of living with an abusive husband.

Adjusting to the end of the relationship is akin to the stages that Elizabeth Kubler-Ross identified in people dealing with death.[19] There is a period of denial. For the abused woman, however, the shock is when she recognizes that she must come to terms with the reality she is beginning to see more clearly. There may be depression. The woman may even try bargaining with herself: "If I could do X, maybe he will change." She conceives imaginary plans—a form of secret strategizing—such as, "I won't demand anything of him, and I'll give him whatever he wants as I get ready to leave." Sometimes the woman repeats herself, obsessively reviewing choices she made and the what-ifs that remain a mystery. It is critical that the therapist not grow impatient with the process. Just as water seeps down to the roots of a tree, it often takes time for the grim realization to sink in. Kind yet firm words are needed.

In one of our sessions Rhonda told me she felt that a part of her had died. Sad as it is, such despair is normal. A part of Rhonda had gone into hiding; the environment needed to be safe before it would come out again. And that is what makes the mourning process helpful—the woman focuses on herself once more. She asks herself, "What do I feel about this? What do I want? Should I tolerate what has been happening?" These questions improve her ability to rely on her thoughts and feelings. They help her to find once more the self that is so desperately in need of nurturing.

WHOSE PROBLEM IS THIS ANYWAY?

The battered woman has blamed herself for the abuse in her marriage. Buying into her husband's script that she is a defective wife or seeking ways in which to empower herself, she lapses into spasms of self-blame. One of the turning points in my work with Rhonda occurred when we discussed how the problem in her marriage was not *her fault*. I used a scene to illustrate my point: "If a man runs into a German shepherd that bites him, does that mean he has a problem with dogs?" This scenario helped Rhonda rename the problem. Andrew was the one with the difficulties, not her. He was the one who couldn't control his temper and lashed out physically. Her "communication" with him was not at issue.

In addition to empathy, reality testing, and education about the nature of upscale violence, the therapy must provide the woman with help in reconstructing her narrative and the meaning she makes of the abuse. In this restructuring, the woman must incorporate concepts that remove the onus from herself. Up to this point her partner was the only person constructing her story with her. Together, and in secrecy, the couple developed a joint meaning system that allowed the abuse to exist in the marriage. Now the therapist influences the patient to reconstruct her story, by virtue of the questions asked and the responses given. Whereas telling a woman she hasn't been abused shuts her down, explaining that what she has called "a communication problem" is abuse opens her up to a whole new view of her life—one that introduces her to opportunities for making new choices as she more clearly grasps the reality she has been living with.

However, while steering the woman away from self-blame, the therapist must also avoid the trap of making her husband out to be the bad guy. This tactic can backfire. The therapist runs the risk of psychologically carrying the client's hurt and anger, and in so doing he or she may end up watching her blissfully return to her abusive husband for another round. It is not just a matter of who is wrong, although domestic abuse is always wrong. It is best to put the problem in the form of choice, so that the woman feels her own power again. Instead of saying how terrible it is to be married to such a man, I often phrase my comments in the following ways:

- "I am sure there have been good times between you, but that's not what I'm hearing about. You sound fearful and unhappy. Do you feel you deserve that?"
- "Do you think you can bear this type of treatment for the rest of your life?"
- "Your husband is not behaving the way a man in love with and committed to his wife behaves. Is that acceptable to you?"

The husband's destructive actions are highlighted in response to the woman's need to cling to the parts of him that swept her off her feet. However, these comments are phrased so that the focus is not on the man's bad behaviors but rather on the woman's responses and the choices she makes based on the reality of the situation.[20]

Slowly, working together with me, Rhonda recognized that she was expending a tremendous amount of energy in anticipating his needs all the time, and that she didn't like it. She saw that it was up to Andrew to make some changes if the marriage was to continue. She started speaking up and kept her boundaries when he became edgy. She insisted so firmly that he get help that he began attending a men's therapy group at their church.

While hopeful, this approach can be risky. Short-term intervention programs (six to twelve weeks) can curb violence in the short run, but research has shown that they may not be effective in the long run. Some men (like Robert) became more sophisticated in their emotional abuse and bullying techniques as a result of participation in treatment.[21] But other men can seem to get better, motivated by the hope of saving their marriage. In these cases the passage of time—more than a few years—would help us to assess the extent and duration of the changes they made.

CAN THIS MARRIAGE BE SAVED?

Women who are in an abusive marriage but still hold the memory of love and want to keep the family intact—that is, women who have every intention of staying often question whether the marriage can be saved. Although I am a strong believer that domestic abuse is criminal and only gets worse unless the perpetrator wants and seeks help, there is no simple answer.

I operate on this premise: *The only way out is out. You get off the path by choosing to do so.* Once the seal of secrecy is broken and even one person voices the unspoken wrongs the woman has endured, she faces a point of inevitability from which she cannot escape. When even the thinnest ray of light penetrates a blackened room, the room is no longer dark. Then the woman's choice becomes one of whether she can tolerate the marriage once it has been made safe or whether she wishes to pursue another path.

Clinicians must be open to all types of endings to their clients' stories. When I first began counseling battered women, I naively directed psychotherapy with one of my clients toward getting her away from her brutal mate. I felt so effective when she left him—what a good patient! But within two weeks she moved in with another man, who treated her far more cruelly than her husband. Leaving is not the only solution, but it is the cultural script that helping professionals adopt most often.[22] I have learned that when I adopt the approach of exhorting a client to leave her abuser no matter what, I may lose the opportunity to work with her within the choices she is making. A basic social work tenet is to "start where the client is" and allow for self-determination.[23]

Besides, staying can feel like an empowering choice for some women.[24] Perhaps the wife is taking steps to protect herself while she keeps her marriage intact. Others may stay as a part of secret strategizing. To think that leaving is the only solution can be arrogant and even disempowering—a Procrustean bed to which all women must conform. Abused women eventually reach the point at which they remember their own strengths and abilities. At this juncture they can make rational decisions about the future, weighing the costs and benefits of leaving as well as examining alternative ways to continue the relationship.[25] For some, compromise may include staying married but with new ground rules, or perhaps a lower level of emotional commitment.

I think that a more important question than, Can this marriage be saved? is, Can this *woman* be saved? Although Rhonda decided to stay with her husband, the work she did in short-term individual therapy was astounding. In only two sessions she realized that the abuse was not her problem and that she was working too hard at second-guessing Andrew. She quickly got into a cost-benefit assessment. She worried about the model she was presenting to her children: she didn't want her daughter to grow up believing it was acceptable for a man to treat his wife as Andrew treated her, and she certainly didn't want to teach her son he had the right to hit a woman. She learned she could choose to control her destiny even if she couldn't control her husband. From this position of power, she decided to stay for the moment and address Andrew's anger rather than be "gripped and muted" by fear of his explosions.

After assessing safety issues and developing a safety plan, the therapist and client should also explore the husband's willingness to change. I have yet to see an abused upscale woman stay with her battering spouse with some modicum of safety and satisfaction if he does not become involved in treatment himself. How does a woman proceed if her husband has stopped the abuse, is seeking help, and wants the marriage to stay viable? She learns to focus on herself first. She practices making demands of him in small increments with the goal of feeling safe and like an equal partner. She recognizes that the marriage will have its ups and downs, and she proceeds cautiously and assesses it daily. She learns to keep to her boundaries, setting up consequences such as leaving if he belittles her again or calling the police if he strikes her once more. She calls the shots for what she's willing to tolerate and is also willing to negotiate with him for change. Although she is patient, she is no longer a victim. However, she must be consistent in enforcing the consequences if they are to work.

Melody stayed with her husband and is pleased with her decision. She told me, "By working in individual therapy and group, I learned that there was a way to be in my marriage and appreciate it with its ups and downs. I gave my husband specific boundaries with specific consequences. I told him I'd divorce him and leave him for good if he didn't change. I guess his love for me and fear of losing me, in addition to the work he has done with his new therapist, have made quite an impact. He rarely barks at me anymore and has never hit me again. We still have rough spots, but I am at least 30 percent checked back in. And I am glad of it."

Perhaps it is only in hindsight that one can know if the abused woman should have tried to salvage her marriage. One fact is certain: a woman cannot and should not remain in a marriage when her own and her children's safety is at stake. On this point the clinician must take a firm stand.

INDIVIDUAL OR MARITAL THERAPY?

A current controversy among clinicians centers on whether treatment should be individual or marital. Virginia Goldner's work at the Ackerman Family Institute has demonstrated that it is possible to work with a couple in which the husband is violent. But she makes clear that

> ours is a therapy that emphasizes the personal responsibility and accountability of both partners. Thus, we believe that women in these relationships must take some responsibility for protecting themselves, given the danger they are in. This is not only a safety issue, although that is paramount. It is also important because an emphasis on personal responsibility gets women engaged in a change process that mobilizes their sense of agency. Although these women have been victims, this does not mean they must be paralyzed by the passivity of the "victim position" ... [a] singular focus [that] has turned out to have galvanizing effects.[26]

I am not so sure this is the best route. I believe that treating the couple at the outset (rather than the woman alone) adds to the moral ambiguity of the situation. It is bad enough that the woman is so quick to blame herself. If her husband is part of the therapy early on, in his defensive effort he will continue to blame her or accuse her of being oversensitive and demanding. Canadian researcher Donald Dutton concurs. He has written that marital work with a man who has a history of relationship violence may be a "conflict-generator" and that individual work (which might include group and/or individual therapy) should come first for both husband and wife.[27]

I believe that a woman needs the certainty of the safety afforded her by individual treatment as she sorts out her life and recognizes that the abuse she has endured is inappropriate, unacceptable, and criminal. Coming as part of a couple at first robs her of the opportunity to hear the other voices she so desperately needs to hear—voices that echo her own small inner voice that has been silenced by an entitled husband who turns the tables and a close-minded society that tells her that what she is living doesn't exist.

Those in favor of treating domestic abuse via marital therapy believe the therapist can create the inner boundaries the couple needs to reach a place of safety. I maintain that for such safety to occur both partners must be engaged in individual work first. There blame cannot be shifted freely. The men learn they have choices other than to be abusive and strike, and the women learn they have choices other than to accept the abuse and stay. While in many cases separating breeds increased violence, staying is often not the answer either. Most often, when the woman starts her own therapy and becomes stronger, she is better able to install her own boundaries as to what she will tolerate. She may even be willing to involve the police and legal systems, which can quickly cool her husband's behavior. And sometimes taking action on her own behalf pushes him to wake up and seek help instead of repeating his violent pattern with his wife or his next unsuspecting victim.

Marital therapy does not provide the battered woman the kind of safety she needs for rebuilding her strength and finding her identity. The consequences may be severe if she is truthful in a couple's session. She may be too afraid. Moreover, many upscale batterers can be charming and persuasive and may convey a far different image of themselves to the therapist than the one that reflects the woman's reality at home.

However, I have found it useful on occasion to meet the abusive husband with his wife for a single session or two, although I make it clear from the outset that I won't be treating them as a couple—I just want to learn more about the woman and her situation. If the husband is not requesting to come in and the wife asks me how to invite him to a session, I say to her, "Tell him that it would be helpful in my work with you if he could fill out the story. It's only for one or two visits." However, if the woman is currently in physical danger or she reports her husband as consistently explosive, I do not request such a meeting.

I gain a great deal of collateral information about the relationship from these meetings, such as how willing the husband is to change his behavior, whether he feels remorseful, and how he treats and feels about his wife. Sometimes these interviews signal what is to come. For instance, Steve cried in my office and expressed deep affection for Melody. He never meant to be so hurtful and was frightened at the prospect of losing her. Melody and Steve have stayed together and continue to work on their relationship. Steve's therapy focuses on his use of anger, his management of it, and the underlying issues causing him to lash out at Melody. His behavior since our initial meeting has markedly improved.

Jacqueline's husband, Brian, came in with her for two sessions but shifted from being mute and sullen to angry and defensive, complaining that his wife was selfish and didn't understand him. Brian went for help and briefly stopped drinking but never worked on the issues that caused him to be abusive and destructive. The couple divorced.

GROUP SUPPORT

The abused upscale woman is best served by individual therapy coupled with group treatment. In individual work she need not reveal herself too quickly. It is also an opportunity for her to pull together her thoughts and feelings so that when other external voices echo her private reality she is able to integrate their message. Group work offers her a sense of universality (she is not the only person in her class experiencing abuse), as well as empathy, support, and a chance to normalize her situation. As psychiatrist Judith Herman has said in her work on recovery from trauma: "Once the sense of basic safety has been reestablished, the survivor needs the help of others in rebuilding a positive view of the self. The regulation of intimacy and aggression, disrupted by the trauma, must be restored."[28]

The interaction of the speaker and listeners in the group is vital. The abused woman's narrative is reshaped by the questions others ask her, as well as by their observations and recognition. One woman had a breakthrough during the early weeks of her participation in group. Owing to the other members' curiosity and empathy about her survival skills and ingenuity, Emily suddenly reframed her story. At a climactic moment she looked up wide-eyed and said, "So it wasn't my fault. I was actually courageous!"

By incorporating other voices with her own, the group member becomes accustomed to making choices and relying on increasing inner strength. Group therapy gives her a safe space in which to learn or relearn social skills and to examine how she relates to others. Because I have seen the dramatic impact of group work on this population, I typically see a woman for three to six sessions and then suggest group treatment, either instead of or in addition to her individual work.

In our women's group Jacqueline often talked about the joys of being alone and "dating herself," and other members quickly picked up on this theme. One amazed group member came in and reported that she had spent the weekend alone and "loved the company." For women who have spent years focusing on the unrealistic demands of a narcissistic partner, it may take some adjustment to give to themselves, but women frequently report an enormous sense of relief once they do.

In a group the battered woman more clearly hears her inner voices, which the therapist and the other women echo. It *is* wrong to be insulted in public. It *was* inappropriate to be thrown out of the tent and humiliated. That shove should *not* have happened no matter what his day was like. Slowly she begins to recognize the realities of her situation. But this recognition is not without a mixture of feelings.

A new identity starts to take hold as strength returns and the love of self takes over. Women who have remained married must learn to take care of themselves. Those who have left their husbands will eventually return to the world of dating. Part of their healing work involves learning to recognize early warning signs of an abusive man and heeding their instincts. This kind of psycho-education can be part of individual therapy. However, in the company of other women they receive valuable feedback about their new experiences. That's why group therapy can be vital for abused women. The wisdom of others at different stages of leaving and reclaiming themselves serves as a travelogue and an advertisement of hope for the woman regaining her strength and her self.

It is also essential to a woman's healing that she develop new social support networks beyond the group, significant relationships within which she can forge or rebuild her eroding identity. Above all, her network should include people to whom she can honestly reveal her situation and who will not deny her reality or judge her. She can also fortify connections with long-standing friends, as long as she consistently learns to pursue healthy, nurturing relationships.

10

The Double-Edged Sword:
How Family, Friends, and Professionals
Can Make Matters Worse

U PSCALE ABUSED WIVES WHO SEEK LEGAL, medical, or mental health services often find themselves revictimized by the neglect, ignorance, and skepticism they encounter there. Even well-meaning helping professionals can unwittingly encourage these women to remain in their marriages. Similarly, well-intentioned friends, family, and clergy sometimes urge a women to "stay the course" for the sake of herself, her children, and God. When a trusted person witnesses emotional or physical abuse but stands by silently for fear of offending the woman, or doubts the woman's account of it, he or she inadvertently retraumatizes her. Many abused women told me they wished that others had named their husband's behavior earlier and had encouraged them to leave. The women's fears of reporting the abuse are legitimized when their help-seeking efforts are met with unresponsiveness; they feel they have nowhere to turn and must suffer alone.

REVICTIMIZATION IN THE CLINICAL
AND SOCIAL SERVICE WORLD

Depending on a therapist's orientation, she or he may not be alert to the signs of violence within a marriage. In fact, a Freudian and a behaviorist interviewing the same new patient may, owing to their divergent points of view, perceive the causes of her problem quite differently and recommend different courses of treatment. Furthermore, if the psychological perspective does not allow for even the possibility of upscale violence, the injured woman is even less likely to be helped.

Many women recounted horror stories about therapists who did not act in their clients' best interest. Kathleen described how her experience in therapy served to compound rather than ease her despairing, suicidal feelings. "I can't believe how many things my therapist didn't ask me," she told me. "And how much I minimized and lied. After these awful things happened with Stuart, I would be so dead inside that I would speak softly, I wouldn't look at anybody."

Although she didn't start out in therapy saying, "I'm an abused wife," she did tell her therapist, "I'm in an unhappy marriage. I'm depressed. I must be doing something wrong." After a physical attack occurred, she would say, "Stuart and I had a really bad fight," as if she were describing two people screaming at each other. "I never explained what happened," she admitted, "but nobody ever asked me. Nobody said, 'Tell me about the fight.' I would have told the therapist about the physical abuse if he'd asked. My therapist never understood the emotional abuse either. I needed to tell him exactly what Stuart said to me, and I never did." It may seem as if Kathleen was taking little responsibility for her own recovery, but an upscale woman who enters therapy to deal with spousal abuse is so vulnerable and mired in her own denial that she may lack the wherewithal to bring up such sensitive issues. It is the therapist's task to do so.

After Kathleen confessed her affair to her husband (to which Stuart replied, "So what? I've had thirty or forty affairs"), she decided she wanted out and began telling others about her situation. "My husband desperately claimed to want to stay married. He said he was going to change. I'd been seeing my individual therapist for almost four years. I finally told him the whole story too. The first time he heard it, he was extremely sympathetic. He said I should get out. But the next week he berated me about how I could leave now that my husband was finally *willing* to work on the marriage. Who the hell did I think I was? What was I going to get? A couple million bucks and just get out? Did I think that was fair? He totally blew me away.

"He said, 'You're really happy you climbed out of this black hole, but you know what? You need to climb *right back into it*, and see if you can *fix* what's in there.' So, weenie that I still was, I took that advice very much to heart, and I decided to stay married." The abusive marriage lasted another two years.

Allison also got inadequate help from her therapist, who could not see through Robert's manipulations and was unwilling to confront the abuse. Allison had insisted on seeking counseling: "I told Robert, 'We're not going to fix this marriage on our own. I'm prepared to leave. Unless you meet me with a third party, I'm not getting back together.' We went to counseling for a year with someone through the church. She was getting her degree in social work, and we were her 'model couple.' Robert learned therapy-speak: what I wanted to hear, how to say it, and what to do. So after a few months, I moved back in with him, and we just let the divorce drop. Things seemed wonderful, but in retrospect, I see now they were just relatively wonderful."

The underlying problems continued. "Sex was still not that great and not that frequent. But at least he came home some nights, and he wasn't ignoring me anymore. He seemed to understand about relationships, and he seemed to hear me when I expressed my concerns. But I was ignoring his *actions*. He was saying what I wanted to hear, but he hit me again. We were in a car, going to the theater, and he punched me in the arm because I was late. I told this to the counselor, and she said, 'Well, obviously it's a communication problem that you two need to work on. Robert, you need to learn how to express your anger in ways that aren't physical.'

"Robert went through this whole hoopla about that's how he and his brothers dealt with their anger. They wrestled on the floor, and that's what he was used to. And then issues with his mom came out in the counseling. Finally, the counselor said to me, 'Basically, I'm here for him. He won't go to counseling by himself. You seem like you're pretty together, so I'm going to have you sit in his sessions, and I'm going to work on Robert.' I thought that was wonderful because it seemed as if he was getting the help he needed. She even put us in front of a one-way mirror at her university, as the model couple, and we helped her earn her degree.

"But she never called what was going on between us abuse. This hitting incident in the car was not abuse to her. And I didn't know any better! She was the expert." Most social work and psychology interns are closely supervised, so this counselor's blunder cannot be reduced to mere inexperience. Even her supervisors and others behind the mirror did not advise the trainee about what to ask—they all missed the abuse. And like Kathleen, Allison viewed her therapist as an "expert"—an assessment that reflected her need more than her ability to accurately judge the counselor's abilities.

Ingrid also complained about the therapist she and Bill had consulted together. "It was awful," she told me. "The first guy said, 'Well, I don't really condone divorce.' He didn't even want to hear what was going on. He looked at me and said, 'Bill doesn't *look* like an abusive husband.' I knew right then this man wasn't worth my time. As soon as I started talking, Bill would interject and slam me right in front of the guy. The therapist would just say, 'Bill, Ingrid can't talk.' That's all!" Finally the therapist asked to see Ingrid alone.

"That's when he began to see what was going on, but I could tell he wasn't even *close* to having a clue about what I was going through. So my lawyer recommended a female therapist, and I started going to her. I went on my own every week, got counseling, and moved out."

Lynne's marriage counselor behaved outrageously, even when the abuse occurred before her very eyes. "Jon didn't like our first therapist," Lynne told me, "but he *did* like the second one, who I didn't particularly like. Once in a session with her he got mad and threw a glass of water on me. But the therapist didn't set any limits. She didn't say, 'Oh, that's totally awful.' She just gave me some Kleenex and continued the session as if nothing had happened. In the next session I asked her, 'Why didn't you do anything?' She said, 'Well, you know, you were both so into it.' I felt this therapist had sided with my husband." Lynne's assessment was correct. Moreover, the therapist was unable or unwilling to intervene as the fight was escalating—a major therapeutic faux pas.

Any therapist can blunder. But mistakes become pernicious if the clinician enters the situation ignorant of the dynamics of domestic abuse, especially among the upscale, or is so rigidly committed to a stance of neutrality (as when Jon threw water on Lynne) that it verges on absurdity. After all, abuse is abuse, and if a therapist sees it in the office, he or she should name it and deal with it.

Typically, the therapeutic error occurs when the clinician unwittingly aligns with the husband's reactions, which the wife frequently minimizes in her early telling of the tale. If the clinician minimizes the events, too, characterizing them as symptoms of "bad communication," the woman is pushed back into the denial that her husband's behavior is not really a problem. She begins to believe that her husband is not at fault and that she is wrong or crazy for feeling so upset. She may then redouble her efforts to preserve the marriage by trying to make him happy. This revision is deplorable because it fits too well with the ambivalence that our culture and many of its helping professionals bring to the notion of upscale violence.

In effect, this response from the therapist results in the woman's revictimization and a reinforcement of her belief that since she has so much going for her, she has no reason or right to complain. She takes refuge in justifications: "He had a hard week." "I shouldn't have pressed him on this." "If only I weren't so demanding." Like the child in the alcoholic family, the woman learns to doubt her perceptions. Unfortunately, a therapist wearing blinders colludes with this disavowal.

By these examples I do not mean to indict the entire profession. Certainly many excellent therapists have helped upscale women deal with their abusive marriages. However, I do want those in the therapeutic community who encounter upscale abuse to examine their reactions. Domestic violence does occur in upper-income and well-educated families, and therapists should be alert to such dynamics.

ACTS OF NEGLECT IN THE MEDICAL PROFESSION

The director of a hospital emergency room I spoke with recently was interested in starting educational programs for his staff so that they could spot and properly treat domestic abuse victims. But not all medical personnel feel that way. When I spoke about upscale violence to the Chicago chapter of the American Medical Association, my sparse audience consisted of ten women and a group of elderly doctors who took my workshop to fulfill their continuing education obligations.

Besides, most battered upscale wives are reluctant to reveal their secret, even to well-intentioned emergency room doctors, especially if they have been able to keep it hidden in so many other, more private, places. Research indicates that the rate at which emergency room doctors detect domestic violence is low.[1] In fact, often they don't catch it. One study found less than 3 percent of women visiting emergency rooms disclosed or were asked about domestic violence by a nurse or physician[2]—this despite estimates that 37 percent of women seeking treatment at emergency rooms have come as a result of injuries inflicted by an intimate.[3] Using protocols to identify and treat victims of spousal violence in emergency rooms increases its identification, according to one study, from 5.6 percent to 30 percent,[4] but too many members of the medical profession still overlook it in the ER and in their offices. Calling the abusive husband "a jerk," as the physician in Sally's case did, is simply not good enough.

Emergency room staff is on the frontlines. They see acutely injured upscale women. Sally went to the ER after Ray broke her jaw. It was the doctor's input about the permanency of her injuries that sobered her into reevaluating her marriage and prompted her to step off the path. Those who are less trained or are afraid to become involved leave the woman to fend for herself.

I have talked with several physicians about their role vis-à-vis upscale abuse. Some initially said that they tended to drop the matter once a woman explained a scar or bruise, so as not to offend her or pressure her: they believed that within the doctor-patient relationship, patients would confide as needed. But at my urging, they have begun to ask follow-up questions in such cases or make comments that indicate their sense that there is more to discuss:

- "How are things going at home, overall?"
- "Sometimes stress in a marriage can manifest in many ways."
- "I know it can be difficult to talk about problems at home, but I am here to listen if you feel like it."
- "You said you fell, but my experience tells me otherwise. You can talk to me."

One doctor had an excellent response: "You seem tense lately. Things okay at home? Sometimes emotional stress and anger can result in different patterns of behavior between husbands and wives. When I see a physically hurt woman, I know from experience it could be the result of abuse at home, which she's afraid to mention. This happens to all sorts of people, even other physicians. If this should ever be the case for you, I hope you'd feel comfortable enough to talk about it with me or someone else."

THE ROAD TO HELL IS PAVED
WITH GOOD INTENTIONS: FRIENDS AND FAMILY

In many instances, battered upscale women turn to loved ones for help, only to be blamed for the violence or urged to stay in or return to the marriage. Sherry's mother and sister, both of the old school and old-fashioned, responded to the news that Sherry's husband had broken her wrist with, "What did you say to provoke him?" Such a response is not unusual. Friends and family, like society at large, are reluctant to acknowledge violence among people they know personally.

Research shows that we interpret violence perpetrated by strangers differently from violence that intimates inflict.[5] Indeed, female victims of domestic violence are six times less likely to report the crime to the police or other officials than those who have suffered at the hands of a stranger.[6] Consider this story: John waits at a bus stop, minding his own business. Fred comes up to him and slugs him. We typically ask: "What's got into Fred?" Fred goes home to his wife, Barbara, who is also minding her own business. He slugs Barbara. A typical response: "What did Barbara do to make Fred angry?"[7] This disparity in reactions is even greater if the upscale man is highly regarded, especially if he gets kudos for being a tiger. We put forth greater efforts to understand the violence of an upscale pillar of the community, and often assume that civility is his true nature and that his attack was an aberration.

When friends and family identify the problem for what it is, refrain from blaming the victim, and offer aid, the abused woman feels vindicated. With her loved ones' validation, she realizes that she didn't instigate the violence. In fact, one of my key findings is that external voices can be crucial in helping the woman to free herself. Bailey's mother and sister were supportive and concurred with her assessments of Peter. Allison's parents took her in, along with her infant. Sally's parents finally understood the scope of their daughter's suffering. It is essential that significant others articulate their concerns. Their outrage should speak to the inner voice of the upscale battered wife. In this way, she can be helped to say, "This *is* happening to me. I must not deny or excuse it *any longer.*"

THE COURTS

An upscale abusive man can use the courts to continue tormenting his wife, even after she has separated from him. Attorney David H. Hopkins told me, "Abusive people, when blocked from carrying out the harassment, often focus on new vehicles—and a well-to-do abuser can sometimes use the litigation process for meritless, baseless, frivolous litigation as a means for further abuse. All too frequently the courts, in an effort to accord the accused batterer all his rights, permit this excessive protraction in the process. They permit the petitioner to be pounded with legal fees—thereby allowing the judicial system to become a vehicle for further harassment. A poorer defendant by definition doesn't have the wherewithal to do it. And the courts don't make the abuser accountable for the costs incurred to protect the woman from these fees. There is need for statutory reform in this area."[8]

This was Allison's experience. "When I left that day on the plane, I thought it was over," she told me. "I had cleared a monumental hurdle, and now my life would be easier. But it was just the beginning. My experience with the court system has been just as rough as my marriage. Here's this man who beats me up and takes away all my money. I'm on welfare because I can't work full-time. I've got to come back to this city every eight days because he has father's rights. He has to see his child for short frequent visits, and I'm responsible for providing the visitation and some sort of bonding. To me it's absolutely ludicrous that he couldn't come here to see my son. How can I work a full-time job that way?

"I won't speak to him without a third party present, so the abuse is subtle. It's all through the courts. All the motions, all the dragging me back into court. Our legal bills are astronomical. Mine alone is $70,000 right now. I don't know where I'm going to get this money. And we haven't even set a trial date. It has been a year since we separated, and it's going to be another two before it's over. The courts are the only way he can communicate his anger to me. He flies his whole family in, and they sit in the courtroom. When I go up on the stand, they laugh at everything I say."

For the upscale, new statutes aimed at addressing the economic imbalance that occurs when a woman uses her legal options to defend herself may deter the man from making frivolous filings. When I asked Hopkins how he counters the husband's moves to pound his wife with legal fees, he told me, "We have sought shifts in legal fees requiring the respondent to pay. In another case we successfully sought an injunction against the respondent filing any pro se pleading in court [an action filed without an attorney] unless he had gotten approval from the chief judge of the division. And there are principles of Illinois law that allow for shifting of legal fees related to frivolous proceedings, where we can go after the attorneys as well. But be aware that these processes are expensive."[9]

Judges' prejudices can compound the wife's difficulties. As Kathleen explained, "Even in court during the divorce, I felt the judge doubted me. Here I was, this lady with millions of dollars, and there was this sense of disbelief like, 'Why would you want to divorce this guy? It can't be that bad because you have so much money, honey.' My own parents had that attitude!" I heard from an attorney firsthand that a prominent judge in domestic violence court said of upscale women, "A little abuse would do some of these women good." The prejudices must also be eliminated from the system as much as possible for the woman to be safe in pursuing protection and recourse. The upscale man receives preferential treatment in the courts and may utilize the system to his advantage. Not all judges are as wise as the one who told the upscale batterer that the statutes had no stipulation that a dentist cannot do time.

THE POLICE AND THE LEGAL SYSTEM

Of all the calls they receive, police dread those involving domestic abuse the most. They are most likely to be hurt during such confrontations because either or both parties often turn their wrath on the attending officers. And since domestic violence is also prevalent among police officers, many may have conflicted feelings when responding to a domestic violence call.[10] Before the mid–1980s,[11] despite the demise of the finger-stitch rule more than a century earlier, many arresting officers still looked to the extent of a woman's injuries—Did she need stitches? Did he break her jaw?—to determine whether they should arrest her husband.

The woman's injuries notwithstanding, there is a correlation between how men perceive the penalties for abuse and how they continue to behave.[12] Lawrence W. Sherman and Richard A. Berk's groundbreaking research in 1984 on domestic assault and police response studied 314 men implicated in misdemeanor spousal assault incidents involving the Minneapolis police. The men were divided into three groups: those who were arrested, those whom the police counseled at the scene, and those whom police separated from the woman they had allegedly assaulted. The arrested men had a recidivism rate of only 13 percent; 18 percent of those who were counseled repeated their offense; and 26 percent of those who were separated from their wives resumed their abuse.[13] These results were so significant that police departments around the country developed policies for mandatory arrest.[14]

Yet in later research Sherman, studying 1,200 cases, found that the recidivism rate was actually higher for arrested men. However, these were subjects who either were deemed socially marginal or lived in poorer communities.[15] In effect, they were men with less to lose.[16] From this we may surmise that mandatory arrest has a greater impact on men in the middle and upper classes—those who have money and prestige. They may be less likely to repeat the offense in the face of the social consequences of arrest.[17] Nevertheless, if wealthy men may have more to lose, it is also the case that their money and influence cushion them in the legal system.

Although such mandatory arrest policies sometimes help and protect abused women, they can also backfire. In fact, they may revictimize the women and children they were meant to protect. According to attorney Leslie Landis, "One of the unintended consequences of mandatory arrest policies has been mutual arrests. When an officer responds to a domestic violence scene, faced with the mandatory arrest policy and a case where the story of each spouse is inconsistent, or when it was not clear who is at fault and both parties were injured, the officer may arrest both parties. This would then lead to the children being placed in temporary protective custody. This has happened so often that there is a new wave in training law enforcement to determine who is the primary aggressor."[18] It is simply not clear exactly how such policies would play out; further examination of them would be well worth the effort.

The *no-drop policy* is another protective approach that has occasionally disappointed. It was initiated in the early 1990s to prevent an abuser from going free if his wife is too intimidated to press charges. Once the original complaint is filed, the woman cannot withdraw it and the charge cannot be dropped. It automatically becomes the state's case. Because domestic violence is considered a criminal offense, victims do not have the right to drop the case, as they do in a civil action.

On the positive side, the no-drop policy can be life-saving because it takes the burden off the woman, who is no longer obliged to decide whether her abuser goes to trial; it is now up to the state. The abuser cannot blame her, nor can his threats have any impact on the pursuit of the charge. This prevents the man from coercing his wife into dropping the charges. The no-drop policy also increases the district attorney's interest in the case. In the past, prosecutors may have been reluctant to get involved in such cases because of their expectation that most women will drop the charges or skip court.

On the other hand, the state's takeover of the case can impinge on the woman's civil liberties. An abused woman may leave her abuser several times prior to leaving him permanently; abusers often use violence, financial control, or threats about the children to compel victims to return.[19] Sometimes the initial charges are the woman's way of entering a frightening legal system that may not always be able to protect her, but that is a means to begin leveraging some power against the abuser. Withholding the option of withdrawing her complaint may reinforce an upscale woman's reluctance to become involved in the courts. When this happens she loses the opportunity both to learn about the legal system and to obtain an order of protection.

As Landis said, "In Chicago we opposed no-drop, as we believe the victim should have her say. We think the victim is aware of the danger she faces, her resources, and her danger level better than anybody else. She could come in, file, get an order of protection, and maybe if she felt that were enough, she could drop the charges—knowing she could always come back. The no-drop cuts this woman off at the pass; she is not allowed to put her toe in the water—it's sink or swim."[20]

Moreover, the no-drop policy means just what it says. No pleas from the woman will cause the charges to be dropped. According to Landis, "in some instances, they have actually jailed women for contempt of court for not testifying against their husbands. Or the woman testified for the defense and the state's district attorney allowed her as a hostile witness and then ripped her apart—further victimizing the person who sought support and safety from the system." Landis believes that upscale women "rarely go to the criminal justice system unless the violence is extremely bad—they usually just go to the divorce courts. If that woman has no say as to whether to prosecute her spouse, it would have an even greater chilling effect, and she would never call the police."[21]

Many a woman chooses to go to divorce court rather than criminal court because she doesn't want her husband—and thus herself and her children—to lose his insurance or the income from his job. With no-drop, a woman can't rethink her decision in light of the potential economic consequences of criminal charges.

Yet, the no-drop policy can serve as a buffer between husband and wife. Attorneys don't have to worry about how the jury regards the woman and her reputation; she doesn't even need to be a witness. This prevents any bias a jury might feel against a victim—especially in the case of the upscale. Jurors need not determine whether she is a worthy victim but rather can focus on her injuries. In fact, in San Diego, prosecutors simply bring in silhouettes of the victims. These drawings sit in court during the trial, reminding the jury that a real person was injured.[22]

Like mandatory arrest and no-drop policies, orders of protection, although also well intended, are not always effective. Despite having obtained a restraining order, victims have been reabused and even killed. In one study nearly 50 percent of the victims who obtained a protection order were reabused within two years.[23] And according to the 1997 Florida Governor's Task Force on Domestic and Sexual Violence, more than 17 percent of domestic homicide victims had filed a protection order against the perpetrator at the time of the murder.[24] Punishment must be certain and severe in order to carry weight with abusive husbands, especially those who are upscale and have the means to manipulate the system.

CONVICTIONS AND CHILD CUSTODY

Like Allison, most upscale abused women deal with their partners in divorce court rather than in a civil or criminal court. As David H. Hopkins explained, "Typically, abuse remains in the closet to a greater or lesser extent until a divorce case starts up. There are many more factors impacting upon the victim, more disincentives not to go forward. Often, a willingness on the part of the victim to deal affirmatively with abuse goes hand in hand with the coming to terms that the marriage is dead." Many upscale women refuse to press charges against their husband because of the financial jeopardy in which it could place them and their children.

However, a woman who opts for divorce court instead of criminal court may present a weaker case than a woman who has pressed charges in the past. A majority of states have adopted statutes requiring courts to consider a record of domestic violence as a factor in custody and visitation determinations. If an upscale abused woman fears for the safety of her children, she may find it in her family's best interest to have her husband arrested and to press charges. Perhaps such a strategy would have saved Allison much heartache.

In the states of Washington and Texas, if the court concludes that a parent has engaged in child abuse or domestic violence, it is precluded from awarding joint legal custody, and it may limit unsupervised time between the offending parent and the child. In Arizona, North Dakota, Oklahoma, and Wyoming, domestic violence is presumed to be contrary to the best interests of the children, and any award of visitation must be designed to best protect the children and the abused parent from further harm. In California, when there is a finding of domestic violence, the courts must consider awarding supervised visitation only. Parents and children may be required to participate in counseling when there is a custody dispute, but the counseling of the parents should be separate if the abused spouse requests it.[25]

According to Pennsylvania, Montana, and Minnesota statutes, if a parent is convicted of certain violent crimes, the court must find that the offending parent does not pose a threat or that it is in the best interest of the child before awarding custody or visitation to the offending parent. Pennsylvania custody statutes require the court to take testimony about the offending parent's domestic violence counseling and any continuing risk to the child before issuing an order of custody to a parent convicted of specific crimes. Prior to the adoption of these provisions, judges routinely concluded that the abuse of a parent by the other was irrelevant in custody proceedings; violence toward one's spouse, presumably, had nothing to do with one's ability to parent adequately.[26]

Custody mediation, in which a neutral, trained mediator, either court-appointed or independent, meets with both parties to assist in their negotiations regarding visitation and support, is another avenue used to resolve these disputes. The National Center for State Courts reports that only a handful of states mandate custody mediation by statute. In several states the courts may not compel mediation of custody disputes in the context of domestic violence. However, feminist scholars and advocates for battered women strongly oppose the imposition of mediation to resolve custody disputes.[27] The only research that squarely addresses the question of whether victims are better protected from future violence by adversarial rather than mediation divorce found that batterers inflict less violence if the divorce is adversarial.[28] Mediation requires cooperation, honest communication, equivalent power, similar investment in the outcome, voluntary participation, and a safe environment. No matter how skillful the mediator, batterers cannot be quickly transformed so that the mediation proceeds with integrity.[29] Custody mediation does not enhance outcomes for battered women and children.[30]

However, despite the potential snags, prejudices, and problems with all these avenues for relief, a woman can often be helped when lawyers, police officers, judges, physicians, clergymen, and clinicians are sensitive to the possibility and complexity of upscale spousal abuse.

IF SOMEONE YOU KNOW IS
AN UPSCALE ABUSED WIFE

It is difficult to be an outside witness to a situation destructive to someone you are close to. If you see a woman you care about inextricably involved with an abusive partner, you may feel helpless. On the one hand, you want to get in there and do something, but on the other hand, you don't want to patronize or alienate her. So what can you do if you observe the abuse but she keeps silent about it?

First and foremost, if you notice injuries, it is imperative that you be direct and ask the woman how she sustained them. Even if her story seems weak, insist that she seek medical attention and offer to go with her. If she is a close friend or relative, rely on the strength and duration of the relationship to say, "I think you're hiding something, and I'm scared for you." If she admits to the abuse, ask whether she filed a police report. Although you don't want to corner her so that she feels like a failure if she doesn't file a complaint, you do want to ask her how she can prevent this from happening again. It is also beneficial to assure her that you know domestic abuse occurs among the upscale. Tell her that it is not her fault nor something to be ashamed of. You may also want to give her the phone numbers of resources in Appendix E. Be prepared for this first effort to seem fruitless. You are making an impact, however, even merely by awakening her consciousness and affirming her reality.

If you only suspect abuse, it's helpful to bring up the subject at an opportune moment. You may fear that the woman will cut off your friendship, become defensive and angry, or push you away. But we know your voice may be key to affirming her fears and recognizing the way off the path. For instance, you might say, "I don't feel comfortable around your husband. Is there something going on between you?" or, "You seem so tense and worried lately. I've really been concerned." Then wait to see if she volunteers information about her situation. If she does, inquire first about her safety and that of her children. Ask her directly, "Are you in danger? Do you think there is a potential for that?" Let her know that domestic abuse only worsens. If she seems in imminent danger, help her to find a safe shelter. Together, call the local domestic violence hotline or coalition so that she can learn about her legal options and how to create a safety plan.

If she resists breaking her silence, you may need to broach the subject more than once. Be clear that you don't mean to intrude, but that you care deeply and wish to be available to help however you can. Eventually let her know that you think she is enduring behaviors that are damaging for her emotionally and physically. You may also offer anecdotes of other women you have known or read about who were in similar upscale abusive marriages. Or you might disclose your own experience to normalize a potential revelation. Speaking by parallel process often opens the door to self-disclosure. And always make it clear you are there to listen and support, not to judge and fix.

It is critical to convey that she is not alone and not to blame. Domestic abuse is criminal as well as dangerous, and no one deserves to be beaten, no matter what the circumstances. She must take care of herself, and you are willing to help her. She does have choices, and the choice of talking about it is the beginning of the healing process. You must reassure her that you will support her as she finds her own way, since she will probably be unprepared to take action immediately. Indeed, she may feel she can't leave the abusive relationship. According to the National Training Center on Domestic and Sexual Violence, the five best things to say to such a victim are:

- I am afraid for your safety.
- I am afraid for the safety of your children.
- It will only get worse.
- I am here for you when you are ready to talk.
- You don't deserve to be abused.
- I will try to help you if you decide you want to leave him.[31]

I also suggest saying the following to the highly educated and upper-income wife:

- It happens everywhere, including to people like us.
- Your secrets run your life. It takes more psychological energy to keep something hidden than to reveal it. It's like telling someone not to think of the word *elephant* for the next five minutes. Try it—it will be all you can think about. Negation takes thought and energy.

- To remain silent lets your husband believe he can get away with such appalling behavior.
- The perks and privileges of your lifestyle are not worth this kind of pain and potential danger.

Tell her about the unique profile of the upscale batterer and show her the lists and questionnaires in the appendices: "Are You an Abused Woman?," "Traits of an Abusive Man," and "Early Warning Signs." As a clinician, I often do so. They give the woman an opportunity to assess her situation objectively. As she begins to agree with a growing number of items, she has difficulty keeping the denial in place. Women are often stunned but also relieved to see the behaviors they have been living with itemized and described. It helps dispel their feeling that this doesn't happen to others and makes them feel less isolated in their predicament.

You may want to help the woman create a safety plan in case her situation worsens. She should have an arranged safe house to go to, where her partner cannot find her. It can be a shelter or a friend's home, as long as the friend understands the need for absolute secrecy. Some women stash a phone in each room of their home so they can call for help, or they and a friend agree to a code word to be used when the danger escalates. The friend then calls the police.

RESOURCES: HOW TO FIND AND USE THEM

Even though upscale battered women seem to have more resources at their disposal than poorer women, the myth that "this doesn't happen to people like us" and professionals' reactions can contribute to inequity. These women may not have equal access to the scarce and valued resources of the multidisciplinary helping system. As I pointed out earlier, lower-income women are far more readily believed when they complain about domestic violence, and upscale men may even benefit from society's protective attitude toward them. According to Deborah Tucker, executive director or the National Training Center on Domestic and Sexual Violence, "Police are cautioned to be careful when dealing with a perpetrator of means with connections. When we advocate for consistent policy and procedure in intervening in domestic violence, we protect everyone—battered women and police officers—from the influential batterer."[32]

However, help is available. Appendix E lists national resources that are an abused woman's first step toward getting the help she needs. Some of these national organizations publish books listing comprehensive shelter, hotline, and legal resources throughout the country. If those organizations can't accommodate the need, they should be able to refer the caller to other resources. At the very least, the phone number to keep on hand is 1-800-799-SAFE (7233). This is the number of the National Domestic Violence Hotline, a national twenty-four-hour hotline that provides immediate response, offering referrals as well as support.[33]

PART FOUR

Aftermath

11

Life Goes On

T HE WOMEN I INTERVIEWED were universally positive about my project. "I think what you're doing is important," one woman told me during our initial phone contact. "If I can make a difference, I'd really like to," said another. In fact, every participant in my study told me that although she had long kept her abusive marriage shrouded in secrecy, she was now willing to share her story in the hope it would help others. Some of these women also expressed a desire for retribution. "He shouldn't get away with this," one told me. "Maybe this will let other women find out about creeps like him" and "I hope he can be exposed for the world to see" were among the denunciations I heard during the prescreening phase of the study. After finishing my research and writing, I followed up with many of these women to learn how their worlds and lives had evolved since our initial meeting.

ALL THE KING'S HORSES

What happens to the woman after she gets off the path? Can her splintered sense of self, the remnants of her identity, be put back together again? Certainly, a battered woman who has escaped is much changed by the experience of seeking help and empowering herself to recognize that nobody deserves to be abused. Some of the domestic violence movement's strongest supporters are survivors themselves.[1] They learned firsthand about the inherent dangers of staying and about the way out. Yet despite the bitterness that some women are left with, most of the women I have studied have improved their lives. The majority have divorced, some have remarried, and a few stayed in their marriages, having taken successful steps to stop the abuse. But they have all moved on. As Judith Herman writes: "Having come to terms with the traumatic past, the survivor faces the task of creating a future. She has mourned the old self that the trauma has destroyed; now she must develop a new self . . . develop new relationships. . . . In accomplishing this work, the survivor reclaims her world."[2]

WHERE ARE THEY NOW?

Many women escape their abusers or change their lives and go forward stronger, smarter, and more self-protective. Their scars, physical and emotional, remain an important part of who they are, although they aren't necessarily held back by them. I reinterviewed the participants in my study from three months to five years after our initial contact. The women who remarried told me their new husbands are dramatically different from their previous spouses. Although they describe their current husbands in glowing terms, it is sad that the traits they *so* treasure in their new partners—kindness, respect, safety, trust, honesty, and flexibility—are qualities that every women should expect from a mate.

Sally's divorce became final, but her physical injuries remain. Her adult children are doing well and are close to her. She has little contact with Ray. Her growing success in a new public relations career has slowly helped her rebuild self-confidence. She is dating again and marvels at how wonderful sex is with her current lover. She nurtures relationships with close girlfriends whom she claims are invaluable and continues to give lovely dinner parties, but without the old tension and fear. Still, she feels sad much of the time and is in psychotherapy, mourning the youth she believes she squandered in a violent marriage. "I can never get back what was taken from me," she told me sadly.

Some of the women who divorced had great difficulty disentangling themselves from their husbands. Allison moved in with her parents who live in a different state. This led to an extremely difficult visitation schedule and an arduous custody battle that went on for four years. She received valuable support from a local domestic violence shelter where she participated in an ongoing woman's group. Despite her having to go on welfare for a short time to help with daily expenses and the costly struggle of keeping up with the often frivolous battles that Robert's legal counsel waged (with money provided by Robert's family), Allison and her steadfast attorney won not only sole custody of her child but also the right to live out of state from her husband.

Allison recently found a good job as a staff writer at a major magazine and also continues to freelance. Her peers have recognized her talent, and she is starting to feel good about herself again. She has moved into her own apartment with her child and has recently returned to the world of dating—with her "eyes wide open for early warning signs" as she assesses the qualities of new suitors. With the seemingly interminable custody and divorce wars finally behind her, Allison is now happy with her life, but she is still trying to understand how she ever became involved with Robert in the first place.

As soon as Jacqueline filed for divorce, Brian engaged in excessive behavioral outbursts. He called me, demanding to know why she was leaving him; he called her in an intoxicated state many times and showed up drunk, pounding on her door in the middle of the night. He finally returned the signed divorce papers, but they were wrinkled and torn, perhaps an artistic gesture symbolizing what her filing had done to their union. His explosions frightened her, and she was prepared to file an order of protection if they continued or if she felt her personal safety threatened. My women's psychotherapy group was a source of external support as she recognized she was on the path and could leave it.

"I've gotten much stronger," she said. "I look back and wonder how I tolerated Brian for so long. My life is much better now, even if it's less comfortable materially. I love my little studio apartment—it is all mine." Although she has not yet started dating, she tells the group that she feels like she is "dating herself" and says she really enjoys the company!

Irene finally completed her arduous divorce, relying on her attorney's skills to carry her through. Carl used devious legal tactics against her in order to protect his assets, but in the end her attorney prevailed and she received a nice settlement. Unfortunately, Irene has since been diagnosed with breast cancer, and these days she focuses most of her energy on her health. Even before her illness, however, she often felt depressed, relying on her family for emotional support. She still feels shocked at the dissolution of her marriage, which had begun as a high school romance. "After the public humiliation, I came home and thought to myself, 'My God! Why did you think this man had an *ounce* of love for you? I would never do that to anyone.' Looking back on it, I would have liked myself a lot better if I had gone through with the divorce when the abuse first started," she admitted.

After leaving her husband, Sherry, the thirty-four-year-old attorney, pursued criminal and civil action against him for breaking her wrist. But because of his business connections and family fortune, the lawyers on both sides seemed to act in ways that were beneficial to him. She wondered whether he used his vast wealth to pay off her attorneys and his family's power and social prominence to sway the judge. In fact, in a bitter twist, her civil attorneys obtained minimal funds for her from her husband's homeowner's insurance (the final act of violence occurred at his ranch) but did not collect their legal fees from her well-heeled spouse. They applied the meager insurance settlement toward their legal bill and in the end presented her with a bill for the balance! She negotiated for them to waive the remaining fees but left the experience feeling understandably bitter.

In retrospect, Sherry felt that she had gone up against the "good old boy" network and lost. It gave her a firsthand lesson in the type of lawyer she didn't want to be. Her divorce is still pending, but she has no contact with her husband. She spent several years in individual therapy and then turned her healing efforts toward *pro bono* work with domestic violence survivors. She is currently in a relationship she believes has serious potential. Her new partner is a psychologist, and she ironically notes that he never demands that she "weigh in." They work out together, and he admires her body.

Bailey, too, experienced a difficult divorce. Peter was stunned when she summoned up the gumption to leave him. At first he was frightened, but then, like the injured narcissist he is, he became angry and tried to retaliate. Bailey's recovery included a drawn-out, publicly hostile divorce. Despite Peter's entitled behavior in the courts (he appealed every judgment that awarded her alimony and was determined to win his case, no matter how much it cost either of them in legal fees), Bailey prevailed. This triumph reaffirmed her sense of justice.

Bailey remains in advertising and found renewed success as an executive in a major New York firm. She recently married Ted, a gentle and intelligent man who owns an art gallery in the suburbs. Ted's annual income is about $100,000, considerably less than Bailey's. Although she had always believed that she needed to marry someone who earned at least as much as she did, she told me, "I'm happy now. I've found peace in my life I've never known." Although she lost the chauffeur, the staff, and the large entourage, she has not suffered materially. She owns a beautiful house in the country and a stylish condo in Manhattan. Peter continues to work in advertising, but at a smaller firm. Bailey has heard through the grapevine that his volatile and vitriolic behavior at work and in romance has not abated.

Ingrid also remarried and describes herself as content. Her new husband is a businessman, and she reports that he is "a joy to live with." They negotiate everything; he is kind and reasonable. She still stays close to the women who supported her while she struggled to free herself from her abusive husband, but for the most part she has put that chapter behind her. "I did without a lot for those three years before I remarried," she told me. "I didn't have everything I wanted. Jeffrey did, because I didn't want him to think anything had changed. But when I got up in the morning and had that peace of mind . . . that was the greatest gift I could have given myself. It was better than any vacation, any beach, any shopping spree I'd ever been on. I had no fear. I did it on my own and I felt good. Everyday I wake up and say, 'Thank you, God.'" Ingrid still has some contact with Bill regarding their son, and they are amicable if distant. She is planning to become pregnant with her new mate.

Kathleen has also remarried and lives comfortably although not as affluently as before. She remains on good terms with her ex-husband; their custody arrangement has worked well, providing consistency and safety for their children. Stuart continues his extravagant partying lifestyle, jumping in and out of relationships, but he no longer directs his rage at Kathleen. He has found new victims who seem willing to put up with it. She works as a physical therapist but also volunteers at a domestic violence shelter where she co-leads a group for abused women. "I remember all too clearly my desperate loneliness when I left Stuart, and how others helped me during that time," she told me. "My involvement at the shelter makes me feel I'm giving back."

Julia was among the women who opted to stay married. She and Marc resolved to change the tenor of their marriage when they decided to move back to Germany, Marc's birthplace. He was offered a chair at a renowned school and asked her to make this move for the sake of his career as well as the opportunity for them to begin anew. After much reflection, Julia decided to try one last time, but only if Marc agreed to counseling for his angry and violent outbursts. Hoping to save the relationship with his children as well as his marriage, Marc consented. The renewed closeness with his parents and siblings also seemed to have a mediating effect.

At the same time Julia became more assertive, the result of individual counseling and her participation in a women's group. She continues to paint and is preparing for another one-woman show in Europe. Her children went to therapy for a time to help them adjust to the move and to the violence they had witnessed between their parents. Although Julia reports that her marriage is better than it had ever been, she also believes she has the strength to leave Marc if he were to revert to abusiveness.

Rhonda participated in psychotherapy for only a few months but experienced profound shifts. In recognizing that the problem was neither hers nor a reflection on her, she became significantly more assertive with Andrew. She told herself she could make it on her own, but for the moment she wanted to fall in love with her husband again and open the channels of communication between them. When she voiced her concerns, Andrew was shaken by her perceptions of him. She urged him to participate in a men's counseling group sponsored by their local church, and surprisingly he agreed. He has been "on good behavior" so far, and she feels guardedly optimistic. She continues periodically with her psychotherapy and may join a woman's group in the future. "I'm committed to speaking up," she told me. "I'm never going to feel cowed by my husband's moods again." Rhonda believes that Andrew is devoted to their family, but she is willing to confront him should he become abusive again. Although she asserted, "If he ever hits me, I'll leave him," she is convinced that he won't hurt her anymore.

WOMAN TO WOMAN

The best advice often comes from sad experience. I asked my interviewees to reflect on their experiences and what they'd learned. I asked them, "What would you tell a woman in your situation, or what do you wish someone had told you?" They responded with heartfelt candor:

Allison advised, "Trust your intuition and stop rationalizing so much. Abusive people need to be told they're wrong. Whether or not society condones it, abuse isn't normal. Women need to be more aware of the subtle cues about what is and isn't abuse. If something seems wrong or hurtful, don't ignore it. *Examine* it, pay attention to it. Very seldom do these things get better, especially if your husband doesn't want to change. There's a whole round of verbal abuse, but if he hits you, if it gets physical, you have to leave. I tolerated and rationalized far too much. I did that partly because we were so educated and affluent, and Robert and his family were so charming and refined. Somewhere much earlier along the line he should have been told to stop. The fact that society tolerates this and condones it and sometimes attributes it to 'communication problems' is not right."

Kathleen emphasized the importance of leaving the marriage. "Don't let the money and status keep you in an abusive situation," she said. "Abuse may be more hidden because you have money. You can stay at a hotel instead of a shelter and hush it up. Even if friends and family disdain you for 'coming out' about it, you must take care of yourself. I know that I lost the 'magic kingdom' and security when I left, but I have rediscovered my serenity and inner sense of safety. No money or power can replace that. I would encourage every woman to get help. Go to a support group. When you see people that look a lot like you going through the same situation, it is very heartening.

"*Talk*," she urged. "Talk to other people, talk to therapists, talk to the girl who works next to you so that you understand what you're living through isn't *normal*. You need to see that this isn't going on in everyone's marriage. There's a certain way husbands and wives should treat each other. In our women's group we talk about exactly what happened. How did it start? What did he say? What did you say? You get it out so you can hear that what the person is doing isn't normal."

Sally reflected on her doubts about her ability to be self-sufficient. "Looking back now, I see I probably could have made it, and it would have been better for my children if I'd left Ray. I would have survived it. At that point I couldn't function; I was depressed. Sometimes it was difficult for me to get out of bed in the morning. I would have an anxious feeling, not knowing what the day would bring. But women today are in a much better position. They can make a living. They're better educated. They can earn as much as a man and provide security for their children without a man. I don't think a male is even necessary. I was brought up and lived through an era when you felt the man was the major factor in raising a child and having a home. But the world is different today. I certainly wouldn't want to see my daughter go through this. Certainly not."

Ingrid cautioned others to think carefully before they get involved with someone. "Read the signs and obey your gut before you get into the relationship," she warned. "Don't try to gloss over your husband's behavior or look through rose-colored glasses. You have to see the signs, however little they are. I'm married for the second time. My life is totally different now. The feelings I have for the man I'm with, the way he treats me, the amount of respect he shows me, the tone of voice he uses . . . it's totally different. A woman who feels she needs the lifestyle—she should know that she can do it on her own. That's really the key. Maybe she can't make that kind of money by herself. But it doesn't matter; it's not important. What counts is having peace of mind for herself and her kids. I wake up every morning and thank God I have that now."

Bailey was the most articulate. "When you are in these relationships," she explained, "you believe that you will lose everything. Why? Because you've lost your sense of self. So you worry, and you never really imagine what your life will be like afterward. You just think it will be bleak. But in fact, my life ended up well. I still have a more-than-comfortable home in the country, an apartment in the city, vacations, cars—maybe none of the ultra-luxury I had before, but still a rather privileged existence—on *my own* salary! I couldn't see it when it seemed so hard to get out of the marriage; I thought I was going to have to give up everything.

"My advice to others is, first trust your gut! If it doesn't feel good, something is wrong. If you can't tell even your sister about your unhappiness, you are in the wrong marriage. (In my case, the isolation was so complete, I just pretended about the kind of life I was living.) Make mini-escapes. These are important. I rented another house ten miles from where we lived, just in case he had an eruption. He didn't know I did this, and I used it only a few times. But just knowing it was there was a relief. I would sometimes go there overnight but tell Peter I was traveling on business. I would be alone and give myself a breather from the pain and tension of the marriage. I really wouldn't do anything there—but at least I had no fear. My time at the house allowed me to see life differently for a few hours. If your husband can't reach you, there is a window of calm, and you can feel how bad it is to go back to him. You start remembering who you are. Many abusive husbands take away who you are. I used to have a wonderful sense of humor. I lost that—I forgot I was funny. So I guess the last thing I would advise others—and I think this is most important: Find yourself again, whatever it takes."

WHAT IS NEEDED

Prevention is often the first line of defense against any illness or problem. How do we prevent domestic abuse, especially with a population that keeps its dangerous secrets behind closed doors?

Change must begin on an individual level. This requires education. If upscale women are more aware that such a problem exists among them, they will better recognize the early warning signs that indicate future abuse in their relationship. Perhaps educational efforts should begin with both genders at the grade school level. At a young age and with the help of national educational and advertising campaigns, boys and young men can learn that it is not "cool" to beat, bully, and belittle their women. And women can learn how to spot potential warning signs and heed their inner voices before they become enmeshed in a damaging relationship.

Helping professionals in the medical, psychological, and legal fields must also be educated. If we professionals accept that domestic abuse occurs among the highly educated and well-to-do, if we can adopt the term *upscale violence* and make it part of our lexicon, that will lend legitimacy to the experience of the women who endure it. If you can name an experience, you are in a better position to recognize it. And perhaps, if the helping professions legitimize the phenomenon of upscale domestic violence, more women will break their isolation, go public, and get help. This would change the rate and frequency with which these women report domestic violence and give us a better sense of its true incidence.

An even more daunting challenge is posed by the changes that need to be made in society more broadly. Upscale abused women cannot be marginalized by their own efforts to maintain secrecy or society's compliance in denying that the problem exists. Shelters and hotlines should be sensitized to their particular issues, and perhaps centers geared to this population should be established.[3] Psychiatric and medical professionals must become aware that upscale violence exists.[4] Moreover, police in upscale neighborhoods need training specific to treating calls from this population. I can still hear the excerpt from Nicole Brown Simpson's 911 call replayed so often during the trial. Her voice was no less frightened, no less distraught, than that of a woman of lesser means. The post-beating pictures she had secured in her safe deposit box were no more glamorous than the post-attack photos of any battered wife.

Society must support women in exposing their dangerous secrets. The notion that "silence is violence" takes on a whole new meaning for the upscale: their silence keeps them bound on the path of abuse. We must be clear that it does happen "to people like us." Although you believe you know a couple well, the face they show in public may be very different from the private hell they live at home.

EPILOGUE

I hope that this work opens doors for highly educated and upper-income battered women who have been prisoners in their pampered communities, that it helps society take a new look at the scope of battering and how it affects "people like us," and that it encourages these women to step forward and step off the path.

I hope that this work has made you a bit uncomfortable—the beginning of a paradigm shift. The familiar models no longer apply. Most important, I hope this work helps women understand their own role in staying on the path. By examining the choices they made we intend neither to condemn nor to blame them, but to show them how to escape. Choice is a liberating possibility that gives them a new direction, new hope, new options.

I remember a metal sculpture I once saw at a craft fair. So much was said in so little with this piece. It was a small birdcage. Inside, a female figure leaned against the bars. She was tormented, looking out at the freedom that lay just beyond her reach. But the direction the figure was gazing in was the unfortunate choice—because the door to this little prison, which was directly behind the stick figure, was wide open.

So it is for the upscale abused wife. All she needs is to turn her thinking around to see that there are ways out, that her choices are making a difference, that the direction in which she is looking is often what determines her fate. It empowers her as a future survivor. Yes, societal support and a new lens are needed—but that can only happen as these women step forward and begin to find their voices in the population of abused women, voices that are heard and taken just as seriously as any others. Their pain is no less real, their fears no less valid.

I hope this work beckons to these women, like the song from the old children's game: "Come out, come out, wherever you are . . ." You are not alone.

APPENDIX A

FIGURE A.1   Comparison of Participants' Marital and Postmarital Household Incomes

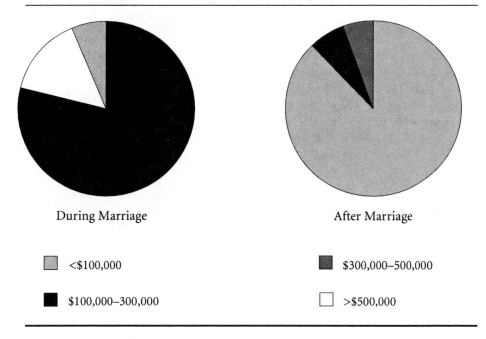

During Marriage

After Marriage

<$100,000

$100,000–300,000

$300,000–500,000

>$500,000

TABLE A.1 Comparison of Participants' Marital and Postmarital Ranked Neighborhoods of Residence

Name of Participant[a]	Marital Neighborhood of Residence[b]	Postmarital Neighborhood of Residence[b]
Allison	5,[c] 146, 23, 245, 274	Out of State
Carol D.	78, 66	9
Ellen	4	4
Ida J.	112	84
Ingrid	50	50
Irene	94, 103, 66	66
Karen L.	58	155
Kathleen	4	4
Molly N.	5, 1462	23, 245
Lynne	58	58
Sally	66	66
Ursula V.	9, 168	9, 168
Winnie X.	9, 168, 23, 245, 27	30
Paula	3	3
Mean	74	72

Source: Based on median household income as determined from 1990 Census data as reported by the Northeastern Illinois Planning Commission.

[a]All names are fictitious. Names given to participants who appear in this book are in italics. Names assigned to other participants in the study are not italicized.

[b]As per 1990 Census data, ranking 77 metropolitan area and 263 suburban neighborhoods from 1 to 340 according to median household income, with 1 being the highest rank and 340 being the lowest.

[c]Numbers in bold italics represent neighborhood rank solely among the 77 metropolitan area neighborhoods. All other numbers represent merged Census rankings among the 77 metropolitan area and 263 suburban neighborhoods. (Total # = 340.) A comma indicates that the participant moved to a new neighborhood.

APPENDIX B

Are You an Abused Woman?

Typical Somatic Symptoms and Complaints

- Appetite disturbance—loss of appetite or overeating
- Asthma
- Chest, back, pelvic pain
- Choking sensation
- Chronic pain
- Digestive problems
- Fatigue
- Gastrointestinal upset
- Headaches
- Hyperventilation
- Injuries, bruises
- Insomnia
- Nightmares, often violent
- Premature aging

Typical Emotional Symptoms and Complaints

- Agitation
- Anxiety
- Depression or symptoms of depression
- Despairing
- Doubts of your sanity; self-doubt
- Drug or alcohol use or abuse; possibly overdose; other addictive behaviors
- Dysphoria
- Embarrassment
- Evasiveness
- Experiences the man as omnipotent
- Extreme emotional reactivity
- Fearfulness—feeling frightened or in constant state of terror
- Feeling like you deserve the abuse
- Feeling out of control
- Feeling worthless
- Feelings of loss and grief
- Frequent crying
- Guilt
- Homicidal ideation
- "Hooked on hope"
- Hopelessness
- Humiliation
- "If only" thoughts
- Inability to relax
- Isolation, feelings of being isolated
- Jumpiness
- Lack of energy
- Learned helplessness
- Loneliness
- Low self-esteem
- Nervousness
- Often accompanied by male partner
- Passive
- Post-traumatic stress disorder (PTSD) symptoms
- Powerlessness
- Self-blaming
- Shame
- Shyness
- Suicidal ideation; suicide attempts
- Warm memories are now cold

Other Characteristics

- You are actively engaged in changing your life
- You assess your reality continuously and make choices
- You are brave.
- You are capable, creative, intelligent, and resourceful.
- You have a high tolerance for cognitive dissonance.

- You have learned not to ask for help "because it is a waste of time."
- You have learned to be realistic.
- You can be manipulative.
- You are persevering.
- You are self-sufficient.
- You are capable of surmounting highly unfavorable conditions.

Traits Unique to the Upscale Abused Woman

Themes in Courtship and Marriage

- You had Cinderella-type beliefs about love and marriage.
- You felt a power imbalance but more sure of yourself—"raised a rung"—when you were with him.
- He made you feel intimidated or inferior.
- It felt like magic being with him; you were "transported," swept off your feet.
- You were impressed by his charisma and personality style.
- You were impressed with his socioeconomic standing and money.
- You were impressed with his prestige and power.
- He pursued you.

- There was little or no history of abuse in your family of origin or previous relationships.
- You had money concerns or came from a lower-income family.
- He rushed you into making a commitment.
- You idealized him.
- For some he was their first sexual encounter.
- You were susceptible because you were going through a major life event or change prior to meeting him.
- You were susceptible because you were lonely and alone prior to meeting him.
- You ignored or justified the early warning signs that he would be capable of abuse.

Coping Strategies

- Belief in the myth that "this doesn't happen to people like us"
- Denial
- Drug or alcohol use
- Embarrassment and shame over being seen as a failure, leading to further isolation ("I made my bed so . . .")
- Idealization of the situation
- Isolation and secret keeping
- Justification by explanation

- Keeping quiet; "playing possum"
- Avoiding discussion with him over issues, outbursts, problems
- Narrative construction that allows for abuse
- Secret strategizing
- Self-blame
- Vigilant watching; scanning to predict
- Wanting to believe; maintaining hope against hope

APPENDIX C

Traits of an Abusive Man

Typical History

- He fears abandonment.
- He felt insufficiently loved as a child.
- He has had few good experiences with women.
- He has a history of battering.
- He may have been abused as a child.
- He may have witnessed abusive, violent behavior between his parents as a child.

Typical Psychological and Personality Profile

- Charismatic, charming, and seductive
- Difficulty with anger management (although sometimes he manages his anger quite well outside the house)
- Employment problems
- Entitlement—may show narcissistic entitlement
- Feels oppressed by life's circumstances
- Financial problems
- Hypersensitive to real or perceived criticism
- Impulsive
- Intimacy problems; jealous, possessive
- Jeckyll-Hyde personality
- Lacks feelings of guilt or shame
- Low frustration tolerance
- Low self-esteem
- Male supremacist attitudes—imposes strict domestic roles and refuses to help out with child-rearing tasks
- Manipulative
- Minimizes or denies the abuse—some never apologize
- Misogynistic—hates women
- Narcissistic personality or borderline personality or traits
- Negative self-image
- Patriarchal beliefs—including domestic role structures
- Unpredictable; patterns can be impossible to discern

Other Behavioral or Interpersonal Characteristics

- Blames spouse; accepts little responsibility for his own behavior
- Controlling behavior (which may seem like concern at first)
- Cruel to animals or children
- Dependent on the relationship, sometimes excessively
- Destroys objects, including his partner's personal (treasured) possessions
- Drug or alcohol use, gambling, or other addictive behaviors

- Emotionally and physically abusive
- Feels harassed and frustrated by spouse, family, job
- Humiliates his partner in all arenas of her life
- Isolates her from friends and family
- Intense courtship; often living together within first three months of meeting
- Intrusive
- Makes continuous demands on his partner
- Possessive; dictates his partner's clothing style or behavior toward other men
- Presents good side to win an argument or sway others' opinions of him
- Presents good side to win allegiance of others who may be intervening
- Promotes his partner's dependency
- Refuses to perform domestic duties

- Relentless—overkill is common
- Selfish, self-absorbed
- Shifting sands or gaslighting
- Threatens violence or murder
- Thoughtless, selfish sexual partner
- Turns tables (another way to blame spouse)
- Unable to provide nurturing support to his partner and children
- Unfaithful
- Unrealistic expectations
- Uses force during arguments
- Uses rape or "playful" force in sexual relations
- Verbally and psychologically abusive
- Views violence as a problem-solver/ tension release and a way to get what he wants

Traits Unique to the Upscale Abusive Male

- There is no honeymoon phase after a violent episode or an emotionally abusive tirade (or short-lived post-abuse "honeymoon"); he refuses to apologize, even after brutal attacks.
- He is arrogant, a trait fostered by society's response to his standing and accomplishments.
- He believes that he is "special" and should associate only with other special or high-status people (or institutions), the only ones who understand him.
- He blames his wife for any household mishap, whatever the cause.
- He creates shifting sands—constant, conflicting, and contradictory shifts in expectations.
- Narcissistic rage is his reaction to real or perceived slights and injuries.
- He feels impunity regarding his behavior and mood swings.
- He has a grandiose sense of self-importance and a sense of entitlement (unreasonable expectations of especially favorable treatment or automatic compliance with his wishes).
- He has fantasies about his achievements: unlimited success, power, brilliance, beauty, or ideal love.
- An important, successful, and well-educated figure, he is admired in his community and profession and is often well liked.
- He is interested only in his own sexual gratification and disregards his wife's needs. Some men feel entitled to engage in multiple extramarital affairs.
- He is charming but interpersonally exploitative (takes advantage of others to achieve his own ends).
- He often envies others or believes that others are envious of him.
- He is self-absorbed and lacks empathy for others–that is, he is unwilling to recognize or identify with the feelings and needs of others. He sees significant others as an extension of his self; his partner is there to meet his needs, and he expects her to respond perfectly.

- His demands about how his wife should look or behave are not necessarily clear, discrete, or consistent.
- He makes demeaning attacks on his wife's femininity, sexuality, appearance, and maternal behavior.
- His demands and expectations of others are unrealistic.
- He needs to be in control of others in every situation.
- He requires excessive admiration and recognition.
- He is terrified of not being respected by others.
- He turns the tables and blames his wife for his behavior.
- He uses his money and power as leverage or threat and to win legal battles, pursue frivolous and meritless lawsuits, and wage vicious custody struggles.
- He reacts violently to his wife's pregnancies and believes that the child is an interloper.

APPENDIX D

Early Warning Signs

- The man dominates the woman verbally, criticizing and belittling her, throwing her off balance, or causing her to doubt her own worth and abilities.
- He makes all plans, neither inquiring about her desires nor gathering input from her.
- He alone sets the sexual pace, initiating all contacts and rejecting any of her sexual approaches.
- He makes most of the decisions about the future and announces them to her instead of including her in planning and decisionmaking. He refuses to compromise or negotiate on major decisions.
- He is moody, making it difficult for her to predict what the next encounter with him will be like.
- He is chronically late without apology or remorse.
- He determines when they can discuss issues, if at all; he repeatedly justifies this control by claiming that he "hates conflict."
- He is hostile toward others as well as her; typical behaviors are unjustified rage, ar-

rogance, controlling behavior, pouting and withdrawal of affection, and sudden coldness and rejection.
- His father was abusive to his own wife.
- He demands control over his partner's contacts with friends and family and her finances.
- He publicly humiliates her, sometimes starting with "put-down" humor; rather than apologizing when she protests, he urges her to "get a thicker skin!" or "lighten up!"
- He slaps, pushes, or hits her.
- He exhibits rage, arrogance, pouting, or withdrawal if not given his way.
- He is suddenly cold or rejecting.
- His temper seems uncontrolled, and he manifests unprecipitated anger at others.
- He is highly critical of his partner.
- He makes comments meant to make the woman feel unsure of herself.
- He is verbally domineering.
- He flaunts his relationships other women.

APPENDIX E

Domestic Violence Resources

National Domestic Violence Hotline
1-800-799-SAFE (1-800-799-7233)

State Organizations

Alabama Coalition Against Domestic
    Violence
P.O. Box 4762
Montgomery, AL 36101
Phone: 334–832–4842
Fax: 334–832–4803

Alaska Network on Domestic Violence
    and Sexual Assault
130 Seward St., Room 209
Juneau, AK 99801
Phone: 907–586–3650
Fax: 907–463–4493

Arizona Coalition Against Domestic
    Violence
100 West Camelback Rd., Suite 109
Phoenix, AZ 85013
Phone: 602–279–2900
Fax: 602–279–2980
E-mail: acadv@goodnet.com

Arkansas Coalition Against
    Domestic Violence
1 Sheriff Lane, Suite C
North Little Rock, AR 72114
Phone: 501–812–0571
Fax: 501–812–0578
E-mail: ssigmon@arkansas.net

Coalition to End Domestic
    and Sexual Violence
2064 Eastman Ave., Suite 104
Ventura, CA 93003
Phone: 805–654–8141
Fax: 805–654–1264
24-hour hotline: 805–656–1111
Spanish hotline: 800–300–2181
TDD: 805–656–4439

California Alliance Against
    Domestic Violence
926 J St., Suite 1000
Sacramento, CA 95814
Phone: 916–444–7163
Fax: 916–444–7165

Statewide California Coalition
    for Battered Women
818–787–0072

Colorado Coalition Against Domestic
    Violence
P.O. Box 18902
Denver, CO 80218
Phone: 303–831–9632, 888–778–7091
Fax: 303–832–7067
E-mail: ccadv@ix.netcom.com

Connecticut Coalition Against Domestic
  Violence
100 Pitkin St.
East Hartford, CT 06108
Phone: 860–282–7899
Fax: 860–282–7892

DC Coalition Against Domestic Violence
513 U St. NW
Washington, DC 20001
Phone: 202–783–5332
Fax: 202–387–5684

My Sister's Place
P.O. Box 29596
Washington, DC 20017
24-hour hotline: 202–529–5991
Administrative office: 202–529–5261

Delaware Coalition Against Domestic
  Violence
P.O. Box 847
Wilmington, DE 19899
Phone: 302–658–2958
Fax: 302–658–5049

Hotlines by county:

24-hour bilingual line: 888-LAC-C571
  (888–522–2571)
New Castle: 302–762–6110
Kent and Sussex: 302–422–8058

Florida Coalition Against
  Domestic Violence
308 East Park Ave.
Tallahassee, FL 32301
Phone: 850–425–2749, 800–500–1119
Fax: 850–425–3091

Georgia Advocates for Battered
  Women and Children
250 Georgia Ave. SE, Suite 308
Atlanta, GA 30312
Phone: 404–524–3847, 800–643–1212
Fax: 404–524–5959

Georgia Coalition on Family Violence, Inc.
1827 Powers Ferry Road
Building 3, Suite 325
Atlanta, GA 30339
Phone: 770–984–0085
Fax: 770–984–0068

Hawaii State Coalition Against Domestic
  Violence
98–939 Moanalua Rd.
Aiea, HI 96701–5012
Phone: 808–486–5072
Fax: 808–486–5169

Idaho Coalition Against Sexual and
  Domestic Violence
815 Park Blvd., Suite 140
Boise, ID 83712
Phone: 208–384–0419, 888–293–6118
Fax: 208–331–0687
E-mail: domvio@micron.net

Illinois Coalition Against Domestic Violence
801 S. 11th St.
Springfield, IL 62703
Phone: 217–789–2830, 800–677–2830
Fax: 217–789–1939
E-mail: ilcadv@springnet1.com

Chicago Mayor's Office
  Domestic Violence Hotline
877–863–6338

Friends of Battered Women
  and Their Children
P.O. Box 5185
Evanston, IL 60204
Phone: 773–274–5232
Fax: 773–274–2214
Hotline: 800–603–HELP
E-mail: info@afriendsplace.org

Indiana Coalition Against
  Domestic Violence
2511 E. 46th St., Suite N-3
Indianapolis, IN 46205
Phone: 317–543–3908, 800–332–7385
Fax: 317–377–7050

Iowa Coalition Against Domestic Violence
2603 Bell Ave., Suite 100
Des Moines, IA 50321
Phone: 515–244–8028, 800–942–0333
Fax: 515–244–7417

Kansas Coalition Against Domestic Violence
220 S.W. 33rd St.
Topeka, KS 66611
Phone: 785–232–9784
Fax: 785–232–1874
Statewide hotline: 888-END-ABUSE

Kentucky Domestic Violence Association
P.O. Box 356
Frankfort, KY 40602
Phone: 502–695–2444
Fax: 502–695–2488

Louisiana Coalition Against
  Domestic Violence
P.O. Box 77308
Baton Rouge, LA 70879–7308
Phone: 225–752–1296
Fax: 225–751–8927

Maine Coalition to End Domestic Violence
170 Park St.
Bangor, ME 04401
Phone: 207–941–1194
Fax: 207–941–2327

Maryland Network Against
  Domestic Violence
6911 Laurel Bowie Rd., Suite 309
Bowie, MD 20715
Phone: 301–352–4574, 800-MD-HELPS
Fax: 301–809–0422

Jane Doe Inc./Massachusetts
  Coalition Against Sexual Assault
  and Domestic Violence
14 Beacon St., Suite 507
Boston, MA 02108
Phone: 617–248–0922
Fax: 617–248–0902

Michigan Coalition Against
  Domestic and Sexual Violence
3893 Okemos Road, Suite B-2
Okemos, MI 48864
Phone: 517–347–7000
Fax: 517–347–1377

Minnesota Coalition for
  Battered Women
1821 University Ave. W., Suite S-112
St. Paul, MN 55104
Metro area hotline: 651–646–0994
Phone: 651–646–6177
Fax: 651–646–1527
E-mail: mcbw@pclink.com

Mississippi Coalition
  Against Domestic Violence
P.O. Box 4703
Jackson, MS 39296–4703
Phone: 601–981–9196, 800–898–3234
Fax: 601–981–2501
E-mail: mcadv@misnet.com

Missouri Coalition Against
  Domestic Violence
415 E. McCarty St.
Jefferson City, MO 65101
Phone: 573–634–4161
Fax: 573–636–3728

Women's Support and
  Community Services
2838 Olive St.
St. Louis, MO 63103
Hotline: 314–531–2003
Office: 314–531–9100

Montana Coalition Against
    Domestic and Sexual Violence
P.O. Box 633
Helena, MT 59624
Phone: 406–443–7794
Fax: 406–443–7818

Nebraska Domestic Violence
    and Sexual Assault Coalition
825 M St., Suite 404
Lincoln, NE 68508–2253
Phone: 402–476–6256, 800–876–6238
Fax: 402–476–6806

Nevada Network Against Domestic Violence
100 W. Grove, Suite 315
Reno, NV 89509
Phone: 775–828–1115, 800–500–1556
Fax: 775–828–9991

SAFE House
18 Sunrise Dr., Suite G-70
Henderson, NV 89014
Phone: 702–451–4203
Fax: 702–451–4302
E-mail: safe@intermind.net

New Hampshire Coalition Against
    Domestic and Sexual Violence
P.O. Box 353
Concord, NH 03302–0353
Helpline: 603–225–9000 (outside of New
    Hampshire)
Phone: 603–224–8893, 800–852–3388 (in
    New Hampshire)
Fax: 603–228–6096

New Jersey Coalition for Battered Women
2620 Whitehorse/Hamilton Square Rd.
Trenton, NJ 08690
For battered lesbians: 800–224–0211
    (in New Jersey only)
Phone: 609–584–8107
Fax: 609–584–9750
TTY: 609–584–0027 (9:00 A.M.–5:00 P.M.,
    then into message service)

New Mexico State Coalition Against
    Domestic Violence
P.O. Box 25266
Albuquerque, NM 87125
Legal helpline: 800–209-DVLH,
    800–773–3645 (New Mexico only)
Phone: 505–246–9240
Fax: 505–246–9434
E-mail: nmcadv@nmcadv.org

New York State Coalition Against
    Domestic Violence
79 Central Ave.
Albany, NY 12206
Phone: 518–432–4864, 800–942–6906
Fax: 518–463–3155

Victim Services
2 Lafayette St.
New York, NY 10007
Headquarters: 212–577–7700
Fax: 212–385–0331
Hotline: 800–621-HOPE (4673)
    (New York City only)
TDD: 212–233–3456, 800–810–7444

North Carolina Coalition Against
    Domestic Violence
301 W. Main St.
Durham, NC 27701
Phone: 919–956–9124
Fax: 919–682–1449

North Dakota Council on
    Abused Women's Services
State Networking Office
418 E. Rosser Ave., Suite 320
Bismarck, ND 58501
Phone: 701–255–6240, 800–472–2911
    (North Dakota only)
Fax: 701–255–1904

Ohio Domestic Violence Network
4041 N. High St., Suite 400
Columbus, OH 43214
Phone: 614–784–0023, 800–934–9840
Fax: 614–784–0033

Action Ohio Coalition for Battered Women
614–221–1255

Oklahoma Coalition Against
   Domestic Violence and Sexual Assault
2525 NW Expressway, Suite 208
Oklahoma City, OK 73116
Phone: 405–848–1815, 800–522–9054
Fax: 405–848–3469

Oregon Coalition Against Domestic
   and Sexual Violence
659 Cottage St. N.E.
Salem, OR 97301
Phone: 503–365–9644, 800–622–3782
Fax: 503–556–7870

Pennsylvania Coalition Against
   Domestic Violence/National
   Resource Center on Domestic Violence
6440 Flank Dr., Suite 1300
Harrisburg, PA 17112–2778
Phone: 717–545–6400, 800–932–4632
Fax: 717–545–9456

Laurel House
P.O. Box 764
Norristown, PA 19404
Phone: 800–642–3150
Hotline: 800–642–3150
Fax: 610–275–4018
E-mail: LaurelHaus@aol.com

Comisión para los Asuntos
   de la Mujer (Puerto Rico)
(Also known as Coordinadora
   para la Paz de la Mujer)
787–722–2907

Rhode Island Coalition Against
   Domestic Violence and Sexual Assault
422 Post Rd., Suite 202
Warwick, RI 02888
Phone: 401–467–9940, 800–494–8100
Fax: 401–467–9943

South Carolina Coalition Against
   Domestic Violence and Sexual Assault
P.O. Box 7776
Columbia, SC 29202–7776
Phone: 803–256–2900, 800–260–9293
Fax: 803–256–1030

South Dakota Coalition Against
   Domestic Violence and Sexual Assault
P.O. Box 141
Pierre, SD 57501
Phone: 605–945–0869, 800–572–9196
Fax: 605–945–0870

South Dakota Network Against
   Family Violence and Sexual Assault
800–430-SAFE
Resource Center of Aberdeen, SD
24-hour crisis line: 605–226–1212,
   888–290–2935

Tennessee Task Force Against
   Domestic Violence
P.O. Box 120972
Nashville, TN 37212
Phone: 615–386–9406, 800–356–6767
Fax: 615–383–2967

Texas Council on Family Violence
P.O. Box 161810
Austin, TX 78716
Phone: 512–794–1133, 800–525–1978
Fax: 512–794–1199

Utah Domestic Violence Advisory Council
120 N. 200 W.
Salt Lake City, UT 84103
Phone: 801–538–9886, 800–897-LINK
Fax: 801–538–3993

Women Helping Battered Women
    (Vermont)
802–658–1996, 800–228–7395

Women's Rape Crisis Center (Vermont)
800–489–7273

Vermont Network Against Domestic
    Violence and Sexual Assault
P.O. Box 405
Montpelier, VT 05601
Phone: 802–223–1302
Fax: 802–223–6943
E-mail: vnadvsa@sover.net

Virginians Against Domestic Violence
2850 Sandy Bay Rd., Suite 101
Williamsburg, VA 23185
Phone: 757–221–0990, 800–838-VADV
Fax: 757–229–1553

Women's Resource Center (Virgin Islands)
809–776–3966

Women's Coalition of
    St. Croix, Virgin Islands
340–773–9272

Washington State Coalition Against
    Domestic Violence
8645 Martin Way N.E., Suite 103
Lacey, WA 98516
Phone: 360–407–0756
Fax: 360–407–0761
TTY: 360–407–0767
E-mail: wscadv@cco.net

Washington State Domestic Violence
    Hotline
Phone: 800–562–6025
E-mail: csn@willapabay.org

West Virginia Coalition Against Domestic
    Violence and Sexual Assault
Elk Office Center
4710 Chimney Dr.
Charleston, WV 25302
Phone: 304–965–3552
Fax: 304–965–3572

Wisconsin Coalition Against
    Domestic Violence
307 S. Paterson St., Suite 1
Madison, WI 53703
Phone: 608–255–0539
Fax: 608–255–3560

Wyoming Coalition Against Domestic
    Violence and Sexual Assault
710 Garfield, #242
P.O. Box 236
Laramie, WY 82073
Phone: 307–755–5481, 800–990–3877
Fax: 307–755–5482

Family Service Centre of Ottawa-Carleton
    (Canada)
119 Ross Ave.
Ottawa, ON K1Y 0N6
Phone: 613–725–3601
Fax: 613–725–5651
TTY: 613–725–3605
E-mail: fscoc@intranet.on.ca (081298)

National Organizations

Battered Women's Justice Project
Minnesota Program Development
4032 Chicago Avenue South
Minneapolis, MN 55407
Phone: 612–824–8768, 800–903–0111, ext. 1
Fax: 612–824–8965

Center for the Prevention of Sexual and
    Domestic Violence
936 N. 34th St., Suite 200
Seattle, WA 98103
Phone: 206–634–1903
Fax: 206–634–0115

Family Violence Prevention Fund
383 Rhode Island St., Suite 304
San Francisco, CA 94103–5133
Phone: 415–252–8900
Fax: 415–252–8991

Health Resource Center on
    Domestic Violence
Family Violence Prevention Fund
383 Rhode Island St., Suite 304
San Francisco, CA 94103–5133
Phone: 800–313–1310
Fax: 415–252–8991

National Battered Women's Law Project
275 7th Ave., Suite 1206
New York, NY 10001
Phone: 212–741–9480
Fax: 212–741–6438

National Coalition Against
    Domestic Violence
Policy Office
P.O. Box 34103
Washington, DC 20043–4103
Phone: 703–765–0339
Fax: 202–628–4899

National Coalition Against
    Domestic Violence
P.O. Box 18749
Denver, CO 80218–0749
Phone: 303–839–1852
Fax: 303–831–9251
Website: www.ncadv.org

National Clearinghouse on
    Marital and Date Rape
2325 Oak St.
Berkeley, CA 94708
510–524–1582

National Network to End Domestic Violence
666 Pennsylvania Ave., S.E.
Suite 303
Washington, DC 20003
Phone: 202–543–5566
Fax: 202–543–5626

National Resource Center on Domestic
    Violence/Pennsylvania Coalition
    Against Domestic Violence
6400 Flank Dr., Suite 1300
Harrisburg, PA 17112
Phone: 800–537–2238
Fax: 717–545–9456

National Training Center on
    Domestic and Sexual Violence
2300 Pasadena Drive
Austin, TX 78757
Phone: (512) 407-9020

Resource Center on Domestic Violence,
    Child Protection, and Custody
    (a resource center for professionals
    and agencies only)
National Council of Juvenile and Family
    Court Judges
P.O. Box 8970
Reno, NV 89507
Phone: 800–527–3223
Fax: 775–784–6160

Other U.S. Organizations

Children's Defense Fund
25 E St. N.W.
Washington, DC 20001
202–628–8787

National Abortion and Reproductive
   Rights Action League
1156 15th St. NW, Suite 700
Washington, DC 20005
Phone: 202–973–3000
Fax: 202–973–3096

National AIDS Network
P.O. Box 13827
Research Triangle Park, NC 27709
National AIDS Hotline: 800–342–2437
TTY: 800–243–7889
Spanish hotline: 800–344–7432

National Coalition for Low-Income Housing
1012 14th St. NW, Suite 1200
Washington, DC 20005
202–662–1530

National Council on Child Abuse and
   Family Violence
1155 Connecticut Ave. NW, Suite 400
Washington, DC 20036
202–429–6695, 800–222–2000

National Helpline National Committee for
   the Prevention of Elder Abuse
c/o Institute on Aging Medical Center of
   Central Massachusetts
119 Belmont St.
Worcester, MA 01605
508–793–6166

National Women's Political Caucus
1275 K St. NW, Suite 750
Washington, DC 20005–4051

WHISPER (Women Hurt in Systems of
   Prostitution Engaged in Revolt)
P.O. Box 56796
St. Paul, MN 55165
612–644–6301

International Organizations

Human Rights Watch, Womenights Project
1522 K St. NW, Suite 910
Washington, DC 20005
202–371–6592

International Women's Rights Action Watch
Humphrey Institute of Public Affairs,
   University of Minnesota
301 19th Ave.
South Minneapolis, MN 55455

United Nations Development
   Fund for Women (UNEFEM)
304 E. 45th St.
New York, NY 10017
212–906–6400

Appendix F
Study Instruments

Demographic Questionnaire

This questionnaire is designed to obtain some basic information about you.
All results are confidential and will remain anonymous.
Please answer the following questions as indicated:

Age: _____

Neighborhood: _____ (during marriage); _____(now)

Ethnic Background: (optional) _____

Marital History:

How long did you know your husband prior to marriage? _____

How long were you married? _____ (actual); _____(legal)

How long were you separated prior to the divorce? _____

Was this a first marriage for you? _____ Second or more?_____

First marriage for your ex-husband?_____ Second or more?_____

Have you remarried since the divorce? _____

How long after? _____ Are you currently still remarried? _____

Educational Level (highest degree held):

Please be specific on the discipline of your degree (e.g., Bachelor in Fine Arts, Master in Business Administration, or Ph.D. in Psychology, etc.) _____

_____

Degrees: _____ (premarriage); _____(during); _____(after)

Husband's Degrees: _____ (premarriage); _____(during); _____(after)

Children:

Number of children (indicate male or female and ages) from marriage:

_____

Number of children (indicate male or female and ages) premarriage:

_____

Number of children (indicate male or female and ages) after marriage:

_____

Yearly Household Income Level (prior to divorce or separation):

(If unsure, estimate category and put a star (*) near your response)

Under $100,000_____ $100,000–300,000_____

$300,000–500,000_____ over $500,000_____

Approximate percentage of income from your earnings:_____

Approximate percentage of income from your spouse's earnings:_____

Approximate percentage of income from other sources
    (e.g., trust funds, dividends, estates, etc.):_____

Current Yearly Household Income Level:

(If unsure, estimate category and put a star (*) near your response)

Under $100,000_____ $100,000–300,000_____

$300,000–500,000_____ over $500,000_____

Approximate percentage of income from your earnings:_____

Approximate percentage of income from your spouse's earnings:_____

Approximate percentage of income from other sources
    (e.g., trust funds, dividends, estates, etc.):_____

Current Employment:

Are you currently employed?_____ If so, how many hours per week?_____

Is it considered full-time, part-time, or something else?_____

Type of work/job title: _____

Do you do volunteer work?_____ If so, how many hours per week?_____

Husband's type of work/job title (during marriage):

_____

Counseling Experience:

"I have never engaged in counseling or psychotherapy services." _____

"I have engaged in counseling or psychotherapy services." _____

When? (dates and duration)_____

Counseling took place:

Before I was married_____ (and/or) after I was married_____

Before the abuse began_____ (and/or) after the abuse began_____

THANK YOU FOR TAKING THE TIME TO ANSWER THIS QUESTIONNAIRE.

Interview Guide (Interview Questions and "Leads")

The interview may be conceptualized as a natural history of abuse, the participant or narrator "telling her story."

1) How did the relationship start?
2) Abuse in a marriage can include physical battering, emotional cruelty, psychological torment, or mental coercion. It can come out in behaviors such as ignoring, withdrawal, berating, humiliation, inducing fear or terror, physical neglect, verbal or physical attacks, beating, damaging of property, and homicide. Can we talk about ways that these forms of abuse apply to your relationship? Can you tell me when the violence started, what triggered it?
3) When did the abuse start? Was there a watershed event, a turning point? How did it happen? When was the first time he hit you? What led up to it? Give examples (background).
4) What did you do? Give examples (detailed chronology and responses).
5) How did the abuse develop? (development of abuse).
6) How did it end? (decisions, turning points, actions taken).
7) Is there anything you would like to tell another woman who is persevering in an abusive marriage? Is there anything you wish someone had told you earlier in your marriage?

NOTES

Chapter 1

1. Although all names and identities have been disguised and altered to protect the anonymity of the women who shared their stories, the stories themselves and quotations from them are *not* fictitious and remain true to the content and process of the narratives.

2. This statistic reflects how many women experience a serious assault by an intimate partner during an average twelve-month period; see American Psychological Association, *Violence and the Family: Report of the American Psychological Association Presidential Task Force on Violence and the Family* (Washington, D.C.: American Psychological Association, 1996), 10. By contrast, conservative estimates indicate that one million women suffer nonfatal violence by an intimate each year; see Bureau of Justice Statistics, *Violence Against Women: Estimates from the Redesigned Survey* (NCJ–154348), Bureau of Justice Statistics Special Report (Washington, D.C.: Bureau of Justice Statistics, August 1995), 3.

3. Commonwealth Fund, *First Comprehensive National Health Survey of American Women* (1993), as cited by Bureau of Justice Statistics' Clearing House and National Victim Center, personal communication, January 10, 1996, Arlington, Va. Other estimates range from every nine seconds (the 1997 estimate of the Family Prevention Fund of the National Coalition Against Violence, most often quoted among domestic violence coalitions around the country) to every fifteen seconds.

4. "The two largest samples reveal a lower incidence of conjugal violence to be associated with higher income, as is widely believed"; L. Okun, *Woman Abuse: Facts Replacing Myths* (Albany: State University of New York Press, 1986), 46.

5. Ibid., 48. Even correcting for class differences in reporting styles, "there remains a higher resultant rate of conjugal violence among the lower classes in the available studies."

6. R. J. Gelles, *The Violent Home: A Study of Physical Aggression Between Husbands and Wives* (Beverly Hills, Calif.: Sage Publications, 1974).

7. M. A. Straus and R. J. Gelles, *Physical Violence in American Families: Risk Factors and Adaptations to Violence in 8,145 Families* (New Brunswick, N.Y.: Transaction Publisher, 1990), 196.

8. U.S. Department of Justice, *The Sourcebook of Criminal Justice Statistics* (Washington, D.C.: U.S. Department of Justice, 1997), 1998.

9. This number was actually consistent with L. Walker's finding that 50 percent of all married women suffer physical abuse from their husbands at least once in their marriage; L. Walker, *The Battered Woman* (New York: Harper & Row, 1979).

10. This imperative also reflects how women in our culture perceive their roles and functions, specifically those pertaining to the maintenance of stability in their domestic relationships. Ac-

cording to Jessica Benjamin, "The unbreachable line between public and private values rests on the tacit assumption that women will continue to preserve and protect personal life, the task to which they have been assigned. . . . The public rationality necessitates that woman's different voice be split off and institutionalized in the private sphere." J. Benjamin, *The Bonds of Love: Psychoanalysis, Feminism, and the Problem of Domination* (New York: Pantheon, 1988), 197.

11. R. T. Sigler, *Domestic Violence in Context: An Assessment of Community Attitudes* (Lexington, Mass.: Lexington Books, 1989), 7.

12. D. Kurz, "Emergency Department Responses to Battered Women: Resistance to Medicalization," *Social Problems* 34 (1987): 69–81.

13. C. Warshaw, "Limitations of the Medical Model in the Care of Battered Women," *Gender and Society* 3 (1989): 505–17.

14. G. L. Bundow, "Why Women Stay," *Journal of the American Medical Association* (Resident Forum) 267, no. 23 (June 17, 1992): 3229. Bundow exhorts health care professionals to "educate yourselves as well as your colleagues and community about domestic violence. Try not to make value judgements. Your interaction with an abused patient has an incredible effect on her; she is searching for someone to believe her and, if possible, to offer an alternative. An attack by a loved one is an emotionally shattering experience. She needs compassion, not criticism or condescension."

15. For example, the bibliography of my dissertation cited 280 works on domestic abuse.

16. The results of a comprehensive review of all literature on domestic abuse found one study that specifically included women of upper socioeconomic and educational levels: L. Walker, "The Battered Woman Syndrome Study," in D. Finkelhor, R. J. Gelles, G.. T. Hotaling, and M. A. Straus, eds., *The Dark Side of Families: Current Family Violence Research* (Newbury Park, Calif.: Sage Publications, 1983), 31–48. According to an early poll by Louis Harris, as cited in another article focused on domestic violence among the middle and upper classes, wife abuse is actually *equally* common among upper and lower income families, and slightly more prevalent among middle income families, R. Stark and J. McEvoy III, "Middle Class Violence," *Psychology Today* 4, (November 1970), 52–54, 110–12.

17. For consistency in the study, I confined the sample population to women who were abused within marriage, and therefore to women who were already divorced or in the process of divorcing. I also chose women who were already out of their abusive marriages because I thought that they might be more likely to talk about their stories than women still living in abusive marriages.

18. Because this study is qualitative—the preferred methodology for obtaining an in-depth understanding of any phenomenon—it includes fewer subjects, owing to the emphasis on obtaining rich, detailed data on participants' lives; R. R. Martin, "Life Forces of African-American Elderly Illustrated Through Oral History Narratives," in E. Sherman and W. J. Reid, eds., *Qualitative Research in Social Work* (New York: Columbia University Press, 1994), 190–99. Based on prior qualitative studies, a sample of twelve to fifteen gives adequate variety to the qualitative researcher's analysis of the experience and inner meanings of being in an abusive marriage (see C. K. Riessman, "Making Sense of Marital Violence," in C. K. Riessman, ed., *Qualitative Studies in Social Work Research* (Thousand Oaks, Calif.: Sage Publications, 1994), 112–32. Each interview may be viewed as a revelation of one aspect of the world being studied.

19. Future research will uncover whether this concept of the path of the upscale abused wife is in any way applicable to women of other socioeconomic statuses.

20. "Because the domestic violence field has been dominated largely by sociologists," Patricia Resick suggests, "the majority of the research done has been attempting to construct theories of violence. . . . Relatively little of the domestic violence research has focused on victims' reactions or therapeutic issues"; P. A. Resick, "Sex Role Stereotypes and Violence Against Women," in V. Frank and E. D. Rothblum, eds., *The Stereotyping of Women* (New York: Springer, 1983), 230–56, 238.

21. It is important that future research be aimed at comparing the narratives and patterns of different socioeconomic groups of abused women.

22. This would probably be the case if any of the insights from this study were to be used as lenses across all populations as well.

23. These profiles will describe patterns of behavior and common styles of interaction as well as personality traits.

Chapter 2

1. It is noteworthy that few studies have been done on abused women of any economic level from a qualitative perspective.

2. A. Jones and S. Schecter, When Love Goes Wrong: *What to Do When You Can't Do Anything Right* (New York: HarperCollins, 1992); L. Walker, *The Battered Woman* (New York: Harper & Row, 1979); L. Walker, "The Battered Woman Syndrome Study" in D. Finkelhor, R. J. Gelles, G. T. Hotaling, and M. A. Straus, eds., *The Dark Side of Families: Current Family Violence Research* (Newbury Park, Calif.: Sage Publications, 1983), 31–48.

3. S. F. Turner and C. H. Shapiro, "Battered Women: Mourning the Death of a Relationship," *Social Work* 31, no.5 (September-October 1986): 372–76.

4. Leslie Landis, personal communication, June 12, 1993.

5. Susan Weitzman and Kirsten Levin, Chicago Abuse Awareness League, "Put up Yer Dukes," letter to the editor, *Chicago Tribune*, September 13, 1992.

6. C. Gilligan, *In a Different Voice: Psychological Theory and Women's Development* (Cambridge, Mass.: Harvard University Press, 1982).

7. M. F. Belenky, B. M. Clinchy, N. R. Goldberger, and J. M. Tarule, *Women's Ways of Knowing: the Development of Self, Voice, and Mind* (New York: Basic Books, 1986).

Chapter 3

1. S. Brownmiller, *Against Our Will: Men, Women, and Rape* (New York: Simon & Schuster, 1975).

2. P. A. Resick, "Sex Role Stereotypes and Violence Against Women," in V. Franks and E. D. Rothblum, eds., *The Stereotyping of Women* (New York: Springer, 1983), 235.

3. L. Okun, *Woman Abuse: Facts Replacing Myths* (Albany: State University of New York Press, 1986), 2.

4. E. A. Hecker, *A Short History of Women's Rights* (Westport, Conn.: Greenwood Press, 1914).

5. Ibid.; Okun, *Woman Abuse*, 2; M. Roy, ed., *Battered Women: A Psychosociological Study of Domestic Violence* (New York: Van Nostrand Reinhold, 1977).

6. Okun, *Woman Abuse*, 2.

7. Ibid.

8. Hecker, *A Short History of Women's Rights.*

9. Ibid.; Roy, *Battered Women.*

10. K. H. Hofeller, *Social, Psychological, and Situational Factors in Wife Abuse* (Palo Alto, Calif.: R & E Research Associates, 1982).

11. Okun, *Woman Abuse*, 4.

12. T. Davidson, *Conjugal Crime* (New York: Hawthorne Books, 1978), 103; Okun, *Women Abuse*, 3.

13. Okun, *Woman Abuse*, 3.

14. Ibid.

15. Pleck, *Domestic Tyranny*, 29.

16. Okun, *Woman Abuse*, 4.

17. Ibid.

18. Ibid., 2.

19. L. Gordon, *Heroes of Their Own Lives: The Politics and History of Family Violence* (New York: Penguin Books, 1988); Pleck, 79–87.

20. D. G. Dutton, *The Domestic Assault of Women: Psychological and Criminal Justice Perspectives* (University of British Columbia Press, 1995); Roy, *Battered Women*, 8888.

21. J. S. Mill, *The Subjection of Women* (New York: D. Appleton, 1870), 63–65.

22. Roy, *Battered Women.*

23. Pleck, *Domestic Tyranny*, 83.

24. D. G. Dutton, *The Domestic Assault of Women*, 24: "During the first quarter of the twentieth century the perception of family violence as a serious crime began to diminish. With the creation of family courts and social casework, criminal justice system sanctions against family crime came to be viewed as inhumane and outmoded. There was an attitudinal shift toward rehabilitation and family privacy."

25. Physical abuse was seen as a manifestation of "family disorganization" and "domestic discord." "They held that differences in the attitudes and circumstances of each spouse created discord, which surfaced whenever the couple faced a difficult decision. The couple was told that neither spouse was to blame, which further dimmed the spotlight on wife beating and the criminal nature of the act"; Pleck, *Domestic Tyranny*, 148.

26. Gordon, *Heroes of Their Own Lives*, 280.

27. Pleck, *Domestic Tyranny*, 125–34.

28. Ibid.

29. Ibid., 137.

30. Hofeller, *Social, Psychological,and Situational Factors in Wife Abuse.*

31. S. Freud, "The Unconscious and Conscious Reality," in *The Interpretation of Dreams,* translated, revised, and edited by James Strachey (New York: Avon, 1965); C. Brenner, *An Elementary Textbook of Psychoanalysis* (New York: Anchor Books, 1974).

32. Hofeller, *Social, Psychological, and Situational Factors in Wife Abuse.*

33. Resick, "Sex Role Stereotypes and Violence Against Women," 237.

34. Dutton, *The Domestic Assault of Women*, 218–49.

35. Karen Horney, a psychoanalyst who pursued her medical career despite the wishes of her sea captain father, rejected the idea of penis envy. She said that masochism is abnormal and should not be encouraged, and she defined it as a set of adult attitudes and behaviors rather than an inclination developing out of infancy. It is manifested, she proposed, by the inhibition

of self-assertion and aggression, a weak, helpless, or inferior self-image, self-sacrifice, submission, feelings of being exploited, and using weakness and helplessness as a means of enticing men. She branded masochism a fixed ideology about womanhood that serves to reconcile women to their subordination and plants in them a belief that masochism represents a fulfillment they crave as well as a desirable and commendable ideal toward which they should strive; E. Pleck, *Domestic Tyranny,* 159–60.

36. B. Friedan, *The Feminine Mystique* (New York: W. W. Norton, 1974), 45.

37. Gordon, *Heroes of Their Own Lives.*

38. Pleck, *Domestic Tyranny,* 188; 195.

39. Okun, *Woman Abuse,* 7; Pleck, *Domestic Tyranny,* 185.

40. R. E. Dobash and R. P. Dobash, *Violence Against Wives* (New York: Free Press/Macmillan, 1979).

41. L. Walker, "Battered Women," in A. M. Brodsky and R. T. Hare-Mustin, eds., *Women and Psychotherapy: An Assessment of Research and Practice* (New York: Guilford Press, 1980).

42. S. Brownmiller, *Against Our Will: Men, Women, and Rape* (New York: Simon & Schuster, 1975).

43. Walker, "Battered Women" (1980).

44. J. Benjamin, *The Bonds of Love: Psychoanalysis, Feminism, and the Problem of Domination.* (New York: Pantheon, 1988).

45. Ibid.

46. M. A. Straus, "Conceptualization and Measurement of Battering: Implications for Public Policy," in M. Steinman, ed. *Woman Battering: Policy Responses* (New York: Norton, 1991); R. J. Gelles, and M. A. Straus, *Intimate Violence* (New York: Simon & Shuster); S. K. Steinmetz and M. A. Straus, eds., *Violence in the Family* (New York: Harper & Row, 1924).

47. B. Friedan, *The Feminine Mystique* (New York: Norton, 1974).

48. D. G. Dutton, *The Domestic Assault of Women: Psychological and Criminal Justice Perspectives* (Vancouver: University of British Columbia Press, 1995); Walker, *The Battered Woman* (1979); Walker, "The Battered Woman Syndrome Study," in D. Finkelhor, R. J. Geller, G. T. Hotaling and M. A. Straus, eds., *The Dark Side of Families: Crime and Family Violence Research* (Newbury Park, CA: Sage Publications, 1983): 31–48.

49. M. Seligman, "Frustration and Learned Helplessness," *Journal of Experimental Psychology Animal Behavior Processes* 104, no. 2 (April 1975): 149–57.

50. D. G. Dutton, *The Domestic Assault of Women: Psychological and Criminal Justice Perspectives* (University of British Columbia: Allyn and Bacon, 1988); Walker, *The Battered Woman* (1979).

51. Walker, *The Battered Woman* (1979), 47: "The learned helplessness theory has three basic components: information about what will happen; thinking or cognitive representations about what will happen (learning, expectation, belief, perception); and behavior toward what does happen."

52. Benjamin, *The Bonds of Love.*

53. D. G. Dutton and S. Painter, "Patterns of Emotional Bonding in Battered Women: Traumatic Bonding," *International Journal of Women's Studies* 8, no. 3 (September–October 1985): 363–75.

54. D. G. Dutton and S. Painter (1993), 1: "[After] assessing 50 battered women and 25 emotionally abused women who had left their relationships, . . . essential features of the [bat-

tered woman] syndrome were present and significantly interrelated. . . . The concept of inter-mittency of abuse is proposed as an alternative to the cycle of violence theory as main con-tributor to the syndrome"; D. G. Dutton and S. Painter, "The Battered Woman Syndrome: Effects of Severity and Intermitting of Abuse," *American Journal of Orthopsychiatry* 63 (no. 4): 614.

55. S. Weitzman, "Upscale Violence and the Dynamics of Toxic Relationships," unpublished paper read at NASW Conference, Lake County, Ill., November 18, 1994.

56. D. L. Graham, E. Rawlings, and N. Rimini, "Survivors of Terror: Battered Women, Hostages, and the Stockholm Syndrome," in K. Yllo and M. Bograd, eds., *Feminist Perspectives on Wife Abuse* (Newbury Park, Calif.: Sage Publications, 1988), 217–33.

57. Dutton, *The Domestic Assault of Women*, p. 94.

58. Ibid.

59. J. R. Meloy, *Violent Attachments* (New York: Jason Aronson, 1992).

60. S. Freud, "Remembering, Repeating, and Working Through," in *The Standard Edition of the Complete Psychological Works of S. Freud* (London: Hogarth Press, 1912).

61. S. Slipp, ed., *Curative Factors in Dynamic Psychotherapy* (New York: McGraw-Hill, 1975); Brenner, *An Elementary Textbook of Psychoanalysis*.

62. Brenner, *An Elementary Textbook of Psychoanalysis*.

63. Anna Freud's concept of identification with the aggressor as so applied is cited by D. G. Dutton: "In a life-and-death situation with a powerful authority figure, the ego identifies with the aggressor-authority to avoid punishment and anxiety" (Dutton, *The Domestic Assault of Women*, 94).

64. B. Engel, *The Emotionally Abused Woman* (New York: Fawcett, 1990).

65. P. Giovacchini, *Treatment of Primitive Mental States* (New York: Jason Aronson, 1979).

66. S. F. Turner and C. H. Shapiro, "Battered Women: Mourning the Death of the Relation-ship," *Social Work* 31, no. 5 (September-October 1986): 372–76.

Chapter 4

1. It is not uncommon for a woman in her middle years to look back on the dream of the ideal relationship she harbored, one that often included how her mate would take care of her needs on many levels. This is discussed in Gail Sheehy, *Passages: Predictable Crises of Adult Life* (New York: Dutton, 1976).

2. E. Fromm, *The Art of Loving* (New York: Harper, 1956).

3. J. E. Gedo and A. Goldberg, *Models of the Mind* (Chicago: University of Chicago Press, 1973); A. Goldberg, "Translation Between Psychoanalytic Theories," paper presented at the sci-entific meeting of the Chicago Psychoanalytic Society, Chicago, January 24, 1984.

4. M. McMahon, "A Study of Selfobject Functions Among Heterosexual Couples" (Ph.D. diss., Institute for Clinical Social Work, Chicago, 1991).

5. J. R. Greenberg and S. A. Mitchell, *Object Relations in Psychoanalytic Theory* (Cambridge, Mass.: Harvard University Press, 1983), 353; H. Kohut, *Restoration of the Self* (New York: In-ternational Universities Press, 1977).

6. E. Person, *Dreams of Love and Other Fateful Encounters* (New York: Penguin Books, 1988).

7. It should be noted that since the narratives I analyzed and the stories of all the women I worked with were told from the woman's perspective, any ways these men idealized their part-ner are largely unknown to me. Only two women volunteered that their future husbands ide-alized them in any way. For example, Allison, reported that her husband "started showing me

off. . . . I was a Ph.D." Another woman reported that her future husband "was fascinated to find out who I was. But I didn't know it at the time."

8. Like someone with an impaired or underdeveloped self, the immature woman is still developing her identity and sense of who she is. Owing to undeveloped or under-developed intrapsychic structures to provide selfobject functions (for example, self-esteem regulation, soothing, and so on), the impaired or unripened person is significantly more dependent on others to provide the functions she is not equipped to provide for herself. In an attempt to attain the necessary selfobject functions, to feel cohesive, and to experience the deficits being "filled in," this woman turns to the abuser-partner, who provides her with an experience that keeps her energized; McMahon, "A Study of Selfobject Functions Among Heterosexual Couples."

9. It is unclear what to make of this statistic. All the virgins had experienced some sort of abuse as children, mostly along the lines of being emotionally or physically abused by their parents. (This history of abuse does not include sexual abuse, about which I did not inquire.) Only two had witnessed domestic violence between their parents. Is there some connection between first sexual encounters and history of abuse? It seems that there might be, and further study would illuminate this connection. Perhaps a woman, already fearful of abuse, seeks to bond with a man who will protect her. For some women there may indeed be a repetition compulsion drawing them to the same type of abusive relationship with which they grew up. But for the majority of the upscale abused wives I have known and worked with, childhood experience of abuse was surprisingly not a predisposing factor.

10. M. C. Froelke, "Living Out Loud," *Chicago* (September 1999): 56–68, 56.

Chapter 5

1. It is ironic that several women in my study as well as in my practice have referred to this character in *The Shining* to describe the look on their husband's face prior to becoming abusive.

2. Walker, *The Battered Woman* (1979).

3. This theoretical lens does not include women who stay in toxic relationships because of intractable external situations related to children, religious beliefs, cultural constraints, finances, and so on, but rather is aimed at women who, on the surface, are free to either remain in or leave the abusive relationship.

4. H. Kohut, *Restoration of the Self* (New York: International Universities Press, 1977).

5. Weitzman, "Upscale Violence and the Dynamics of Toxic Relationships."

6. E. Mishler, *Research Interviewing: Context and Narrative* (Cambridge, Mass.: Harvard University Press, 1986).

7. D. Polkinghorne, *Narrative Knowing and the Human Sciences* (Albany: State University of New York Press, 1988); J. Palombo, "Narratives, Self-Cohesion, and the Patient's Search for Meaning," *Clinical Social Work Journal* 20, no. 3 (Fall 1992): 249–70.

8. The philosophy of Nelson Goodman as cited in J. Bruner, *Actual Minds, Possible Worlds* (Cambridge, Mass.: Harvard University Press, 1986).

9. J. Palombo, "Incoherent Self-Narratives and Disorders of the Self in Children with Learning Disabilities," *Smith College Studies in Social Work* 64, no. 2 (March 1994): 129–52, 194.

10. M. F. Belenky et al., *Women's Ways of Knowing* (New York: Basic Books, 1986).

11. C. Saari, *The Creation of Meaning in Clinical Social Work* (New York: Guilford Press, 1991).

12. D. Saleeby, "Culture, Theory, and Narrative: The Intersection of Meanings in Practice," *Social Work* 39, no. 4 (July 1994): 351–59: "The stories . . . [they] tell, the constructions they

devise about their lives, sometimes propel them down dead ends or dangerous paths. . . . [As Joan Laird claimed,] occasionally such stories assume the status of myth" (356).

13. *Emplotment* is when a person becomes embroiled in someone else's story line, such as the young man whose father, grandfather, and great-grandfather were all physicians, and so the expectation is that he will be a doctor too. He goes to medical school, even though he has creative talents and dreams of being an artist, and he becomes depressed as he remains emplotted in the life script his elders created; J. Palombo, "Gender as a Theme in Self Narratives," *The Journal of Analytic Social Work* 2, no. 2 (1994): 3–24. The term was originally conceived by the French existential philospher Paul Ricoeur; it is referred to in A. P. Kerby, *Narrative and the Self* (Bloomington: Indiana University Press, 1991).

Chapter 6

1. Deborah Tucker, personal communication, January 13, 2000.

2. H. E. Marano, "Why They Stay: A Saga of Spouse Abuse," *Psychology Today* 29, no. 3 (May–June 1996): 59. Many researchers concur that the woman's risk of serious injury or death increases dramatically at the time of separation; see D. G. Saunders and A. Browne, "Domestic Homicide," in R. T. Ammerman and M. Hersen, eds., *Case Studies in Family Violence* (New York: Plenum Press, 1991), 379–402; Dutton, *The Domestic Assault of Women* (Boston: Allyn & Bacon, 1988).

3. Bureau of Justice Statistics, *Female Victims of Violent Crime* (Bureau of Justice Statistics Report, 1991).

4. Bureau of Justice Statistics, *Violence Against Women: Estimates from the Redesigned Survey* (NCJ–154348), Bureau of Justice Statistics Special Report (August 1995), 4.

5. Florida Governor's Task Force on Domestic and Sexual Violence, Florida Mortality Review Project (1997), 47 (table 17).

6. E. Stark and A. Flitcraft, "Killing the Beast Within: Woman Battering and Female Suicidality," *International Journal of Health Services* 25, no. 1 (1995): 43–64.

7. D. J. Sonkin, D. Martin, and L. E. Walker, *The Male Batterer: A Treatment Approach* (New York: Springer, 1985); A. Browne, *When Battered Women Kill* (New York: The Free Press, 1987).

8. D. Ellis, "Post-Separation Woman Abuse: The Contribution of Lawyers as 'Barracudas,' 'Advocates,' and 'Counsellors,'" *International Journal of Law and Psychiatry* 10, no. 4 (1987): 403–4.

9. F. Hart, "A Sudden Silence: An Analysis of the Psychological Literature on Battering Men, 1982 to 1990," *Resources for Feminist Research/Documentation* 20, no. 3–4 (Fall–Winter 1991): 103–4.

10. L. Bowker, *Beating Wife Beating* (Lexington, Mass.: Lexington Books, 1983).

11. Metropolitan Nashville Police Department Domestic Violence website (2000).

12. H. Kohut, *Restoration of the Self* (New York: International Universities Press, 1977).

13. C. Brenner, *An Elementary Textbook of Psychoanalysis* (New York: Anchor Books, 1974). Freud uses the term *cathexis* to denote our investment of psychological energies in objects of attachment, such as people, places, and events.

14. E. Fromm, *The Art of Loving* (New York: Harper, 1956).

15. The Stone Center is devoted to the study of women, women's behaviors, and effective treatment modalities that respect the diversity of women's development and internal makeup.

16. J. B. Miller, *Toward a New Psychology of Women* (Boston: Beacon Press, 1986), 11.

17. Walker, "Battered Women," (1980).

18. Miller, *Toward a New Psychology of Women*, 11; M. F. Belenky, et al., *Women's Ways of Knowing* (New York: Basic Books, 1986).

19. C. Gilligan, *In a Different Voice* (Cambridge, Mass.: Harvard University Press, 1982).

20. J. Herman, *Trauma and Recovery* (New York: Basic Books, 1997): "Disclosures can be highly empowering. . . . The power of the disclosure rests in the act of telling the truth" (200).

21. H. E. Marano, "Why They Stay: A Saga of Spouse Abuse," *Psychology Today* 29, no. 3 (May–June 1996): 59.

22. D. Vaughan, *Uncoupling* (New York: Oxford University Press, 1986).

23. J. Laird, "Women and Stories: Restorying Women's Self-Construction," in M. Mc-Goldrick, C. M. Anderson, and F. Walsh, eds., *Women in Families: A Framework for Family Therapy* (New York: Norton, 1989), 427–50, 427.

24. L. Walker, "Battered Women" (1980).

25. David H. Hopkins, personal communication, January 24, 2000.

Chapter 7

1. M. Elbow, "Theoretical Considerations of Violent Marriages, *Social Casework* 58, no. 9 (November, 1977): 515–26; D. Martin, *Battered Wives* (San Francisco: Glide Publications, 1976); P. A. Resick, "Sex Role Stereotypes and Violence Against Women," in V. Frank and E.D. Rothblum, eds., *The Stereotyping of Women* (New York: Springer, 1983); L. Walker, *The Battered Woman* (New York: Harper & Row, 19979).

2. M. A. Straus, R. J. Gelles, and S. K. Steinmetz, *Behind Closed Doors: Violence in the American Family* (New York: Anchor Books, 1981); R. J. Gelles, *The Violent Home: A Study of Physical Aggression Between Husbands and Wives* (Beverly Hills, Calif.: Sage Publications, 1974).

3. Straus, Gelles, and Steinmetz, *Behind Closed Doors*.

4. Ibid.

5. M. Roy, ed., *Battered Women* (New York: Van Nostrand Reinhold, 1977). Roy interviewed 150 women randomly selected from 1,000 cases at the Abused Women's Aid in Crisis (AWAIC) center. Her sample included a population that reflected a cross-section of socioeconomic statuses, duration of relationships, family histories, frequency of violence, and onset and degree of violence. It would be interesting to learn how and whether Roy's nine factors are replicated in a population composed solely of upper-income women.

6. L. Walker, "The Battered Woman Syndrome Study," in D. Finkelhor et al., *The Dark Side of Families* (Newbury Park, Calif.: Sage Publications, 1983). Walker was interested in learning as much as possible about the nature of domestic violence from the perspective of the battered woman. In her study, she hypothesized that battered women develop psychological sequelae that can be considered to constitute a battered woman syndrome; that experiences in childhood and those from living in an abusive relationship have an impact on a woman's state; and that these experiences interfere with the woman's ability to stop the violence once the man initiates it (in other words, learned helplessness). Independent variables included class, race, childhood experiences (such as battering in the childhood home and incest), and whether a woman was currently in an abusive relationship or had been out of one for more or less than one year. Dependent variables were women's perceptions of abuse, violent behavior, women's sense of locus of control, perceptions about female sex role stereotypes, emotional stability,

and women's experience of degree of terror. Walker's sample consisted of self-identified battered women who lived in a six-state region. Most of the women were intelligent and well educated; 25 percent were in professional occupations. A woman was considered eligible to participate if she reported that she was battered at least twice by a man with whom she had an intimate or marital relationship. Geographic distribution was constructed to allow for natural selection, but correcting for under-representation of groups could be done when necessary. Direct contact was made with minority groups to encourage participation.

7. D. N. Kyriacou, D. Anglin, E. Taliaferro, S. Stone, T. Tubb, J. A. Linden, R. Muelleman, E. Barton, and J. F. Kraus, "Risk Factors for Injury to Women from Domestic Violence," *New England Journal of Medicine* 34, no. 2225 (December 16, 1999): 1892–98. The study, using a standardized questionnaire, encompassed eight large university-related emergency rooms, and was based on responses from 256 women who had been intentionally injured and 659 controls who were treated for other conditions in the emergency room.

8. J. Marquis, "Alcohol, Job Woes Cited in Domestic Violence," *Los Angeles Times*, December 16, 1999, sec. 1, p. 3.

9. Straus, Gelles, and Steinmetz, *Behind Closed Doors*, 113. Interestingly, and as one might predict about violence in a family system, "the couples who did not hit each other had the lowest rates of abusive violence toward their children" (115).

10. L. Okun, *Woman Abuse* (Albany: State University of New York Press, 1986), 62. It should also be noted that when both spouses were included in assessing the impact of the 'double whammy' effect, "a marriage involving a person who [grew up in a violent home] is much more likely to be the scene of violent battles than are other marriages. In fact, depending on which sex and which measure of violence is used, these marriages are *from five to nine times more likely to be violent* [italics sic]" than a marriage whose partners did not experience the double whammy; Straus, Gelles, and Steinmetz, *Behind Closed Doors*, 114.

11. Okun, *Woman Abuse*, 166.

12. D. G. Saunders, "A Typology of Men Who Batter: Three Types Derived from Cluster Analysis," *American Orthopsychiatry* 62, no. 2 (1992): 264–75.

13. Okun, *Woman Abuse*, 68.

14. N. S. Jacobson and J. M. Gottman, *When Men Batter Women* (New York: Simon and Shuster, 1998).

15. N. S. Jacobson, "Domestic Violence: What Are Marriages Like?" Paper read at American Association for Marital and Family Therapy conference, Anaheim, CA, October 1993.

16. D. G. Dutton, with S. K. Golant, *The Batterer* (New York: Basic Books, 1995), 28.

17. Ibid.

18. Ibid., 26.

19. Ibid., 29–33.

20. Ibid., 33–38.

21. Ibid., 140–55.

22. American Psychiatric Association, *Diagnostic and Statistic Manual of Mental Disorders*, 4th ed. (*DSM-IV*) (Washington, DC: American Psychiatric Association, 1994), 280–81.

23. Ibid., 275.

24. Dean Joseph A. Walsh, Loyola University School of Social Work, Chicago, personal communication, December 17, 1999.

25. E. Hamilton, *Mythology* (New York: Penguin, 1969), 87–88.

26. American Psychiatric Association, *DSM-IV*, 282.

27. Ibid.

28. H. Kohut and G. Cocks, eds., *The Curve of Life: The Correspondence of Heinz Kohut, 1923–1982* (Chicago: University of Chicago Press, 1994), 24.

29. Miriam Elson, personal communuication, January 24, 2000; see also M. Elson, *Self Psychology in Clinical Social Work* (New York: W.W. Norton, 1988), 252–53; Elson, ed., *The Kohut Seminars: On Self Psychology and Psychotherapy with Adolescents and Young Adults* (New York: W.W. Norton, 1987); Elson, "Self-pity, Dependence, Manipulation, and Exploitation: A View from Self Psychology" in *The 25th Annual of Psychoanalysis* 25 (1999): 5–16.

30. Miriam Elson, personal communications, December, 1999. Elson is also a well-respected author of papers and two books on self psychology, a lecturer, and a gifted analytic clinician in her own right.

31. Ibid.

32. M. Gunther, "Aggression, Self Psychology, and Health," in A. Goldberg, ed., *Advances in Self Psychology* (New York: International Universities Press. 1980), 167–92, 178.

33. Ibid.

34. M. Tolpin, "Corrective Emotional Experience: A Self Psychological Re-evaluation," in A.Goldberg, ed., *The Future of Psychoanalyis* (New York: International Universities Press, 1983), 363–79.

35. How the upscale male with NPD functions in abusive relationships is a fertile ground for investigation, as it has not been conceptualized in this manner until now. I am planning not only to study this phenomenon but to explore further the internal dynamics of these men.

36. This may or may not be true for the lower-income batterer as well; there have been no studies to date of the sense of entitlement held by male batterers of any socioeconomic statues. Research has focused on conflicts related to educational differences, economic problems and overcrowding, alcohol abuse, and so on.

37. This unpredictability is not atypical of battering behavior. "For the vast majority of couples in our sample, it was extremely difficult to predict when the batterer would strike"; Jacobson and Gottman, *When Men Batter Women*, 62.

38. Sarah Buel, personal communication, January 6, 2000. The case, Commonwealth vs. Gravina, 1991, 1992, was tried and convictions were obtained in the Quincy Court District in the State of Massachusetts.

39. This, too, is a worthwhile focus for further comparative study.

40. I suspect that this pattern with regard to meals and housekeeping may be present in abusive marriages of all socioeconomic groups. Again, this would only be better understood through future comparative studies.

41. Okun, *Woman Abuse*, 51.

42. H. Kohut, keynote address given at the Fourth Annual International Conference on the Psychology of the Self, San Francisco, California, 1981.

43. K. Nelson, "Cognition, Context and Culture," in K. Nelson, ed., *Making Sense: The Acquisition of Shared Meaning* (New York: Academic Press. 1985), 249–65.

44. Margareta Hydén did a study in Sweden inquiring about why men and women remain in marriages where violent episodes repeatedly occur, and how repeated abuse occurs in a relationship predicated on trust; Hydén, "Woman Baattering as a Marital Act: Interviewing and Analysis in Context," in C. K. Riessman, ed., Qualitative Studies in Social Work Research (Thousand Oaks, Calif.: Sage Publications, 1994), 95–112. Using a methodology similar to Catherine Kohler Riessman's in analyzing the meaning-making of divorcing women—see Riessman, *Di-*

vorce Talk: Women and Men Make Sense of Personal Relationships (New Brunswick, N.J.: Rutgers University Press, 1990)—Hydén explored how a husband and wife make sense of their partici- pation in violent episodes, how they characterize, reflect, make sense of, and interpret the mean- ing of battering events for their marriage. She interviewed twenty couples who had reported domestic violence to the police and analyzed their narrative accounts of the pre-history, the vi- olent act, and the aftermath. Her hypothesis (borne out by subsequent findings from the inter- views) was that men and women characterize and reflect on domestic violence differently; the view they shared was that while woman beating was immoral and wrong, wife beating was per- ceived as a marital act within the social context of marriage, and hence, was acceptable. It was the social context that contributed to the meaning the couple made of the battering. Hydén also examined the gap between action and expectation, and how justifications and excuses are de- veloped. It should be noted that Hydén did not define wife abuse operationally but rather de- termined abuse as per what constituted the action for participants in her study. Over two years, seven out of the twenty couples stayed together, and most redefined what happened. The rest separated or divorced, and in subsequent interviews Hydén's interviewees reported that the in- terviews had made a synergistic contribution to their review and reevaluation of their life story and their efforts to take new actions to change the narrative. Hydén states that she witnessed dramatic unfoldings and reinterpretations during the research, which speaks to the potential impact of researching narratives and narrative work.

45. Sarah Buel, personal communication, January 6, 2000.

46. David H. Hopkins, personal communication, January 24, 2000.

47. L. H. Bowker, *Beating Wife Beating* (Lexington, Mass.: Lexington Books, 1983); J. R. Chapman and M. Gates, eds., *The Victimization of Women* (Beverly Hills, Calif.: Sage Publica- tions, 1978); T. Davidson, *Conjugal Crime* (New York: Hawthorne Books, 1978); R. E. Dobash and R. Dobash, *Violence Against Wives* (New York: Free Press, 1979); R. Langley and R. Levy, *Wife Beating: The Silent Crisis* (New York: Dutton, 1977); D. Martin, *Battered Wives* (San Fran- cisco: Glide Publications, 1976); E. Stark and A. Flitcraft, "Violence Among Intimates: An Epi- demiological Review," in V. B. Hasselt, ed., *Handbook of Family Violence* (New York: Plenum, 1988), 293–318.

48. J. Herman, *Trauma and Recovery* (New York: Basic Books, 1997), 81.

Chapter 8

1. New York Victim Services web site (December 1999).

2. National Clearinghouse on Child Abuse and Neglect Information, "In Harm's Way: Do- mestic Violence and Child Maltreatment," monograph (Washington, D.C.: U.S. Department of Health and Human Services, 1999).

3. Although studies have suggested the predictive impact of growing up in a violent home, several significant study areas have yet to be explored. Specifically, research on the children of upscale violence and, more generally, longitudinal studies on the psychological impact of growing up with domestic assault.

4. This project, part of a community pediatric clinic, is a collaborative team training model with police to learn about how to intervene when kids are exposed to violence. In effect since 1991 (and now a model for other communities across the nation), this twenty-four-hour-a-day service deals with post-traumatic stress disorder as well as other sequelae to exposure to do- mestic abuse. People in this program are lower-income. The rich in New Haven, according to

Berkman, rarely report domestic abuse; they hire private professionals to help them, or they live far enough apart from others that the domestic abuse may easily go undetected.

5. Miriam Berkman, personal communication, September 9, 1999.

6. "Mothers have a child abuse rate that is 75 percent greater than the rate of fathers"; M. A. Straus, R. J. Gelles, and S. K. Steinmetz, *Behind Closed Doors* (New York: Anchor, 1981), 213.

7. E. Peled, "Supporting the Parenting of Battering Men: Issues and Dilemmas," unpublished manuscript 1996.

8. B. E. Carlson, "Outcomes of Physical Abuse and Observation of Marital Violence Among Adolescents in Placement," *Journal of Interpersonal Violence* 6 (1991): 526–34; V. Stagg, G. D. Wills and M. Howell, "Psychopathology in Early Childhood Witnesses of Family Violence," *Topics in Early Childhood Special Education* 9 (1989): 73–87.

9. Miriam Berkman, personal communication, September 9, 1999.

10. Specific recommended works on the effects of witnessing domestic abuse for children include: H. M. Hughes, "Psychological and Behavioral Correlates of Family Violence in Child Witness and Victims." *American Journal of Orthopsychiatry* 58 (1988): 77–90; H. M. Hughes, D. Parkinson, D. and M. Vargo, "Witnessing Spouse Abuse and Experiencing Physical Abuse: A 'Double Whammy'?" *Journal of Family Violence,* 4 (1989): 197–209; M. P. Jaffee, D. A. Wolfe, and S. K. Wilson, *Children of Battered Women* (Newbury Park, Calif.: Sage Publications, 1990); J. R. Kolbo, "Risk and Resilience among Children Exposed to Family Violence," *Violence and Victims* 11 (1996):113–128; G. Margolin, "Effects of Domestic Violence on Children." In P. K. Trickett and C. J. Schellenbach, (eds.), *Violence against Children in the Family and Community* (Washington, D.C.: American Psychological Association, 1998), 57–102; G. Margolin, and R. S. John, "Children's Exposure to Marital Aggression." In G. K. Kantor and J. L. Jasinski (eds.) *Out of the Darkness: Contemporary Perspectives on Family Violence.* (Thousand Oaks, Calif.: Sage Publications, 1997): 90–104; E. Peled, "The Experience of Living with Violence for Pre-Adolescent Witnesses of Woman Abuse," unpublished doctoral dissertation, University of Minnesota, 1993; V. Stagg, G. D. Wills and M. Howell, "Psychopathology in Early Childhood Witnesses of Family Violence," *Topics in Early Childhood Special Education,* 9 (1989): 73–87; Straus, Gelles and Steinmetz, *Behind Closed Doors.*

11. J. L. Edleson, "Problems Associated with Children's Witnessing of Domestic Violence," Violence Against Women Online Resources (1997, revised April 1999), 1. See also Edleson, "Children's Witnessing of Adult Domestic Violence," *Journal of Interpersonal Violence* 14 , no. 8 (August 1999): 839–70.

12. G. T. Hotaling and D. B. Sugarman, "An Analysis of Risk Markers in Husband to Wife Violence: The Current State of Knowledge," *Violence and Victims* 1 (1986).

13. Bureau of Justice Assistance, *Family Violence: Interventions for the Justice System,* NCJ-144532 (Washington, D.C. : U.S. Department of Justice, 1993).

14. American Psychological Association, *Violence and the Family: Report of the American Psychological Association Presidential Task Force on Violence and the Family* (Washington, D.C.: American Psychological Association, 1996), 80.

15. Ibid., 40.

16. Florida Governor's Task Force on Domestic and Sexual Violence, *Florida Mortality Review Project* (1997), 45 (table 11).

17. Ibid., 51 (table 28).

18. National Council of Juvenile and Family Court Judges Family Violence Department, *Effective Intervention in Domestic Violence and Child Maltreatment Cases: Guidelines for Policy and Practice* (Reno, NV: National Council of Juvenile and Family Court Judges, 1998), 10.

19. K.G. Evans, "If Mom's Battered, Kids Suffer," *Children's Advocate (Action Alliance for Children)* (July-August 1997).

20. New York Victim Services web site (December 1999).

21. A. Freud, "Indications and Contraindications for Child Analysis," in *Problems of Psychoanalytic Training, Diagnosis and the Technique of Treatment:The Writings of A. Freud,* vol. 7 (New York: International Universities Press, 1968), 110–23, 115.

22. S. Marans, "Psychoanalysis on the Beat: Children, Police, and Urban Trauma," *The Psychoanalytic Study of the Child* 51, (1996): 522–41, 533.

23. S. Marans and A. Adelman, "Experiencing Violence in a Developmental Context." in J. Osofsky, ed., *Children in a Violent Society* (New York: Guilford Press, 1997), 202–22, 202–3.

24. Edleson, "Problems Associated with Children's Witnessing of Domestic Violence."

25. Ibid., 1.

26. Ibid., 2.

27. National Research Council, *Understanding Child Abuse and Neglect* (Washington, D.C.: National Academy Press, 1993).

28. Evans, "If Mom's Battered, Kids Suffer."

29. Margolin, "Effects of Witnessing Violence on Children."

30. Cited in National Clearinghouse on Child Abuse and Neglect Information, "In Harm's Way," 3. Others have found that children suffering from the "double whammy" obviously show more behavior problems; L.A. McClosky, A.J. Figueredo and M.P. Koss, "The Effects of Systemic Family Violence on Children's Mental Health," *Child Development* 66 (1995): 1239–61.

31. Hughes, Parkinson and Vargo, "Witnessing Spouse Abuse and Experiencing Physical Abuse"; McClosky et al., "The Effects of Systemic Family Violence on Children's Mental Health"; L. Silvern, J. Karyl, L. Waelde, W.F. Hodges, J. Starek, E. Heidt and K. Min, "Retrospective Reports of Parental Partner Abuse: Relationships to Depression, Trauma Symptoms and Self-esteem Among College Students," *Journal of Family Violence* 10 (1995): 177–202.

32. Silvern et al., "Retrospective Reports of Parental Partner Abuse."

33. National Council of Juvenile and Family Court Judges Family Violence Department, *Effective Intervention in Domestic Violence and Child Maltreatment Cases,* 10.

34. D. Sinclair, *Understanding Wife Assault: A Training Manual for Counselors and Advocates* (Toronto, Ontario: Ontario Government Bookstore, Publications Services Section, 1985).

35. Domestic Violence and Incest Resource Centre (DVIRC) web site (September 1997).

36. New York Victim Services web site (December 1999).

37. Ibid.

38. J. Herman, *Trauma and Recovery* (New York: Basic Books, 1997), 33.

39. Silvern, et al., "Retrospective Reports of Parental Partner Abuse."

40. DVIRC web site (September 1997).

Chapter 9

1. "Not only is it portrayed [in women's magazines] as a private problem, but most often it is the victim's problem. The dominant individual perspective that places responsibility on the

victim normalizes the idea that the victim should be held responsible for solving the problem"; N. Berns, "My Problem and How I Solved It: Domestic Violence in Women's Magazines," *Sociological Quarterly* 40, no. 1 (Winter 1999): 85–108.

2. In addition to being apprehensive about facing her problem, many an abused woman comes to the therapist with apprehensions of another sort. As Judith Herman notes: "Though the traumatized patient feels a desperate need to rely on the integrity and competence of the therapist, she cannot do so, for her capacity to trust has been damaged by the traumatic experience. . . . Until proven otherwise, she assumes that the therapist cannot bear to hear the true story of the trauma. . . . [She also may] mistrust the motives of any therapist who does not back away"; J. Herman, *Trauma and Recovery* (New York: Basic Books, 1997), 138.

3. "The deepening of connection is also apparent within the therapeutic relationship. The therapeutic alliance now feels less intense, but more relaxed and secure. . . . The patient has a greater capacity for self observation and a greater tolerance for inner conflict"; ibid., 205.

4. It is noteworthy that de Beauvoir was working on *She Came to Stay* at precisely the time when Sartre was writing *Being and Nothingness*. For an intriguing discussion of intellectual priority, see K. Fullbrook and E. Fullbrook, *Simone deBeauvoir and Jean-Paul Sarte: The Remaking of A Twentieth Century Legend* (New York: Basic Books, 1994).

5. S. deBeauvoir, *She Came to Stay.* New York: W.W. Norton, 1954), 61.

6. J.-P. Sartre, *Being and Nothingness* (New York: Washington Square Press, 1953), 86–116.

7. Ibid., 96.

8. S. Weitzman, "The Abused Woman: A Look Through A Sartrean-Existential Lens," unpublished manuscript, 1997.

9. L. Walker, *The Battered Woman* (New York: Harper & Row, 1979); Walker, "The Battered Woman Study," in D. Finkelhor et al., eds., *The Dark Side of Families* (Newbury Park, Calif.: Sage Publications, 1983).

10. J. Riviere, *The Ideal Reader* (New York: Meridian Books, 1960).

11. A. Modell, *Object Love and Reality: An Introduction To a Psychoanalytic Theory of Object Relations* (New York: International Universities Press, 1968).

12. S. Novey, *The Second Look: the Reconstruction of Personal History in Psychiatry and Psychoanalysis* (Baltimore, Maryland: The Johns Hopkins Press, 1968).

13. By comparison, Freudian theory asserts that our recollections are pure representations of what we experience, but that sometimes, because they are too painful, our defense mechanisms (i.e., repression) filters the degree and content so that they are tolerable. Freud suggests that individuals need to break through the repression and free themselves from these painful life experiences. This is not the case with the narrative perspective; J. Bruner, *Actual Minds, Possible Worlds* (Cambridge, Mass.: Harvard University Press, 1986).

14. J. Bruner, "Life as Narrative," *Social Research* 54 (1987), 11–32; J. Bruner, "The Narrative Construction of Reality," *Critical Inquiry* 18 (Autumn, 1991), 1–21; K. S. Gergen, *The Concept of Self* (New York: Holt, Rinehart, and Winston, 1971); Gergen, M. "Narrative Structures in Social Explanation" in C. Antaki, ed., *Analyzing Everyday Explanation: A Casebook of Methods* (Newbury Park, Calif.: Sage Publications, 1988), 94–112; K. Nelson, "Cognition, Context and Culture,"in K.Nelson, ed., *Making Sense: the Acquisition of Shared Meaning* (New York: Academic Press,1985), 249–65; Novey, *The Second Look: the Reconstruction of Personal History in Psychiatry and Psychoanalysis;* J. Palombo, J., "Narratives, Self-Cohesion, and the Patient's Search for Meaning," *Clinical Social Work Journal* 20, no. 3 (Fall 1992): 249–70; J. Palombo, "Incoher-

ent Self-Narratives and Disorders of the Self in Children With Learning Disabilities," *Smith College Studies in Social Work* 64, no. 2 (March 1994),129–52; D. Polkinghorne, *Narrative Knowing and the Human Sciences* (Albany: State University of New York Press, 1988); C. Saari, *The Construction of Meaning in Clinical Social Work* (New York: Guilford Press, 1991); D. Saleeby, "Culture, Theory, and Narrative: The Intersection of Meanings in Practice," *Social Work* 39, no. 4 (July 1994): 351–59; R. Schafer, *Aspects of Internalization* (Madison, Connecticut: International Universities Press, 1990).

15. J. Bruner, "Life as Narrative," *Social Research* 54 (1987), 11–32.

16. J. Benjamin, *The Bonds of Love* (New York: Pantheon, 1988).

17. Walker, "The Battered Woman Syndrome Study."

18. S.F. Turner and C.H. Shapiro, "Battered Women: Mourning the Death of a Relationship" *Social Work* 31, no. 5 (September-October 1986): 372–76.

19. E. Kuebler-Ross, *On Death and Dying* (New York: Macmillan, 1969).

20. A. Jones and S. Schecter's *When Love Goes Wrong: What to Do When You Can't Do Anything Right: Strategies for Women with Controlling Partners* (New York: HarperCollins, 1992) examines the function of the man's violent behaviors as well as the woman's responses and how she views herself and the situation.

21. American Psychological Association, *Violence and the Family: Report of the American Psychological Association Presidential Task Force on Violence and the Family* (Washington, D.C.: American Psychological Association, 1996), 85.

22. E. Peled, Z. Eisikovits, G. Enosh and Z. Winstok, "Choice and Empowerment for Battered Women Who Stay: Toward a Constructivist Model," *Social Work* 45, no. 1 (January 2000): 9–24.

23. F. P. Biestek, *The Principle of Client Self-Determination In Social Casework* (Washington, D.C.: Catholic University of America Press, 1951): F. P. Biestek, *Casework Relationship* (Chicago: Loyola University Press, 1957); F.P. Biestek and C.C. Gehrig, *Client Self Determination in Social Work: A Fifty Year History* (Chicago: Loyola University Press, 1978); Hollis, F. *Casework: A Psychosocial Therapy* (New York: Random House, 1972): H.H. Perlman, *Relationship, The Heart of Helping People* (Chicago: University of Chicago Press, 1979); H.H. Perlman, "The Problem Solving Model in Social Casework," in R.W. Roberts and R.H. Nee, eds., *Theories of Social Casework* (Chicago: University of Chicago Press, 1970).

24. Ibid.

25. Jones and Schecter, *When Love Goes Wrong.*

26. V. Goldner, "The Treatment of Violence and Victimization in Intimate Relationships," *Family Process* 37, no. 3 (Fall 1998): 263–86, 276.

27. D. G. Dutton, *The Domestic Assault of Women* (Vancouver: University of British Columbia Press, 1995), 266.

28. Herman, *Trauma and Recovery*, 63.

Chapter 10

1. J. Abbott, R. Johnson, J. Koziol-McLain, and S. R. Lowenstein, "Domestic Violence Against Women: Incidence and Prevalence in an Emergency Department Population," *Journal of the American Medical Association* 273, no. 22 (June 1995):1763–67, 1766.

2. Ibid.

3. Bureau of Justice Statistics, *Violence-Related Injuries Treated in Hospital Emergency Departments (NCJ–156921),* Bureau of Justice Statistics Special Report (August 1997), 5.

4. Children's Safety Network, *Domestic Violence: A Directory of Protocols for Health Care Providers* (1992).

5. J. Fagan and S. Wexler, "Crime at Home and in the Streets: The Relationship Between Family and Stranger Violence," *Violence and Victims* 2, no. 1 (Spring, 1987): 5–23.

6. American Psychological Association, *Violence and the Family: Report of the American Psychological Association Presidential Task Force on Violence and the Family* (Washington, D.C.: American Psychological Association, 1996), 10.

7. Fagan and Wexler, "Crime at Home and in the Streets."

8. David H. Hopkins, personal communication, January 24, 2000.

9. Ibid.

10. Leslie Landis, personal communication, January 3, 2000.

11. D.G. Dutton, *The Domestic Assault of Women: Psychological and Criminal Justice Perspectives* (Vancouver, B.C.: University of British Columbia Press, 1995), 224–25. "Decisions to arrest were most strongly influenced by victim injuries, which accounted for 85 percent of the variance in composite arrest decisions," as per a study published by Waaland and Keeley in 1985: P. Waaland and S. Keeley, "Police-Decision Making in Wife Abuse: The Impact of Legal and Extralegal Factors," *Law and Human Behavior* 9, no. 4 (1985): 355–66.

12. D.C. Carmody and K.R. Williams, "Wife Assault and Perceptions of Sanctions." *Violence and Victims,* 2 (1987): 25–38; P. G. Jaffe, D.A. Wolfe, A. Telford and G. Austin, (1986). "The Impact of Police Charges in Incidents of Wife Abuse." *Journal of Family Violence,* 1, no. 1 (March 1986): 37–49.

13. Evidence suggests that mandatory arrest is the best way to address spousal abuse. "We know from the Schulman (1979) and Straus, Gelles, and Steinmetz (1981) surveys that the likelihood of repeat violence is high (66% without police intervention). . . . Sherman and Berk (1984) found that recidivist assault within six months has a 28% to 37% likelihood when police attend and do not make an arrest . . . [thus] a case can be made for police arrest for putative wife assault"; Dutton, The Domestic Assault of Women [1995], 237.

14. R. J. Gelles (1993). "Constraints Against Family Violence: How Well Do They Work?" *American Behavioral Scientist* 36, no. 5: 575–86; Dutton, *The Domestic Assault of Women,* 238.

15. L. W. Sherman, J. D. Schmidt, D. P. Rogan, D. A. Smith, P. R. Gartin, E. G. Cohn, D. J. Collins, and A. R. Bacich , "The Variable Effects of Arrest on Criminal careers: the Milwaukee Domestic Violence Experiment," *Journal of Criminal Law and Criminology,* 83, no. 1 (1992): 137–61.

16. Leslie Landis, personal communication, January 3, 2000.

17. E. S. Buzawa and C. G. Buzawa, eds., *Do Arrests and Restraining Orders Work?* (Newbury Park, Calif.: Sage Publications, 1996), 48–49.

18. Leslie Landis, personal communication, January 3, 2000.

19. American Bar Association, Commission on Domestic Violence: Myths and facts on Domestic Violence," www.abanet.org (1999), 1.

20. Leslie Landis, personal communication, January 3, 2000.

21. Ibid.

22. Ibid.

23. Buzawa and Buzawa, *Do Arrests and Restraining Orders Work?* 46 (table 15). In another study, 60 percent of women who obtained orders of protection reported violations within one year of filing, 10; 240.

24. Florida Governor's Task Force on Domestic and Sexual Violence, *Florida Mortality Review Project* (1997).

25. New York Task Force on Women in the Courts, 1987.

26. Ibid.

27. C. S. Bruch, "And How Are the Children? The Effects of Ideology and Mediation on Child Custody Law and Children's Well-Being in the U.S.," *Family and Conciliation Courts Review* 30, no. 1 (January 1992): 112–34.

28. D. Ellis, "Post-Separation Woman Abuse: The Contribution of Lawyers as 'Barracudas,' 'Advocates' and Counsellors,'" *International Journal of Law and Psychiatry* 10, no. 4 (1987): 403–11; D. Ellis and L. Wight, "Estrangement, Interventions, and Male Violence toward Female Partners," *Violence and Victims* 12, no. 1 (Spring 1997): 51–67.

29. M. Pagelow, "Effects of Domestic Violence on Children and Their Consequences for Custody and Visitation Agreements," *Mediation Quarterly* 7, no. 4 (Summer 1990): 347–63.

30. Bruch, "And How Are the Children?" 1988.

31. National Training Center on Domestic and Sexual Violence, "Five Things to Say to a Victim Who Feels She Cannot Leave," handout (1999).

32. Deborah Tucker, personal communication, January 13, 2000.

33. In addition, most local and state bar associations have a lawyer referral service and will recommend two or three lawyers or legal clinics in the community that specialize in domestic violence cases and may provide pro bono legal assistance.

Chapter 11

1. "The sense of participation in meaningful social action enables the survivor to engage in. . . battle. . . from a position of strength. . . The survivor also gains satisfaction from the public exercise of power in the service of herself and others. . . . Her particular battle becomes part of a larger, ongoing struggle to impose the rule of law on the arbitrary tyranny of the strong." J. Herman, *Trauma and Recovery* (New York: Basic Books, 1997), 210–11.

2. Ibid., 196.

3. Deborah Tucker, personal communication, January 13, 2000: "Many people perceive battered women's shelters as for the disadvantaged. And because we ourselves in the [battered women's] movement have not reached out to women in the group you're discerning [the upper-income and highly educated], they just don't know where to turn."

4. Perhaps the *DSM-IV* should give the entire nature of domestic abuse some credence by having an entry called "battered woman syndrome" or "post-traumatic reaction to domestic abuse," as opposed to marginal mention within the appendix of the work (as pointed out in Herman, *Trauma and Recovery*, 118.)

REFERENCES

Abbott, J., Johnson, R., Kozial-McLain, J., and Lowenstein, S. R. 1995. "Domestic Violence Against Women: Incidence and Prevalence in an Emerging Dependent Population." *Journal of the American Medical Assocaition* 223, no. 22 (June 1995): 1763–67.

American Bar Association. Commission on Domestic Violence. 1998. "Myths and Facts about Domestic Violence." ABA web site, www.abanet.org/domviol/myths.html.

American Psychiatric Association. 1994. *Diagnostic and Statistical Manual of Mental Disorders.* 4th ed. Washington, D.C.: American Psychiatric Association.

American Psychological Association. 1996. *Violence and the Family: Report of the American Psychological Association Presidential Task Force on Violence and the Family.* Washington, D.C.: American Psychological Association.

Beauvoir, S. de. 1954. *She Came to Stay.* New York: Norton.

Becker, H. 1960. "Notes on the Concept of Commitment." *American Journal of Sociology* 66 (July): 32–40.

Belenky, M. F., Clinchy, B. M., Goldberger, N. R., and Tarule, J. M. 1986. *Women's Ways of Knowing.* New York: Basic Books.

Benjamin, J. 1988. *The Bonds of Love: Psychoanalysis, Feminism, and the Problem of Domination.* New York: Pantheon.

Berns, N. 1999. "My Problem and How I Solved It: Domestic Violence in Women's Magazines," *Sociological Quarterly* 40, no. 1 (Winter 1999): 85–108.

Biestek, F. P. 1951. *The Principle of Client Self-Determination In Social Casework.* Washington, D.C.: Catholic University of America Press.

———. 1957. *Casework Relationship.* Chicago: Loyola University Press.

Biestek, F. P., and Gehrig, C. C. 1978. *Client Self Determination in Social Work: A Fifty Year History.* Chicago: Loyola University Press.

Blackman, J. 1989. *Intimate Violence: A Study of Injustice.* New York: Columbia University Press.

Bowker, L. H. 1983. *Beating Wife Beating.* Lexington, Mass.: Lexington Books.

Bowlby, J. 1969. *Attachment.* Vol. 1 of *Attachment and Loss.* New York: Basic Books.

———. 1973. *Separation.* Vol. 2 of *Attachment and Loss.* New York: Basic Books.

Brenner, C. 1974. *An Elementary Textbook of Psychoanalysis.* New York: Anchor Books.

Browne, A. 1987. *When Battered Women Kill.* New York: Free Press.

Brownmiller, S. 1975. *Against Our Will: Men, Women, and Rape.* New York: Simon & Schuster.

Bruch, C. S. 1992. "And How Are the Children? The Effects of Ideology and Mediation on Child Custody Law and Children's Well-Being in the United States." *Family and Conciliation Courts Review* 30, no. 1 (January 1992): 112–34.

Bruner, J. 1986. *Actual Minds, Possible Worlds.* Cambridge, Mass.: Harvard University Press.

_____. 1987. "Life as Narrative." *Social Research* 54:11–32.

_____. 1991. "The Narrative Construction of Reality." *Critical Inquiry* 18 (Autumn): 1–21.

Bundow, G. L. "Why Women Stay." *Journal of the American Medical Association* (Resident Forum) 267, no. 23 (June 17, 1992): 3229.

Bureau of Justice Assistance. 1993. *Family Violence: Interventions for the Justice System.* (NCJ-144532). Washington, D.C.: U.S. Department of Justice.

Bureau of Justice Statistics. 1991. *Female Victims of Violent Crime.* Bureau of Justice Statistics Report.

_____. 1995. *Violence Against Women: Estimates From the Redesigned Survey (NCJ–154348).* Bureau of Justice Statistics Special Report. August.

_____. 1997. *Violence-Related Injuries Treated in Hospital Emergency Departments (NCJ–156921).* Bureau of Justice Statistics Special Report. August.

Burns, N. 1989. "Standards for Qualitative Research." *Nursing Science Quarterly* 2:44–52.

Buzawa, E. S., and Buzawa, C. G., eds. 1996. *Do Arrests and Restraining Orders Work?* Newbury Park, Calif.: Sage Publications.

Carlson, B. E. 1991. "Outcomes of Physical Abuse and Observation of Marital Violence among Adolescents in Placement." *Journal of Interpersonal Violence* 6: 526–34.

Carmody, D. C., and Williams, K. R. 1987. "Wife Assault and Perceptions of Sanctions." *Violence and Victims,* 2: 25–38.

Chapman, J. R., and Gates, M., eds. 1978. *The Victimization of Women.* Beverly Hills, Calif.: Sage Publications.

Charmaz, K. 1990. "'Discovering' Chronic Illness: Using Grounded Theory." *Social Science Medicine* 30, no. 11: 1161–72.

Children's Safety Network. 1992. *Domestic Violence: A Directory of Protocols for Health Care Providers.* Vol. 1.

Davidson, T. 1978. *Conjugal Crime.* New York: Hawthorne Books.

Davis, L. 1987. "Battered Women: The Transformation of a Social Problem." *Social Work* 32, no. 4 (July-August): 306–11.

Dobash, R. E., and Dobash, R. P. 1979. *Violence Against Wives.* New York: Free Press.

Domestic Violence and Incest Resource Centre (DVIRC). web site. September 1997.

Dutton, D. G. 1988. *The Domestic Assault of Women: Psychological and Criminal Justice Perspectives.* Boston: Allyn & Bacon.

_____. 1995. *The Domestic Assault of Women: Psychological and Criminal Justice Perspectives.* Vancouver: University of British Columbia Press.

Dutton, D. G., with Golant, S. K. 1995. *The Batterer.* New York: Basic Books.

Dutton, D. G., and Painter, S. 1985. "Patterns of Emotional Bonding in Battered Women: Traumatic Bonding." *International Journal of Women's Studies* (September-October): 8, no. 4:363–75.

_____. 1991. "Traumatic Bonding: The Development of Emotional Attachments in Battered Women and Other Relationships of Intermittent Abuse." *Victimology* 6, no. 1–2:139–55.

_____. 1993. "The Battered Woman Syndrome: Effects of Severity and Intermittency of Abuse." *American Journal of Orthopsychiatry* 63, no. 4:614–22.

Edleson, J. L. 1997. Revised April 1999. "Problems Associated with Children's Witnessing of Domestic Violence," Violence Against Women Online Resources web site, http://www.vaw.umn.edu.

Elbow, M. 1977. "Theoretical Considerations of Violent Marriages." *Social Casework* 58, no. 9 (November): 515–26.

Ellis, D. 1987. "Post-Separation Woman Abuse: The Contribution of Lawyers as 'Barracudas,' 'Advocates,' and 'Counsellors'" *International Journal of Law and Psychiatry* 10, no. 4. 403–11.

———. 1999. "Children's Witnessing of Adult Domestic Violence," *Journal of Interpersonal Violence* 14, no. 8 (August): 839–210.

Ellis, D., and Wight, L. 1997. "Estrangement, Interventions, and Male Violence toward Female Partners" *Violence and Victims* 12, no. 1 (Spring): 51–67.

Elson, M. 1988. *Self Psychology in Clinical Social Work*. New York: Norton.

Elson, M., ed. 1987. *The Kohut Seminars on Self Psychology and Psychotherapy with Adolescents and Young Adults*. New York: Norton.

———. 1999. "Self-pity, Dependence, Manipulation, and Exploitation: A View from Self Psychology." In *Annual of Psychoanalysis* 25: 5–16.

Engel, B. 1992. *The Emotionally Abused Woman*. New York: Fawcett/Columbine.

Evans, K. G. 1997. "If Mom's Battered, Kids Suffer." *Children's Advocate (Action Alliance for Children)*. July-August.

Fagan, J., and Wexler, S. 1987. "Crime at Home and in the Streets: The Relationship between Family and Stranger Violence," *Violence and Victims* 2, no. 1 (Spring 1987): 5–23.

Finkelhor, D., Gelles, R. J., Hotaling, G. T., and Straus, M. A., eds. *The Dark Side of Families: Current Family Violence Research*. Newbury Park, Calif.: Sage Publications.

Fleming, J. B. 1979. *Stopping Wife Abuse: A Guide to the Emotional, Psychological, and Legal Implications for the Abused Woman and Those Helping Her*. New York: Anchor/Doubleday.

Florida Governor's Task Force on Domestic and Sexual Violence. 1997. Florida Mortality Review Project.

Flynn, J. P. 1977. "Recent Findings Related to Wife Abuse." *Social Casework* 58 (January): 13–20.

Forward, S., and Torres, J. 1987. *Men Who Hate Women, and the Women Who Love Them*. New York: Bantam.

Friedan, B. 1974. *The Feminine Mystique*. New York: Norton.

Freud, A. 1968. "Indications and Contraindications for Child Analysis." In *Problems of Psychoanalytic Training, Diagnosis and the Technique of Treatment: The Writings of A. Freud*. Vol. 7. New York: International Universities Press, 1968, 110–23.

Freud, S. 1912. "Remembering, Repeating, and Working Through." *The Standard Edition of the Complete Psychological Works of Sigmund Freud*. London: Hogarth Press.

———. 1965 [1910]. "The Unconscious and Conscious Reality." In *The Interpretation of Dreams*. Translated, revised, and edited by James Strachey. New York: Avon.

Froelke, M. C. 1999. "Living Out Loud." *Chicago* (September 1999): 56–68.

Fromm, E. 1956. *The Art of Loving*. New York: Harper.

Fullbrook, K., and Fullbrook, E. 1994. *Simone de Beauvoir and Jean-Paul Sartre: The Remaking of a Twentieth Century Legend*. New York: Basic Books.

Gedo, J. E., and Goldberg, A. 1973. *Models of The Mind*. Chicago: University of Chicago Press.

Gelles, R. J. 1974. *The Violent Home: A Study of Physical Aggression between Husbands and Wives*. Beverly Hills, Calif.: Sage Publications.

———. 1979. *Family Violence*. Beverly Hills, Calif.: Sage Publications.

_____. 1993. "Constraints against Family Violence: How Well Do They Work?" *American Behavioral Scientist* 36, no. 5: 575–86.

Gelles, R. J., and Cornell, C. P.. 1990. *Intimate Violence in Families.* 2d ed. Newbury Park, Calif.: Sage Publications.

Gelles, R. J., and Straus, M. A. 1988. *Intimate Violence.* New York: Simon & Schuster.

Gergen, K. J. 1971. *The Concept of Self.* New York: Holt, Rinehart and Winston.

Gergen, M. 1988. "Narrative Structures in Social Explanation." In C. Antaki, ed., *Analyzing Everyday Explanation: A Casebook of Methods.* Newbury Park, Calif.: Sage Publications, 94–112.

Gilligan, C. 1982. *In a Different Voice: Psychological Theory and Women's Development.* Cambridge, Mass.: Harvard University Press.

Giovacchini, P. 1979. *Treatment of Primitive Mental States.* New York: Jason Aronson.

Glaser, B. G., and Strauss, A. L. 1967. *The Discovery of Grounded Theory: Strategies for Qualitative Research.* Chicago: Aldine/Altherton.

Goldberg, A. 1984. "Translation between Psychoanalytic Theories." Paper presented at the scientific meeting of the Chicago Psychoanalytic Society, Chicago, January 24, 1984.

Goldner, V. 1998. "The Treatment of Violence and Victimization in Intimate Relationships." *Family Process* 37, no. 3 (Fall): 263–86.

Gondolf, E. W. 1985. *Men Who Batter: An Integrated Approach for Stopping Wife Abuse.* Holmes Beach, Fla.: Learning Publications.

_____. 1988. *Battered Women as Survivors: An Alternative to Treating Learned Helplessness.* Lexington, Mass.: Lexington Books.

Gordon, L. 1988. *Heroes of Their Own Lives: The Politics and History of Family Violence.* New York: Penguin Books.

Graham, D. L., Rawlings, E., and Rimini, N. 1988. "Survivors of Terror: Battered Women, Hostages, and the Stockholm Syndrome." In K. Yllo and M. Bograd, eds., *Feminist Perspectives on Wife Abuse.* Newbury Park, Calif.: Sage Publications, 217–33.

Greenberg, J. R., and Mitchell, S. A. (1983). *Object Relations in Psychoanalytic Theory.* Cambridge, Mass.: Harvard University Press.

Greenblat, C. S. 1983. "A Hit Is a Hit Is a Hit . . . Or Is It?" In D. Finkelhor, R. J. Gelles, G. T. Hotaling, and M. A. Straus, eds., *The Dark Side of Families: Current Family Violence Research.* Newbury Park, Calif.: Sage Publications.

Guba, E., and Lincoln, Y. S. 1981. *Effective Evaluation.* San Francisco: Jossey-Bass.

Gunther, M. 1980. "Aggression, Self Psychology and Health." In A. Goldberg, ed., *Advances in Self Psychology.* New York: International Universities Press, 167–92.

Hamilton, E. 1969. *Mythology.* New York: Penguin.

Hart, F. 1991. "A Sudden Silence: An Analysis of the Psychological Literature on Battering Men, 1982–1990." *Resources for Feminist Research/Documentation* 20, no. 3–4 (Fall-Winter): 108–14.

Hecker, E. A. 1914. *A Short History of Women's Rights.* Westport, Conn.: Greenwood Press.

Herman, J. 1997. *Trauma and Recovery.* New York: Basic Books.

Hofeller, K. H. 1982. *Social, Psychological and Situational Factors in Wife Abuse.* Palo Alto, Calif.: R & E Research Associates.

Hoff, L. A. 1990. *Battered Women as Survivors.* New York: Routledge.

Holingshead, A. B., and Redlich, F. C. 1958. *Social Class and Mental Illness: A Community Study.* New York: John Wiley.

Hollis, F. 1972. *Casework: A Psychosocial Therapy*. New York: Random House.

Hotaling, G. T., and Sugarman, D. B. 1986. "An Analysis of Risk Markers in Husband to Wife Violence: The Current State of Knowledge." *Violence and Victims* 1:101–24.

Howard, P. F. 1978. *Wife Beating: A Selected Annotated Bibliography*. San Diego: Current Bibliography Series.

Hughes, H. M. 1988. "Psychological and Behavioral Correlates of Family Violence in Child Witness and Victims." *American Journal of Orthopsychiatry* 58:77–90.

Hughes, H. M., Parkinson, D., and Vargo, M. 1989. "Witnessing Spouse Abuse and Experiencing Physical Abuse: A 'Double Whammy'?" *Journal of Family Violence* 4: 197–209.

Hyden, M. 1994. "Woman Battering as a Marital Act: Interviewing and Analysis in Context." In C. K. Riessman, ed., *Qualitative Studies in Social Work Research*. Thousand Oaks, Calif.: Sage Publications.

Jacobson, N. S. 1993. "Domestic Violence: What Are Marriages Like?" Paper read at the American Association for Marital and Family Therapy conference, Anaheim, Calif., October 1993.

Jacobson, N. S., and Gottman. J. H. 1998. *When Men Batter Women*. New York: Simon & Schuster.

Jaffee, P. G., Wolfe, D. A., Telford, A., and Austin, G. 1986. "The Impact of Police Charges in Incidents of Wife Abuse." *Journal of Family Violence* 1, no. 1 (March): 37–49.

Jaffee, P. G., Wolfe, D. A., and Wilson, S. K. 1990. *Children of Battered Women*. Newbury Park, Calif.: Sage Publications.

Jones, A. 1994. *Next Time, She'll Be Dead*. Boston: Beacon Press.

Jones, A., and Schecter, S. 1992. *When Love Goes Wrong: What to Do When You Can't Do Anything Right—Strategies for Women with Controlling Partners*. New York: HarperCollins.

Kantrowitz, R. E., and Ballou, M. 1992. In L. S. Brown and M. Ballou, eds., *Personality and Psychopathology: Feminist Reappraisals*. New York: Guilford Press.

Kelly, L. 1988. *Surviving Sexual Violence*. Minneapolis: University of Minnesota Press.

Kerby, A. P. 1991. *Narrative and the Self*. Bloomington: Indiana University Press.

Kohut, H. 1971. *Analysis of the Self*. New York: International Universities Press.

———. 1977 *Restoration of the Self*. New York: International Universities Press.

———. 1984. *How Does Analysis Cure?* Edited by Arnold Goldberg with Paul E. Stepansky. Chicago: University of Chicago Press.

Kohut, H., and Cocks, G., eds. 1994. *The Curve of Life: The Correspondence of Heinz Kohut, 1923–1982*. Chicago: University of Chicago Press.

Kolbo, J. R. 1996. "Risk and Resilience among Children Exposed to Family Violence." *Violence and Victims* 11: 113–28.

Kuebler-Ross, E. 1969. *On Death and Dying*. New York: Macmillan.

Kurz, D. "Emergency Department Responses to Battered Women: Resistance to Medicalization." *Social Problems* 34 (1987): 69–81.

Kyriacou, D. N., Anglin, D., Taliaferro, E., Stone, S., Tubb, T., Linden, J. A., Muelleman, R., Barton, E., and Kraus, J. F. "Risk Factors for Injury to Women from Domestic Violence." *New England Journal of Medicine* 34, no. 2225 (December 16, 1999) 1892–98.

Laird, J. 1989. "Women and Stories: Restorying Women's Self-Construction." In M. McGoldrick, C. M. Anderson, and F. Walsh, eds., *Women in Families: A Framework for Family Therapy*. New York: Norton. pp. 427–50.

Langley, R., and Levy, R. 1977. *Wife Beating: The Silent Crisis*. New York: Dutton.

Lewis, D. O. 1992. "From Abuse to Violence: Psychophysiological Consequences of Maltreatment." *Journal of the American Academy of Child Adolescent Psychiatry* 31, no. 3 (May): 383–89.

Loewald, H. 1960. "On the Therapeutic Action of Psychoanalysis." *International Journal of Psychoanalysis* 41:16–33.

Loseke, D. R. 1992. *The Battered Woman and Shelters*. New York: State University of New York Press.

Marano, H. E. 1996. "Why They Stay: A Saga of Spouse Abuse," Psychology Today 29, no. 3 (May-June 1996): 57–78.

Marans, S. 1996. "Psychoanalysis on the Beat: Children, Police, and Urban Trauma." *Psychoanalytic Study of the Child* 51: 522–41.

Marans, S., and Adelman, A. 1997. "Experiencing Violence in a Developmental Context." in J. Osofsky, ed., *Children in a Violent Society*. New York: Guilford Press, 202–22.

Margolin, G. 1998. "Effects of Domestic Violence on Children." In P. K. Trickett and C. J. Schellenbach, eds., *Violence Against Children in the Family and Community*. Washington, D.C.: American Psychological Association, 57–102.

Margolin, G., and John, R. S. 1997. "Children's Exposure to Marital Aggression." In G. K. Kanter and J. L. Jasinski, eds., *Out of the Darkness: Contemporary Perspectives on Family Violence*. Thousand Oaks, California: Sage Publications, 90–104.

Marquis, J. 1999. "Alcohol, Job Woes Cited in Domestic Violence." *Los Angeles Times*, December 16, sec. 1, p. 3.

Martin, D. 1976. *Battered Wives*. San Francisco: Glide Publications.

Martin, R. R. 1994. "Life Forces of African-American Elderly Illustrated through Oral History Narratives." In E. Sherman and W. J. Reid, eds., *Qualitative Research in Social Work*. New York: Columbia University Press: 190–99.

McClosky, L. A., Figueredo, A. J., and Koss, M. P. 1995. "The Effects of Systemic Family Violence on Children's Mental Health." *Child Development* 66: 1239–61.

McMahon, M. 1991. "A Study of Selfobject Functions among Heterosexual Couples." Ph.D. dissertation, Institute for Clinical Social Work, Chicago.

Mederer, H. J., and Gelles, R. J. 1989. "Compassion or Control Intervention in Cases of Wife Abuse." *Journal of Interpersonal Violence* 4, no. 1, 25–43.

Meloy, J. R. 1992. *Violent Attachments*. New York: Jason Aronson.

Metropolitan Nashville Police Department Domestic Abuse web site, http://www.nashville.net/ ~police/abuse.

Mill, J. S. 1870. *The Subjection of Women*. New York: Appleton.

Miller, J. B. 1986. *Toward a New Psychology of Women*. Boston: Beacon Press.

Mishler, E. 1986. *Research Interviewing: Context and Narrative*. Cambridge, Mass.: Harvard University Press.

Modell, A. 1968. *Object Love and Reality: An Introduction to a Psychoanalytic Theory of Object Relations*. New York: International Universities Press.

Moewe, M. C. 1992. "The Hidden Violence: For Richer and For Poorer." *Fort Worth Star Telegram*, April 15, p. 6.

Montfalcore, W. R. 1980. *Coping with Abuse in the Family*. Philadelphia: Westminster Press.

Moore, R., and Gillette, D.. 1990. *King, Warrior, Magician, Lover: Rediscovering the Archetypes of the Mature Masculine*. San Francisco: HarperCollins.

Mowrer, E. R., and Mowrer, H. R. 1928. *Domestic Discord*. Chicago: University of Chicago Press.

National Clearinghouse on Child Abuse and Neglect Information. 1999. "In Harm's Way: Domestic Violence and Child Maltreatment." Monograph. Washington, D.C.: U.S. Department of Health and Human Services.

National Council of Juvenile and Family Court Judges. Family Violence Department. 1998. *Effective Intervention in Domestic Violence and Child Maltreatment Cases: Guidelines for Policy and Practice.* Reno, Nev.: National Council of Juvenile and Family Court Judges.

National Research Council. 1993. *Understanding Child Abuse and Neglect.* Washington, D.C.: National Academy Press.

Nelson, K. 1985. "Cognition, Context and Culture." In K. Nelson, ed., *Making Sense: The Acquisition of Shared Meaning.* New York: Academic Press.

Newberger, E. H., and Bourne, R., eds. 1985. *Unhappy Families.* Littleton, Mass.: PSG Publishing.

New York Task Force on Women in the Courts, 1987.

New York Victim Services web site. December, 1999.

NiCarthy, G., Merriam, K., and Coffman, S. 1984. *Talking It Out: A Guide to Groups for the Abused Woman.* Seattle: Seal Press.

Norwood, R. 1985. *Women Who Love Too Much.* Los Angeles: Jeremy P. Tarcher.

Novey, S. 1968. *The Second Look: The Reconstruction of Personal History in Psychiatry and Psychoanalysis.* Baltimore: The Johns Hopkins Press.

Okun, L. 1986. *Woman Abuse: Facts Replacing Myths.* Albany: State University of New York Press.

Ostrander, S. A. 1984. *Women of the Upper Class.* Philadelphia: Temple University Press.

Owen, C. 1968. *Social Stratification.* London: Routledge & Kegal Paul.

Pagelow, M. 1990. "Effects of Domestic Violence on Children and Their Consequences for Custody and Visitation Agreements." *Mediation Quarterly* 7, no. 4 (Summer): 347–63.

Palombo, J. 1992. "Narratives, Self-Cohesion, and the Patient's Search for Meaning." *Clinical Social Work Journal* 20, no. 3 (Fall 1992): 249–70.

_____. 1994a. "Incoherent Self-Narratives and Disorders of the Self in Children with Learning Disabilities." *Smith College Studies in Social Work* 64, no. 2 (March): 129–52.

_____. 1994b. "Gender as a Theme in Self Narratives." *Journal of Analytic Social Work* 2, no. 2:3–24.

Peele, S., and Brodsky, A. 1975. *Love and Addiction.* New York: Signet/NAL.

Peled, E. 1993. "The Experience of Living with Violence for Preadolescent Witnesses of Woman Abuse." Unpublished doctoral dissertation. University of Minnesota, Minneapolis.

_____. 1996. "Supporting the Parenting of Battering Men: Issues and Dilemmas." Unpublished manuscript.

Peled, E., Eisikovits, Z., Enosh, G., and Winstok, Z. 2000. "Choice and Empowerment for Battered Women Who Stay: Toward a Constructivist Model." *Social Work* 45, no. 1 (January): 9–24.

Perlman, H. H. 1970. "The Problem Solving Model in Social Casework." In R. W. Roberts and R. H. Nee, eds., *Theories of Social Casework.* Chicago: University of Chicago Press.

_____. 1979. *Relationship, The Heart of Helping People.* Chicago: University of Chicago Press.

Person, E. 1988. *Dreams of Love and Fateful Encounters.* New York: Penguin Books.

Pizzey, E. 1974. *Scream Quietly or the Neighbors Will Hear.* London: Penguin Books.

Pleck, E. 1987. *Domestic Tyranny: The Making of Social Policy against Family Violence from Colonial Times to the Present.* New York: Oxford University Press.

Polkinghorne, D. 1988. *Narrative Knowing and the Human Sciences.* Albany: State University of New York Press.

Pressat, R. 1985. *The Dictionary of Demography*. New York: Basil Blackwell.

Prus, R. 1996. *Symbolic Interaction and Ethnographic Research: Intersubjectivity and the Study of Human Lived Experience*. New York: State University of New York Press.

Resick, P. A. 1983. "Sex Role Stereotypes and Violence Against Women." In V. Franks and E. D. Rothblum, eds., *The Stereotyping of Women*. New York: Springer: 230–56.

Rich, A. 1977. "Conditions for Work: The Common World of Women." In S. Ruddick and P. Daniels, eds., *Working It Out*. New York: Pantheon, xiv–xxiv.

Riessman, C. K. 1990a. *Divorce Talk: Women and Men Make Sense of Personal Relationships*. New Brunswick, N.J.: Rutgers University Press.

_____. 1990b. "Strategic Uses of Narrative in the Presentation of Self and Illness: A Research Note. *Social Science and Medicine 30*, no. 11:1195–1200.

_____. 1994. "Making Sense of Marital Violence." In C. K. Riessman, ed., *Qualitative Studies in Social Work Research*. Thousand Oaks, Calif.: Sage Publications: 112–32.

Riviere, J. 1960. *The Ideal Reader*. New York: Meridian Books.

Rosenblatt, A., and Waldfogel, J., eds. 1983. *Handbook of Clinical Social Work*. San Francisco: Jossey-Bass.

Roy, M., ed. 1977. *Battered Women: A Psychosociological Study of Domestic Violence*. New York: Van Nostrand Reinhold.

Saari, C. 1991. *The Creation of Meaning in Clinical Social Work*. New York: Guilford Press.

Saleeby, D. 1994. "Culture, Theory, and Narrative: The Intersection of Meanings in Practice. *Social Work 39*, no. 4 (July): 351–59.

Sampselle, C. M., ed. 1992. *Violence against Women*. New York: Hemisphere.

Sartre, J.-P. 1953. *Being and Nothingness*. New York: Washington Square Press.

Saunders, D. G. 1992. "A Typology of Men Who Batter: Three Types Derived from Cluster Analysis." *American Orthopsychiatry 62* (2): 264–75.

Saunders, D. G., and Browne, A. 1991. "Domestic Homicide." In R. T. Ammerman and M. Hersen, eds., *Case Studies in Family Violence*. New York: Plenum Press: 379–402.

Schafer, R. 1968. *Aspects of Internalization*. Madison, Conn.: International Universities Press.

Schecter, S. 1982. *Women and Male Violence: The Visions and Struggles of the Battered Women's Movement*. Boston: South End Press.

Schulman, M. 1979. *A Survey of Spousal Violence Against Women in Kentucky*. Washington, D.C.: U.S. Department of Justice, Law Enforcement.

Seligman, E. 1975. "Frustration and Learned Helplessness." *Journal of Experimental Psychology Animal Behavior Processes 104*, no. 2 (April): 1499–57.

Sheehy, G. 1976. *Passages: Predictable Crises of Adult Life*. New York: Dutton.

Sherman and Berk 1984. T.K.(FIND IN DUTTON)

Sherman, E., and Reid, W. J., eds. 1994. *Qualitative Research in Social Work*. New York: Columbia University Press.

Sherman, L. W., and Berk, R. A. 1984. "The Specific Deterrent Effects of Arrest for Domestic Assault." *American Sociological Review 49*: 261–72.

Sherman, L. W., Schmidt, J. D., and Rogan D. P. 1992. *Policing Domestic Violence*. New York: Free Press.

Sherman, L. W., Schmidt, J. D., Rogan, D. P., Smith, D. A., Gartin, P. R., Cohn, E. G., Collins, D. J., and Bacich, A. R. 1992. "The Variable Effects of Arrest On Criminal Careers: The Milwaukee Domestic Violence Experiment." *Journal of Criminal Law and Criminology,* 83, no. 1:137–61.

Sigler, R. T. 1989. *Domestic Violence in Context: An Assessment of Community Attitudes.* Lexington, Mass.: Lexington Books.

Silvern, L., Karyl, J., Waelde, L., Hodges, W. F., Starek, J., Heidt, E., and Min, K. 1995. "Retrospective Reports of Parental Partner Abuse: Relationships to Depression, Trauma Symptoms and Self-Esteem among College Students." *Journal of Family Violence* 10: 177–202.

Sinclair, D. 1985. *Understanding Wife Assault: A Training Manual for Counselors and Advocates.* Toronto: Ontario Government Bookstore, Publications Services Section.

Slipp, S., ed. 1975. *Curative Factors in Dynamic Psychotherapy.* New York: McGraw-Hill.

Smith, S. M., Williams, M. B. and Rosen, K., eds. 1990. *Violence Hits Home: Comprehensive Treatment Approaches to Domestic Violence.* New York: Springer.

Sonkin, D. J., Martin, D., and Walker, L. E. 1985. *The Male Batterer: A Treatment Approach.* New York: Springer.

Stacy, W. A., and Shupe, A. 1983. *The Family Secret: Domestic Violence in America.* Boston: Beacon Press.

Stagg, V., Wills, G. D., and Howell, M. 1989. "Psychopathology in Early Childhood Witnesses of Family Violence." *Topics in Early Childhood Special Education* 9:73–87.

Star, B. 1983. *Helping the Abuser: Intervening Effectively in Family Violence.* New York: Family Service Association of America.

Stark, et al 1981. [TK].

Stark, E., and Flitcraft, A. 1988. "Violence among Intimates: An Epidemiological Review," in V. B. Hasselt, ed., *Handbook of Family Violence.* New York: Plenum, 293–318.

———. 1995. "Killing the Beast Within: Woman Battering and Female Suicidality," *International Journal of Health Services* 25, no. 1 (1995): 43–64.

Stark, R., and McEvoy III, J. 1970. "Middle Class Violence," *Psychology Today* 4 (November 1970): 52–54, 110–12.

Steinmetz, S., and Straus, M. A., eds. 1974. *Violence in the Family.* New York: Harper & Row.

Stith, S. M., Williams, M. B., Rosen, K. H., eds. 1990. *Violence Hits Home: Comprehensive Treatment Approaches to Domestic Violence.* New York: Springer.

Straus, M. A., 1991. "Conceptualization and Measurement of Battering: Implications for Public Policy." In M. Steinman, ed., *Woman Battering: Policy Responses.* New York: Norton.

Straus, M. A., and Gelles, R. J. 1990. *Physical Violence in American Families: Risk Factors and Adaptations to Violence in 8,145 Families.* New Brunswick, N.J.: Transaction Publishers.

Straus, M. A., Gelles, R. J., and Steinmetz, S. 1981. *Behind Closed Doors: Violence in the American Family.* New York: Anchor Books.

Taylor, S. J. and Bogdan, R. 1984. *Introduction to Qualitative Research Methods: The Search for Meanings,* 2d Ed. New York: John Wiley.

Tierney, K. J. 1982. "The Battered Women's Movement and the Creation of the Wife Beating Problem." *Social Problems* 29 (February 1982): 207–220.

Tolpin, M. 1983. "Corrective Emotional Experience: A Self Psychological Re-Evaluation," in A. Goldberg, ed., *The Future of Psychoanalyis.* New York: International Universities Press, 363–79.

Turner, S. F., and Shapiro, C. H. 1986. "Battered Women: Mourning the Death of the Relationship." *Social Work* 31, no. 5 (September-October): 372–76.

U.S. Department of Justice. 1997. *The Sourcebook of Criminal Justice Statistics.* Washington, D.C.: U.S. Department of Justice, p. 1998.

Vaughan, D. 1986. *Uncoupling.* New York: Oxford University Press.

Waaland, P., and Keeley, S. 1985. "Police Decision-Making in Wife Abuse: The Impact of Legal and Extralegal Factors," *Law and Human Behavior* 9, no. 4: 355–66.

Walker, L. 1979. *The Battered Woman.* New York: Harper & Row.

_____. 1980. "Battered Women." In A. M. Brodsky and R. T. Hare-Mustin, eds., *Women and Psychotherapy: An Assessment of Research and Practice.* New York: Guilford Press.

_____. 1983. "The Battered Woman Syndrome Study." In D. Finkelhor, R. J. Gelles, G. T. Hotaling, and M. A. Straus, eds., *The Dark Side of Families: Current Family Violence Research.* Newbury Park, Calif.: Sage Publications, 31–48.

Warshaw, C. 1989. "Limitations of the Medical Model in the Care of Battered Women." *Gender and Society* 3: 505–17.

Weitzman, S. 1994. "Upscale Violence and The Dynamics of Toxic Relationships." Paper read at National Association of Social Workers (NASW) Conference, Lake County, Ill., November 18, 1994.

_____. 1997. "The Abused Woman: A Look through a Sartrean-Existential Lens." Unpublished manuscript.

_____. 1998. "Upscale Violence: The Lived Experience of Domestic Abuse among Upper Socioeconomic Status Women." Ph.D. dissertation, Loyola University, Chicago.

Weitzman, S., and Levin, K. 1992. "Put Up Yer Dukes." Letter to the editor. *Chicago Tribune*, September 13.

White, E. C. 1985. *Chain, Chain, Change: For Black Women Dealing with Physical and Emotional Abuse.* Seattle: Seal Press.

Willbach, D. 1989. "Ethics and Family Therapy: The Case Management of Family Violence." *Journal of Marital and Family Therapy* 15, no. 1:43–52.

Wilson, C. F. 1981. *Violence Against Women: An Annotated Bibliography.* Boston: G. K. Hall.

Winters, M. S. 1988. *Laws against Sexual and Domestic Violence.* New York: Pilgrim Press.

Wright, E. O. 1985. *Classes.* London: Verso.

Yllo, K., and Bograd, M., eds. 1988. *Feminist Perspectives on Wife Abuse.* Newbury Park, Calif.: Sage Publications.

INDEX

ABOUT THE AUTHOR

Susan Weitzman, Ph.D., is an institute lecturer at the University of Chicago's School of Social Service Administration and has served as an adjunct professor at Loyola University's School of Social Work. A practicing psychotherapist in Chicago and formerly on staff for twelve years at the University of Chicago's Department of Outpatient Adult Psychiatry, Dr. Weitzman lectures and conducts workshops nationally. She is currently the project manager of a grant from the Department of Justice's Office of Victims of Crime (awarded to the American Professional Society on the Abuse of Children) whose aim is to address the issues involved in treating children who are exposed to violence. Dr. Weitzman was recently nominated for inclusion in the annual *Today's Chicago Woman Magazine* poll of "100 Women Making a Difference." Dr. Weitzman's website is *www.nottopeoplelikeus.com.*